# Reality
## —*and*—
# Wisdom

# Reality

## *and*

# Wisdom

### Exploring the Buddha's Four Noble Truths and the *Heart Sutra*

Lama Migmar Tseten

Wisdom Publications
132 Perry Street
New York, NY 10014 USA
wisdomexperience.org

*Library of Congress Cataloging-in-Publication Data*
Names: Tseten, Migmar, author.
Title: Reality and wisdom: exploring the Buddha's four noble truths and
    the Heart sutra / Lama Migmar Tseten.
Description: First edition. | New York: Wisdom Publications, 2023.
Identifiers: LCCN 2023010662 (print) | LCCN 2023010663 (ebook) |
    ISBN 9781614298328 (paperback) | ISBN 9781614298557 (ebook)
Subjects: LCSH: Four Noble Truths. | Buddhism—Doctrines.
Classification: LCC BQ4230 .T795 2023 (print) | LCC BQ4230 (ebook) |
    DDC 294.3/42—dc23/eng/20230509
LC record available at https://lccn.loc.gov/2023010662
LC ebook record available at https://lccn.loc.gov/2023010663

ISBN 978-1-61429-832-8  ebook ISBN 978-1-61429-855-7

27 26 25 24 23
5 4 3 2 1

Cover design by Marc Whitaker. Interior design by James Skatges.
Typeset by Gopa & Ted2, Inc.

Printed on acid-free paper that meets the guidelines for permanence and durability of the Production Guidelines for Book Longevity of the Council on Library Resources.

Printed in the United States of America.

Please visit fscus.org.

# Contents

The *Four Noble Truths* and the *Heart Sutra* are two of Buddhism's most well-known and important teachings.

The *Four Noble Truths* was the first teaching given by the Buddha after his enlightenment. In it, he explained the cause and result of both samsara and nirvana. Defilements are shown to be the cause that results in suffering. Removing those defilements on the path is the cause which results in nirvana.

The *Heart Sutra* is part of a larger group of sutras known as the *Prajnaparamita*, or Perfection of Wisdom sutras. It is the essence of the Buddha's teachings. Given to bodhisattvas, it is the means by which all buddhas, bodhisattvas, shravakas, and pratyekabuddhas attained realization.

In *Reality and Wisdom*, Khenpo Migmar Tseten explains these important sutras clearly for students who wish to understand them more deeply. Careful study and practice of these important teachings will bring great blessings in one's daily life and Dharma practice.

# Preface

This compilation of teachings combines revised and updated versions of two previously self-published books on the four noble truths and the *Heart Sutra*. The teachings on the four noble truths were conducted over the course of several months at the Sakya Institute in Cambridge, Massachusetts. The classes were then transcribed and adapted to book form.

The teachings on the *Heart Sutra* are based on retreats at Harvard University, MIT, and various Buddhist and yoga centers throughout the United States. These classes were also transcribed and adapted for print.

In an effort to promote the accessibility of these teachings, the transcriptions have been left much as they were. For this reason, the book remains conversational in nature and less formal than a scholarly text.

Whether you are new to Buddhism or a long-time practitioner, hopefully these pages deepen your understanding of the four noble truths and the *Heart Sutra* and inspire your practice. May all sentient beings everywhere be free from suffering.

Lama Migmar Tseten
Cambridge, MA
August 24, 2022

# PART I

The Four Noble Truths and
the Eightfold Path

I

# The First Noble Truth: Suffering

THE FOUR NOBLE TRUTHS are the central teachings of the Buddhist tradition. They provide the framework upon which all Buddhist philosophy and meditation are based. Although we may already be familiar with them, by repeatedly studying them and their sixteen corresponding aspects, our realizations on the spiritual path can become more transformative and profound.

These noble truths are the truth of suffering, the truth of the origin of suffering, the truth of the cessation of suffering, and the truth of the path leading to the cessation of suffering.

These four truths are based on the realizations of Prince Siddhartha, who reached enlightenment to become the Buddha Shakyamuni. It is said that the Buddha's very first teachings after attaining enlightenment were these teachings on the four noble truths.

Prince Siddhartha's early life in India was one of great wealth and privilege. He was given every luxury imaginable, but he soon realized that none of these comforts were bringing him true happiness, and he began to venture outside the palace walls.

On these early trips, the young prince was first exposed to the sufferings of impermanence. As he toured the town, he saw sick, aging, and dying people in the streets. He recognized that, despite all the comforts one may possess, no one can avoid the sufferings of sickness, old age, and death.

As he continued to venture from the palace, Prince Siddhartha also saw a meditator and was introduced to the idea of a spiritual life. This was the moment in which he saw that there was another way to live.

At this point he abandoned his life as a prince and renounced the kingdom. He dedicated his life to spiritual practice and eventually came to the profound realization of enlightenment. Through this awakening he came to recognize the four noble truths, including the noble eightfold path, which outlines the essence of Buddhist practice and provides eight practical instructions that lead to the cessation of all suffering.

These eight interconnected factors are to be developed simultaneously in our lives, and they instruct us on the following ways to live: right view, right intention, right speech, right action, right livelihood, right effort, right mindfulness, and right concentration.

It is essential in our perfection of the practice that we not only comprehend these four noble truths intellectually but also integrate such wisdom into our meditation and into every aspect of our lives.

## Shamatha (Calm Abiding) and Vipashyana (Insight) Meditations

The most effective method to begin cultivating some realization of the first noble truth, the noble truth of suffering, is to begin practicing shamatha meditation. Through gradually training our minds to remain focused on one object of meditation for a period of time, we start to familiarize ourselves with the underlying thought patterns and afflictive emotions that cause so much restlessness and suffering in our lives.

To those who have not done any meditation, shamatha practice may at first sound very easy or relaxing. We are instructed to focus our attention on a single object, most often a blue flower or our breath.

As we begin this practice, we discover it is actually very challenging to sit still. The mind is constantly distracted with racing thoughts and conflicting emotions. What we believed might be relaxing is actually very difficult at first! Our physical bodies are filled with discomfort, and our minds suddenly seem more restless and distracted than ever before. This early stage is crucial to our recognition of the nature of suffering. Through observing this discomfort, we begin to see that we are always running away from these feelings. When we cease to distract ourselves with worldly activities, we notice that there is tremendous suffering just beneath the surface of even a seemingly happy or privileged life.

If we persevere with our shamatha practice for a period of time, we will begin to gain some experience. There are five different levels of realization in shamatha meditation that are compared to different states of water, ranging from the first stage, in which the mind is a waterfall of rushing thoughts, to the fifth stage, in which the mind has attained a state like that of an ocean without waves.

At this fifth level of shamatha meditation, we have reached a stage of very good attention without much distraction and disturbance. When we experience this fifth level of concentration, we will observe that our minds have become very clear and mindful. Now shamatha meditation can become the base on which we further cultivate insight meditation.

With that insight we will begin to see something we have never seen before. We will begin to recognize that what we believed was real in the past is not actually true. Perhaps the four noble truths are called *noble truths* because they help us to move beyond our conditioning toward a more accurate view of the reality of our human existence.

Through very deep insight during meditation, our old view of the nature of our lives begins to fall apart. This can be very frightening without proper training and guidance because all our former conceptions of reality are shattered. Our way of looking at life is completely transformed, and we come to understand that our previous ways of seeing were all based on misperceptions.

Our old view of life was based on lies, on relativity, on false conditioning. With the cultivation of shamatha and insight meditations, we come to deeply understand the profound meaning of the four noble truths, and we are introduced to the path that can lead us beyond the confines of our suffering.

We recognize these noble truths when we first begin to see things with a very clear mind and without any emotions. This perceptual change affects not only how we see ourselves but also how we view all other objects. For the first time we realize that what we have seen and experienced in the past is mostly due to our inner emotional conditions. We understand that we have falsely projected many things onto outer objects as well as onto our own idea of ourselves. As our insight deepens, all these projections start to dissolve. This false reality we have constructed begins to shatter. As we progress from shamatha meditation to the practice of insight meditation, our realizations will counteract many of the misconceptions we have projected onto different objects.

Each of the four noble truths has four different aspects, and we will explore these sixteen aspects more thoroughly through the course of these teachings. Understanding these aspects is based on our insight and on the clarity of each of our minds. As our vision grows purer, these aspects become more apparent.

## Impermanence

The first aspect of the first noble truth is the aspect of impermanence. Impermanence is the understanding that whatever is created due to causes and conditions is subject to decay. Everything is changing, and nothing can remain forever.

In order to understand our own impermanence, we must first examine what we are made of. According to Buddhist philosophy we consist of *five aggregates*, which are the foundation of our current experience. These five aggregates are the form of the physical body, feeling, ideation, formation (which includes all of the other emotions), and mental consciousness. These are the five aggregates that are the basis of all our physical and mental experiences.

Normally in our lives we possess a very strong attachment to the five aggregates. Due to our strong attachment, we have many misconceptions. Although subconsciously at some level we know that we are constantly changing and that we will eventually grow old and die, due to our very strong attachment to our bodies, we remain in denial about our own impermanence.

Although intellectually we understand that whatever is born must decay, due to our attachments we become ignorant of this reality in our daily lives. No one wants to get older. No one wants to get sick. No one wants to experience the death of a loved one. Due to this fear, we create a strong sense of denial around impermanence.

There is a real conflict between our attachment to these five aggregates and the truth of impermanence. No matter how much attachment we may have to our physical bodies, they are constantly changing. Our feelings are changing. Our ideas are changing. Our emotional states are changing. Our consciousness is constantly shifting. All these aggregates are impermanent, and they are continuously in a state of flux.

So the truth of impermanence and change versus our attachment to the five aggregates creates an underlying conflict in our lives. As a consequence, whenever we are confronted with the truth of impermanence, we experience tremendous pain and suffering.

### SUFFERING

The second aspect of the first noble truth is suffering itself. There are three main types of suffering. First, we have the *suffering of suffering,* which includes all the physical illnesses and discomforts. Sickness is called the suffering of suffering because it is adding physical or emotional pain to our underlying state of suffering.

The second type of suffering is the *suffering of change.* The source of this suffering is often very surprising to people. This suffering actually stems from all of our pleasurable experiences and all of our conditional states of happiness.

Nothing in this life can stay the same, but we often remain ignorant of this impermanence. When you fall in love with someone, you expect that blissful state of happiness to be permanent. When the relationship begins to change, when you begin to see your partner's flaws and you start to argue, you experience much suffering.

When you first have a child, you are so excited. You feel that your baby is lovely and has made your life complete. Then when the child gets older and begins to separate from you and becomes a difficult teen-ager, the child can become a source of pain. You miss the early days when your child was an infant, and you wish you could go back to that happy time in your life.

What we fail to see is that our suffering is actually rooted in that original happiness. All of these delightful experiences are actually the suffering of change because they become the causes and conditions for future pain and suffering. Since anything good will inevitably change, our greatest pleasure is already sowing the seeds of loss and disappointment.

The third type of suffering is the *suffering of conditioning*. We will all grow old and die. Nothing in this life can stay the same. Everything will decay and change over time.

This third form of suffering is actually the basis for both the suffering of suffering and the suffering of change. The suffering of conditioning refers to conception and the very beginning of the five aggregates within a person. You could say that from the very moment that we are conceived, we are already beginning to die. Everything in this life is conditioned, and this impermanence is at the root of all our suffering.

These three kinds of suffering become much more intensified when our emotions are involved. If we have no meditation experience, then the changing aspects of our lives will create many difficult feelings for us.

So we see that all three kinds of suffering are magnified because they are related to destructive emotions. The suffering of suffering is related to the destructive emotion of anger. The suffering of change is related to emotions of desire and attachment. And the suffering of conditioning is based on our ignorance.

Suffering is constant in our lives because every moment is filled with change and impermanence. Even when things are going well, we have an underlying fear of our inevitable death. On a deep level we are still trying to distract ourselves from the truth of our conditioned existence.

In our lives we are constantly striving for happiness and pleasure. Everything we do in our lives is motivated by our desire for pleasure and comfort. We are completely driven by our attachments, and we are ignoring the suffering nature of our lives. This ignorance to the causes of suffering and this effort to cling to our pleasurable experiences creates tremendous conflict in us.

When we practice insight meditation, we begin to see deeper and deeper into the nature of our lives. We recognize the truth of change and impermanence. This seeing helps us begin accepting the reality of our lives.

This acceptance happens when we truly understand our attachment as the cause of our emotional pain. We do not want to die, but the nature of life is impermanence. Through meditation, when we begin to accept the truth of suffering and its causes, the conflict at the very core of our existence begins to dissolve.

Only through insight meditation, when our minds are clearer and we are free from destructive emotions, will we see impermanence more clearly. We will begin to see the suffering of conditioned existence.

When we can observe that every moment everything is changing, we can stop clinging to our lives. We can stop living in fear of our own deaths. We can begin to move beyond our ignorance to see the noble truth of suffering.

## INSUBSTANTIALITY AND THE FIVE AGGREGATES

The third aspect of the first noble truth is insubstantiality. Another way for us to understand the truth of suffering is for us to integrate it into our five aggregates. As we have discussed, each person has the five aggregates of form, feeling, ideation, formation, and consciousness. Through developing stronger insight meditation, we come to know the characteristics of all these aggregates.

The first aggregate of form is, of course, what our material body consists of. While we are alive, we have this physical component. This is the aggregate of matter. Once we know the nature of our physical bodies, we will also understand the nature of other people's bodies. Their bodies are impermanent just like ours. This observation will help us to understand how all other material things outside of our bodies are also impermanent.

The Buddha said that as our insight meditation deepens, not only do we see impermanence in ourselves, but we also begin to see impermanence in all living beings. We begin to see impermanence in all material things. By realizing the changing nature of our own bodies, we learn to recognize this impermanence in all sentient beings and all physical matter.

By nature, all physical matter is composed of material atoms. According to Buddhist philosophy, these atoms are comprised of the four basic elements of earth, water, fire, and air. If we look deeper into these atoms, then all material things begin to lose their identification. At the atomic level, what reference do we have with which to identify an object? At the level of the atom, we discover the insubstantiality of all objects.

Generally in our lives, we do not break things down to the atomic level, and instead we assign an identity or label to each object in the material world. Then, based on its usefulness to us, we get attached. It is one thing to enjoy something and to let it go. But if we get emotionally attached to it and then something happens to that object, we will experience so much suffering of change.

The second aggregate is that of feeling. Based on the recognition of our own feelings, we can comprehend that other beings have feelings. If we look closely at feelings, whether they are pleasure or pain, happiness or unhappiness, even neutral feelings, they are all a form of suffering. This is because feelings are based on the five aggregates, and the five aggregates are defiled.

Even a neutral feeling is a form of suffering. Neutral feelings are a result of our underlying ignorance. This ignorance is the basis of all the suffering of suffering and the suffering of change.

Through contemplation we can recognize the insubstantiality of feelings. If we look closely, can we find any lasting feeling? Can we find any substantial or permanent state? The same principles apply to the rest of the five aggregates: ideations, formations, and consciousness. They are all insubstantial.

Insubstantiality is not limited only to material things. Consciousness and emotions are not material. But what is the mind? Even with strong insight, if we look into the mind, we cannot actually find it! The mind loses its identity.

## EMPTINESS

The fourth aspect of the first noble truth is emptiness. When we look deeper into any of the five aggregates, we cannot find lasting evidence of them. They are insubstantial. As our meditation deepens, we begin to go beyond all concepts, beyond all identification of objects, to discover the empty nature of things.

Right now in our lives we have a lot of attachment to objects. Whenever something happens to those objects of attachment, we experience pain and suffering. This is because we have believed that these objects are real and substantial. It is very difficult for us to see the empty nature of things without meditation experience.

An understanding of impermanence can only arise from deep insight meditation experience. Through reflection, we see the impermanent and empty nature of all things. This realization counteracts our misconceptions of reality. We even come to accept and eventually embrace the inevitability of our own death.

By learning to view even our happy feelings as a cause of suffering, we can counteract the misconception that life should always be pleasurable. As long as we are expecting life to be pleasurable, we will constantly be disappointed and experience pain instead. As long as we have emotional attachment to objects, thinking that they are real, we will experience much pain and sadness when we lose them.

To counteract these attachments, we need to develop a profound understanding of the insubstantiality and empty nature of those objects, emotions, thoughts, and even of the mind itself. Reflecting and meditating on each aspect of the four noble truths helps to counteract our misconceptions about reality.

In our lives we cling to the idea of a *self*. Most of what we do in our lives is based on *self-cherishing* because we believe that the self and ego truly exist. As we have discussed, the objects of our attachments are rooted in the five aggregates. This self-cherishing is based on our bodies, our feelings, our ideas, our habitual formations, and our consciousness.

When we look deeper, we discover there is no substance to what we thought existed. That is why emptiness, the fourth aspect of the first noble truth, includes not only the empty nature of ourselves, but of other objects as well. They are all empty. Insubstantiality and emptiness help us to overcome the misconception of self, which is based on our five aggregates.

These aspects also help us to overcome all our ideas of ownership based on our sense of self. Concepts like "my" are based on the idea of the phenomenal self arising from the five aggregates. These notions of "my house" or "my car" arise from misconceptions related to the five aggregates. We each have attachment to ourselves and to the whole universe. It is very important to understand the aspects of insubstantiality and emptiness in order to counteract these attachments.

We can study the four noble truths and gain some intellectual understanding of them. But only when they become true experiences through deep insight meditation will they become noble truths. Through meditation we learn to see these four aspects: impermanence, suffering, insubstantiality, and emptiness. We see these four aspects in ourselves, other beings, and all other things in the conditioned world.

When we see in this way, then we are seeing the first noble truth because we are seeing right through our misconceptions. We are no longer clouded by our desires. We are no longer seeing reality through anger or ignorance.

At this level, we have gone beyond all three afflictive emotions of attachment, anger, and ignorance. We have stopped viewing the world through the lens of these emotions, and we have stopped relating to ourselves and those around us with desire, anger, or indifference. Now we are gaining some wisdom, some equanimity in our experience.

The noble truth or insight means seeing with wisdom; seeing with equanimity that is free from all destructive emotions. We no longer have the inner conditions with which we falsely project our emotions onto an object. The way we see reality will be very different.

That is why it is called a *noble truth*. When we see beyond our delusions, we will realize for the first time that what we saw before was actually defiled. We will realize that our old way of seeing was tainted. It was all based on misconceptions.

The way yogis see, and the way we see now, are two completely different experiences of reality. What we see is based on ignoble perceptions. If we have ignorance, then we will have all the other emotions. Then everything we see will be affected by those other emotions.

But when we can see through our delusions to the noble truth, we recognize that the nature of all our feelings was suffering. Only nirvana is unconditioned and is beyond death. Nirvana is the cessation of feelings that were rooted in the ego. All feelings, even neutral feelings, are rooted in the ego. The seed of these feelings is poisonous. Whatever grows from such a seed is always poisonous.

But through practice, as we recognize the wisdom of the four noble truths, we will see that there is an entirely new way to experience our lives.

# 2

# The Second Noble Truth: The Origin of Suffering

THE SECOND NOBLE TRUTH is the origin of suffering. As we have established in the first noble truth, the nature of conditioned existence is suffering. The second noble truth looks closely at the origins of that suffering.

Origination is subtler because many times we do not see origination directly. There are many misunderstandings and doubts about origination. The Buddha also taught four different aspects related to the second noble truth. These aspects help to clear away our misconceptions related to the origin of suffering.

## CAUSE

The first aspect of the second noble truth is *cause*. This is to help us see the true source of our pain and suffering. When we experience the suffering of suffering in the form of a headache, we feel the pain of that headache, but we do not know what the real causes of it are.

We may go to the doctor and receive many different tests. Sometimes a doctor can offer a solution. Other times a doctor may misdiagnose the source of the headache. There can be many different kinds of headaches. There are migraine headaches. There are stress headaches. Some headaches are a warning sign for a stroke. We feel the pain, but the cause can be many different things.

If we look closely, we can see that pretty much all suffering has some cause. But the causes are complex. They are subtle. There are various durations of time during which we experience such suffering. Sometimes we cannot remember the causes of our suffering because the suffering has extended over many lifetimes.

There are many reasons why our attempts to determine the causes of suffering can lead to misunderstandings. There are many schools of thought. Perhaps the reason why the Buddha taught *cause* as the first aspect of the second noble truth is because there are many people who do not accept the natural law of karma.

From a medical standpoint, doctors may determine the causes for a physical illness and accept those as the original causes of that particular suffering. Doctors do not necessarily accept karma. So if they find an obvious physical explanation for a particular illness, they may see that as the only cause and rarely look deeper at karmic causes and conditions.

Perhaps the majority of people in the world do not accept karma. That means that people accept only what they can prove, only what they can diagnose materially. But if something is immaterial, then how can they find a diagnosis? The purpose of the first aspect of the second noble truth is to emphasize the natural law of karma.

What is the law of karma? Karma refers to cause, condition, and result. And within these three, there is interdependency; there is relativity. That is karma. The natural law of cause and effect has the meaning of relativity and interdependency.

Since we do not see the causes and conditions most of the time, many people do not believe in karma. Some people may say "it's karma" but fail to comprehend the depth of it. Thus, one reason for this first aspect of "cause" is to prove that everything is interdependent and based on cause, condition, and result.

So all three kinds of suffering that we have outlined in the first noble truth are interdependent. They all have causes and conditions. In order to prove this fact, the Buddha taught this first aspect of cause.

We can study all the details of different causes, conditions, and results in the Abhidharmakosha, which is actually the most detailed approach to the four noble truths. Through extensive study of all the causes, conditions, and results, we can prove that everything we experience is actually due to karma. As a result of negative karma, we experience suffering.

Everything we experience is due to the interdependency of cause, condition, and result. The first aspect of the second noble truth is to prove that, although everything has a cause, condition, and result, each particular cause will have its own particular result. We may expect a mango seed to grow into a pomegranate, but it will never happen! The result has to have its own cause and condition.

This is how we can prove that all suffering is caused by negative karma based on negative emotions. We can study the various factors of negative karma. We can study the ten negative karmas, which correspond to physical, verbal, and mental negative emotions. Basically, we can prove that all suffering is due to negative karma created by negative emotions. This demonstrates that all karma is based on specific causes and conditions. The negative emotions are the seeds and suffering is the result.

So through this first aspect of cause, we can study karma in general, as well as the causes and results of negative karma. This first aspect, cause, can prove that everything manifests as a result of this cycle of cause, condition, and result.

## ORIGINATION

The second aspect of the second noble truth is *origination*. Origination here does not mean that karma has an origin or a first cause. Once we've established interdependency and relativity between cause, condition, and result, then within interdependency we cannot find a first cause.

Origination here refers to that cycle where every cause has its own cause, and that cycle keeps repeating again and again.

Each past cause and condition has a present result. Then the present result is the cause and condition for a future result. So this is the cycle through which everything originates. Origination is not to be misunderstood as a first cause. Origination refutes a first cause. It refers to interdependent origination, which means the result becomes the cause for another chain of events.

In this cycle, one thing can be both the result of something in the past as well as the cause of whatever happens next. So that is why things are interdependently continuing all the time.

We could say, then, that origination proves that there is no first cause and also no singular cause. Take for example how one entity can be both a cause and a result. One man can be a son to his father and a father to his son simultaneously. He's one person, but he can be referred to in multiple ways.

In dependent origination, causes are always multiple. They are multiple in the sense that one entity can have different aspects. The entity can be a result, a cause, or a condition, depending on our frame of reference. That is why the second aspect of the second noble truth is to refute the existence of a first cause and a singular cause.

Everything is unfolding in a cycle, and each thing has multiple aspects. Origination supports the very philosophy of interdependency and the law of karma. This aspect of origination refers to multiple causes and conditions as well as to interdependency. The main object is to refute a first cause and a singular cause.

## PRODUCTION

The third aspect of the second noble truth refers to the process of being *produced*. This third aspect is to show that whatever we experience is a direct result of our karma. When we experience suffering, it is because we have participated personally in the creation of that karma.

Whatever suffering we experience is a direct result of our past actions and emotions. Sometimes this extends over multiple lifetimes, so it is difficult for us to see how we have caused it. But it is important to recognize that no one else has produced that karma for us.

When the Buddha taught the four noble truths, he was refuting all theistic religions. He asked the question, "If everything was created by God, then why would a benevolent God create so much suffering?" The Buddha couldn't reconcile these opposing factors.

Thus the Buddha taught that every form of suffering we experience, whether it manifests as feelings of pain or of pleasure, must have been caused by karma that we have personally created.

In order to prove this, the Buddha taught this third aspect of the second noble truth. Being produced means that due to our own karma we are now experiencing such suffering. It has nothing to do with some other force creating such suffering. This is also related with karmic law. The Buddha said that whatever we experience has a direct connection to what we have personally done in the past. All results are due to our own karma and our own emotions.

Another person cannot produce our suffering. We have to have participated in the production of our suffering and pain. To prove that point, the Buddha taught this third aspect of the second noble truth. This third aspect confirms that every experience, every feeling we have, is preceded by our own karma and our own emotions.

## CONDITION

The fourth aspect of the second noble truth is *condition*. There are some religious traditions like Jainism that believe we have a permanent soul. This permanent soul is said to always be at peace even though circumstantially we have pain and suffering. The Jains believe in a soul that is always happy and free from suffering.

To refute such teachings, the Buddha discussed conditions. He observed that the experiences we have are not only due to our causes but also to our conditions. Causes are like the seed, and conditions are like the water, soil, and everything that makes the seed grow. Causes and conditions are very much related to each other and determine the result.

This aspect is mainly to refute a permanent cause. In this way the Buddha is saying that the second noble truth of origination or causation is a product of causes and conditions. As a result of these causes and conditions we experience suffering.

As we have established, the first noble truth is suffering, which includes all three kinds of suffering. The second noble truth examines all the causes and conditions of that suffering. Generally we see that there are three main causes of suffering: ignorance, desire, and anger. Due to ignorance we create karma. Ignorance is the main cause of birth and rebirth. When we die without any awareness or any practice, when we experience overwhelming pain and suffering at the time of death, we tend to lose consciousness. When the elements of our physical bodies are dissolving at the time of death, we often cannot maintain our awareness. That unconsciousness is, in some sense, an experience of that ignorance. Because we become unconscious at the time of dissolution, we cannot maintain wisdom, we cannot maintain awareness.

Out of that lack of awareness, out of that unconsciousness, when we enter the *bardo* or intermediate state after death, those habitual patterns and all the karma that has been impressed on our consciousnesses will take over our minds.

All these afflictive emotions that have been imprinted on our mindstreams will follow us into the bardo. We will carry very strong desire and attachment after death, which will then force our rebirth.

We are conceived and reborn again and again. In that very first moment of conception, when our consciousness is combined with our father's and mother's elements, that is the beginning of the suffering of conditioned nature. The very fact of our birth means we will experience old age and death and will experience the suffering of the conditioned nature of all things.

The Buddhist teachings always discuss death as occurring every moment. Death is "momentary." From the very moment we are conceived we have started toward death because every moment we are changing. We can experience that impermanence in every heartbeat. At any moment that heart can stop, and we can leave this body.

Recently I was talking with a friend who is a doctor. He said that the more he learned about the workings of human physiology, the more amazed he was that we live as long as we do! The more he studied, the more he came to see that our physical bodies are almost like a ticking time bomb. He was amazed that our bodies function as well as they do most of the time. At any moment a human body can stop working.

We have evolved to have this physical body that becomes the basis for the other two kinds of suffering. If we are never born, then we do not have a body. However, due to ignorance, we are conceived. With conception we have physical bodies. Then, with a physical body, we have the three kinds of suffering. Either way, the suffering of suffering and the suffering of change are both based on the suffering of conditioning. The basic suffering of conditioned existence is there all the time, even when we do not actively feel the suffering of change or the suffering of suffering.

Shantideva said in his *Bodhicharyavatara* that most anger is rooted in pain and suffering. When we have physical pain we may become short tempered and impatient. Often we express this anger to the people we are closest to emotionally.

Pain can make adults act like children again. When children have physical pain, sometimes they take it out on their parents. Maybe children think they can get away with expressing anger toward their parents since they feel unconditionally loved by them.

It is a common human trait to try to find someone to blame for our suffering. We try to find some kind of excuse by becoming angry at outer circumstances or at someone in our lives.

The other obvious source of suffering occurs when our desires are not being fulfilled. This may also cause us to become angry. And the desire is there in the first place because we do not see the true nature of the object of our desire.

So we can see how the afflictive emotions are completely interdependent. Desire is there because of ignorance. Unfulfilled desire can cause suffering. Suffering can be the root of anger. They are all interrelated.

The expression of these three afflictive emotions at a mental level generates karma. At the verbal level, when we express these three emotions, that becomes verbal karma. At the physical level, when we express these three emotions through actions, that becomes physical karma.

We can see how karma and those destructive emotions are the causes and conditions for the three kinds of suffering. The more we understand the way causes and conditions operate, the more we can free ourselves from misconceptions about karma.

On a larger scale, when we accept karma, karma can refute all those big philosophical questions about whether a creator god is responsible for our suffering. When we take personal responsibility for creating our own karma, we can begin to recognize how our karma is creating our experiences of the entire universe. This can encourage us to stop blaming outer circumstances and to begin creating causes and conditions for a positive future.

This is not to diminish how interdependent we are. Our personal experiences generated by our individual karma also affect the universe. For this reason it is very important to understand karma.

The Buddha taught that one act of killing can have multiple results. One example is that this act of violence may shorten our lives. Furthermore, if we kill with desire—killing an animal for meat, for example—then that type of killing can increase our desire. If we kill with anger, then that will increase our anger. If we kill with ignorance, that will increase our ignorance.

All these types of killing will also make our habitual pattern of killing stronger. As a result, by killing others, by eliminating their lives, a feeling of lifelessness will pervade our environment—the energy of our external world will be affected. You can really sense this in areas of war or conflict.

If we examine the situation closely, then we will see that there are many factors involved in killing just one sentient being. For this reason, studying the complexities of karma can be very important. The more we study, the more we can clear away doubts and misunderstandings. This in turn will give us more confidence about the natural law of karma.

In this way, these four aspects of the second noble truth—cause, origination, production, and condition—are designed to clear away misunderstandings related with the three kinds of suffering and their causes and conditions.

# 3

# The Third Noble Truth: Cessation

THE THIRD NOBLE TRUTH is the truth of cessation. This truth acknowledges that there can be an end to suffering—that we can reach nirvana. While we may try to understand nirvana intellectually, the state of nirvana is actually beyond our intellect. Without a direct experience of nirvana, it is very difficult for us to comprehend what nirvana is. But we will attempt to explore it as scholars and practitioners in order to comprehend the possibility of freedom from suffering.

I often use the example of sugar. Only those of us who have tasted sugar will truly know what sugar is. We cannot reach this experience through discussion or comparison. No matter how many names we use, or how deeply we go into describing its chemical properties, we cannot duplicate the experience intellectually. Even if we were to write a very big book about what sugar is, it still would not give us that firsthand experience.

What is nirvana? Nirvana is the cessation of suffering. That result can only be reached through practicing the noble eightfold path, which will be presented in our discussion of the fourth noble truth.

The Buddha addressed four different aspects of each of the four noble truths. These four aspects are designed to clear away our doubts and misconceptions.

## CESSATION

The first aspect of the third noble truth of nirvana is *cessation*, which has a meaning of liberation. This first aspect is to clear away any misunderstandings related to whether freedom from suffering is possible.

If we believe that the destructive emotions that are the cause of all our suffering are inherent in human nature, then no matter how much we practice, we will never be free. If we believe that these afflictive emotions are our true nature, then whatever faith we cultivate, whatever spiritual practice we may do, there will still be no possibility of going beyond suffering and the causes of suffering.

The Buddha taught the opposite. He said that humans are fundamentally pure by nature. He taught that all sentient beings are possessed of buddha nature and have the potentialities to become free from suffering and the causes of suffering.

On the topic of human nature there are two basic schools of thought. One school thinks that the nature of humanity is passionate and aggressive. This school thinks that humans are wired for war and conflict, imprinted with fight or flight responses, neuroses, and afflictive emotions. There are some who would argue that these responses are embedded in our genes and cannot be altered.

The other school of thought, which is shared by Buddhists, is that by nature we are pure, compassionate, and wise. While Buddhists understand that the nature of life right now is suffering, and suffering has causes, we also perceive that the nature of our minds is free from suffering and free from the causes and conditions of suffering. That inherent nature is actually nirvana.

In the sutra teachings, the inner space of the mind, that inherent nature, is described as being similar to the sky. When we have clouds and bad weather, we do not see the blue sky in its pristine state. And when we have many disturbing emotions and concepts in our minds, then we cannot see the clarity of our inner space either.

Because of these obscurations, we do not experience nirvana or cessation. Only when we have a very deep meditation session does whatever is unreal, whatever is relative, whatever is fake temporarily dissolve. What remains is the clarity of that inner space.

Outer space is unconditioned. It has been unconditioned for an infinite time in the past. It will be unconditioned for an infinite time in the future. But all the planetary systems, billions of them, come and go. According to the Buddha, these planetary systems are limitless, but none of them are permanent. Only space remains.

Our earth is just one tiny planet, and humans are only one small fraction of the sentient beings on earth. But for us personally, our own experiences are so important that whatever we experience we assume should be a universal truth. We think everyone has to agree with us and has to see reality as we see it. But there is no universal truth to our perceived reality. What we experience is based on our inner conditions. Our individual inner conditions have shaped all of our experiences and have projected a unique experience of the external world.

The universe is limitless. But we interact with the universe based on personal experiences, and those personal experiences are based on our inner conditions. We become convinced that our individual experience must have some universal authority, but that is not the case.

When we discover through meditation that inner space in which we transcend all these objects, and in which inner space and outer space become one, then our experience of everything will change.

When inner and outer space merge, for the first time we have a glimpse of nirvana. In addition, we see the absence of all emotions, including the root destructive emotions of anger, ignorance, and attachment.

In this glimpse of nirvana, we see the possibility of complete freedom from suffering. As long as we have feelings, however, we have suffering. Even a happy feeling is suffering according to the Buddha. Even a neutral feeling is suffering.

As we have discussed, when we have pleasure, we think we are happy.

But that is our misunderstanding of relativity. That is our misunderstanding of karma. Because we experience the result, and we do not see the cause, we think that this is freedom from suffering. But actually karma is such that even those positive feelings can become a cause for negative feelings.

Here in the west when we hear the word *nirvana*, we probably think of Kurt Cobain and his famous band Nirvana from Seattle. Cobain's life was actually an example of the horrible suffering of samsara. He rose to stardom as a very young man. He sold millions of records around the world. But his fame and wealth only fueled his addictions and increased his suffering.

Artists and musicians are very creative people. They are very sensitive. They work on cultivating an inner space through their art that may even feel like nirvana at times. But the method they are applying is often confused, and the attention they receive often serves to reinforce their destructive emotions. As a result, they can fall into terrible states of suffering.

This is what we do in samsara. We try hard to avoid suffering through false methods. In the sixties Western culture erupted in a positive revolution fueled by drug use. Some of these psychedelic drugs had the power to give people a glimpse of nirvana. But that high was quickly followed by the withdrawal. There is no shortcut to nirvana. True freedom from suffering can only be reached through deep meditation practice.

Nirvana is a state of not feeling. Painkillers and recreational drugs have the power to temporarily kill feelings in our nervous systems. All systems are shut down, and that is why we may feel some relief, some freedom from suffering. Feeling is based on ego, and when we forget ourselves, we think we are having a wonderful experience. But relief is only temporary when it is achieved in this way. These drugs are not actually freeing us from any of the underlying afflictive emotions.

Our attention always goes to an area that has pain. When we have a headache, all we can think about is that nagging discomfort. If our feelings have been hurt by a friend, all we can think about is that rejection. However, we generally do not pay attention to areas free from pain.

Drugs can provide a way to forget ourselves. Because we feel a temporary sense of relief, we wonder if it is similar to nirvana. But being momentarily ecstatic or numb, or forgetting ourselves as a result of a drug, has very little in common with the experience of nirvana.

Nirvana is the awareness of a state beyond feeling. The realization of inner space is based on awareness and mindfulness, not distraction. When we go beyond the ego and self, we can become free from the five aggregates.

Nirvana is the cessation of the five aggregates. We go beyond the aggregates of form, feeling, ideation, formation, and consciousness. We go beyond our physical bodies. We go beyond our feelings, ideas, and activities.

How can we do that? I think we can only do that through our awareness. We go beyond the ego and self. And then, in the state beyond ego and self, we experience inner space. When we are fully aware of that inner space, we are experiencing nirvana. We are experiencing the cessation of craving and attachment and of all the feelings related with the five aggregates.

*Cessation* means freedom from all conditioned and unconditioned phenomena. It means freedom from feelings, ideas, and activities, including freedom from our minds and emotions. Cessation is possible because that is the nature of our minds when we see that inner space. In that inner space all the defiled aggregates also dissolve.

So the first aspect of the third noble truth—this aspect of *cessation*—proves that through meditation practice we can experience freedom. Since we can experience cessation, we can know there is liberation. We can know that there is freedom not only from suffering but from the very causes of suffering.

This aspect of cessation can be very useful in combatting our worldly, narcissistic ways of life. It can be used to refute those who do not have any faith in spiritual enlightenment and liberation.

While the Buddha didn't face as much materialism or capitalism as we experience today, there were five prominent non-Buddhist philosophers in India whose misconceptions he faced.

In particular, there was one non-Buddhist school called Charvaka that was very similar to many of our materialistic societies. The Charvakas only believed in this life. They didn't believe in rebirth or karma. Their main purpose in life was to be narcissistic and to pursue pleasure.

The Indian philosopher who founded the Charvaka school had a very clever mind. He developed a theory positing that there is no rebirth and no karma. Thus he argued that we can narcissistically enjoy this moment. He thought the pursuit of pleasure was what life is composed of. To refute such philosophers, the Buddha taught the aspect of cessation, the actual achievement of freedom from suffering.

Today, many humanists have no faith in things that they cannot see or prove. If they do not see rebirth, they do not believe in it. Everything has to be proven based on direct experience. Many of us have not yet been to India, but we believe it exists because others have been there. Among the humanists, there is no belief in any inferential logic. Even today, the Buddha's ancient teachings can help to refute these new belief systems, which do not subscribe to karma or rebirth.

## Pacification

The second aspect of the third noble truth is *pacification*. We may practice meditation for any number of reasons. Meditation in the Western world is often used for therapeutic purposes. If we practice according to Herbert Benson, we are practicing to achieve what he calls *relaxation response*. If we practice meditation according to Jon Kabat-Zinn, then the goal of meditation may be mindfulness-based stress reduction. There are many goals for meditation in our current culture.

If we practice shamatha meditation, then maybe we will experience some peace, but this does not mean that our peace is permanent. Even the best shamatha practitioners only achieve good states of awareness and freedom from actively destructive emotions. But shamatha meditation does not free us from underlying emotions.

Often we misunderstand peace as being equivalent to nirvana. But nirvana is an unconditioned state. It is a permanent state. Even if we experience peace for a lifetime, that does not mean that we have reached a state of nirvana.

Nirvana is unconditioned, and it is a permanent state once we achieve it. The aspect of pacification makes it clear that these temporary peaceful experiences of meditation, like states of meditative absorption in the form and formless realms, are not nirvana.

If we are successful in cultivating shamatha meditation, that meditation can help us experience a more peaceful mind. But if that shamatha is not integrated with mindfulness meditation, then when we wake up from that shamatha we are still prone to destructive emotions and suffering. This second aspect—*pacification*—clarifies that those temporary peaceful states achieved in shamatha meditation are not equivalent to nirvana.

According to Buddhist cosmology, gods such as Brahma are part of the form realm. Merit accumulated through acts of love, compassion, joy, and equanimity can help someone to be reborn in the form realm. For this reason they are sometimes called the abodes of Brahma, the *brahmaviharas*.

Someone who has practiced these virtuous qualities without much wisdom, and who has accumulated lots of merit based on such practices, will have a better chance of being reborn in the form and formless realms.

Within Buddhism the form realm is also called the heavenly realm. But that heaven is not a Buddha realm. That heaven has not gone beyond samsara. Those heavenly beings have been reborn there due to merit and positive karma, but still they are missing the wisdom that transcends samsara. They have peace. They have pleasure and happiness. But that peace and happiness is not nirvana. Nirvana is an unconditioned permanent state of cessation.

## IMMACULATE ACCOMPLISHMENT

The third aspect of the third noble truth is *immaculate accomplishment*. This aspect also signifies accomplishment. When we achieve that inner space of nirvana permanently, then that state is immaculate because we have transcended even the causes and conditions of suffering.

This third aspect is also a clarification on formless beings. Yogis who have more merit are reborn in the form realm, the heavenly realm, which we have just discussed. Meditators who are even more accomplished are reborn in the formless realm. But both the form and the formless beings are still not liberated. They are still not beyond samsara.

In the formless realm, beings do not have physical bodies. They do not have pain or pleasure, happiness or unhappiness. They only have neutral mental feelings and very subtle concepts in the mind.

For this reason, meditation is much deeper in the formless realm. It is a state of absorption, free from all active and gross feelings and thoughts. But the mind maintains a level of attention. This state of absorption is also called *samadhi*.

This third aspect of the third noble truth is to clarify that such states of absorption are not nirvana. Even if formless beings were to remain in samadhi for eons, when they emerge from meditation, suffering could still arise, and they could still experience disturbing emotions. This experience of absorption is not an unconditioned state. Only nirvana is immaculate, pure, and unconditioned.


## GOING BEYOND SAMSARA

The fourth aspect of the third noble truth is *going beyond* or *renouncing* samsara. Samsara is the endless cycle of life and death. This cycle of suffering is depicted by the Buddhist image of the wheel of life. Samsara is not limited to our small planet earth. Due to our karma and emotions, we are reborn again and again in the desire, form, and formless realms, throughout countless planetary systems.

Nirvana is when we go beyond these three realms of samsara. It is full renunciation. As long as we experience feelings of any kind, even of profound peace, we are still not in a state of nirvana. Only when our spiritual practice and meditation have the power to go beyond samsara's three realms will we experience the complete cessation of suffering.

Similarly, as long as we have an ego, we cannot go beyond the three realms. Ego causes the emotions of ignorance, attachment, and anger. Out of these root destructive emotions we create so much karma.

Due to interdependency, we are cycling again and again through countless lifetimes. Only when we see the true nature of ego, only when we are egoless, will we be free from destructive emotions. But as long as we are attached to ourselves, we won't have renunciation. Only when we reverse the wheel of life, only when we overcome ignorance through deep meditation, can we achieve nirvana.

The Buddha taught these four aspects of the third noble truth in order to clear away misunderstandings and doubts about nirvana. Nirvana is reached through the noble eightfold path presented in the fourth noble truth.

# 4

# The Fourth Noble Truth:
# The Path

THE FOURTH NOBLE TRUTH is the noble eightfold path. This path leads to self-awakening and ultimately to the cessation of suffering. It offers us eight principal guidelines to live by. These are right view, right intention, right speech, right action, right livelihood, right effort, right mindfulness, and right concentration.

The term *path* in this context has the meaning of realization based on our practice. Generally in Buddhism we refer to five different levels of the path, starting with the path of accumulation that begins when we take refuge. We accumulate merit by doing our practices again and again, whether they are related with meditation, keeping precepts, or based on wisdom trainings.

Part of the path of accumulation is accumulating merit by doing daily practices. By practicing repeatedly, we counteract negative karma and the actions that cause destructive emotions. Through the path we come to the result, which is the state of nirvana we just discussed. So the path starts with the path of accumulation. Second is the path of application.

As our practice becomes stronger and stronger, we can overcome negative actions and destructive emotions more easily.

Within our minds there is always a conflict between positive and
negative emotions and actions. Before we develop a spiritual practice,
our destructive emotions and negative karma are often strongest. These
negative emotions and actions form habitual patterns and determine
our personalities. But once we commit to the spiritual path, our positive karma and positive emotions grow stronger and stronger through
our practice.

The path of application has four different levels. These are heat,
summit, patience, and excellent Dharma. These levels are the measurement of how much merit we have accumulated and how much negative
karma we have burned off and purified.

When our accumulation of merit becomes very strong and we burn
off all our negative karma, we may see a glimpse of selflessness, a glimpse
of emptiness. That glimpse is our entry into the path of seeing. The
noble eightfold path, which is the essential feature of the fourth noble
truth, is part of the realization of the path of seeing.

When a yogi has a glimpse of emptiness, of selflessness, then for the
first time wisdom can arise. That realization can happen only when we
have purified our negative karma and overcome our active destructive
emotions. Only then may we have a glimpse of emptiness.

## THE PATH OF SEEING: A GLIMPSE OF EMPTINESS

The first aspect of the fourth noble truth is the path of seeing emptiness
or selflessness. Based on this insight, we continue to see that emptiness
or selflessness more and more in our meditation.

This glimpse of emptiness gives us profound understanding and faith
in the path. It invigorates our practice since we become absolutely convinced that we can achieve the result, which is nirvana. It also helps us
to overcome any misconceptions and any false belief in a permanent
self.

When Buddhist yogis perceive the truth of selflessness, they become utterly confident that there is no such thing as a permanent self. The nature of the self is selflessness. This is critical, not only philosophically, but also for proving that there is nirvana, which is the cessation of the self.

This cessation of the self includes the cessation of all five aggregates. Even the fifth aggregate, which is the mind or mental consciousness, also ceases.

When all these defiled aggregates cease, then a yogi will not perceive any permanent self. What is realized instead is the wisdom of selflessness. Only wisdom remains.

This is why the noble eightfold path is important. As we have discussed, there are five levels to the path. There are the two worldly levels of accumulation and application and then three noble levels.

When we speak of these levels in the context of the fourth noble truth, we are generally referring to three *noble* levels of the path: the path of seeing, the path of meditation, and the path of no more learning.

The first worldly level, accumulation, is about recognizing the path. This brings us confidence that there is a way forward that can help us realize nirvana. We realize that through the second worldly level of application we can apply Dharma practice and gain insight. This paves the way for the three noble levels of the path.

The spiritual path is not a linear trajectory. Rather, it is a progression through different states of mind. The path is a method to evaluate and guide our realizations.

## APPROPRIATE OR SUITABLE

The second aspect of the fourth noble truth is *appropriate* or *suitable*. Whenever we have a certain realization, this aspect helps us to see what is possible and what is not possible. For example, when we glimpse our own selflessness, then we see that selflessness is possible and that self-clinging is not appropriate.

If we look within the mind, there are things to be abandoned, and there are things to be realized. But all that is still within the mind. When we go beyond the mind, there is not a thing to realize. Even if we study Buddhist psychology according to the two levels of the Abhidharma, such study cannot encompass all the complexities of the mind.

The mind is very intricate and filled with contradictory thoughts and emotions. Love is in the mind. Hate is also in the mind. Both exist, but they are completely opposite. The same is true with jealousy. Jealousy is there, and joy is also there. All the conflicting emotions are there. There are destructive feelings, positive feelings, and neutral feelings.

As we follow the Buddhist path, we begin to understand that spiritual practice helps us to abandon many negative activities and mental states. Through this process of abandonment and renunciation, we start to make space for great realizations to occur.

If we study our mental activities according to the ancient Buddhist texts of the Abhidharma, we will learn that there are ten basic natural activities of the mind that are always present. There are also negative emotions, such as ignorance and attachment, and positive emotions, such as love and compassion.

Buddhist practice relies on cultivating positive emotions. Through focusing on positive emotions, we learn to gradually overcome negative ones. We are working toward uncovering the natural qualities of the mind, which are wisdom and compassion.

So this aspect of *suitability* means that emotions and mental activities are not permanent. They are there to be transformed. Through practice we abandon that which is to be abandoned, and we begin to see the inherent qualities of the mind.

The mind is very complex. We need the mind in order to accomplish our spiritual journey. But ultimately, through practice, we can achieve nirvana, that state in which the mind ceases to exist.

You may wonder what is left after the mind ceases. What is left is wisdom. When we go beyond the mind, then only wisdom remains. This second aspect of suitability or appropriateness informs our practice. As we progress along the spiritual path, we can use this aspect to determine what must be abandoned and what can be achieved.

## ACHIEVING OR ATTAINING

The third aspect of the path is *achieving* or *attaining*. When we talk about achievement in this context, we do not mean achievement on a mental level. What we are really talking about is achievement based on *wisdom*—recognizing the true nature of the mind. As we abandon negative activities and emotional states, we begin to achieve this inherent wisdom.

The second aspect we just discussed—*suitability*—has more to do with method, with the means of accomplishment. But this third aspect, that of *attainment*, is about achieving nirvana. We are practicing in order to achieve freedom from suffering.

When we go beyond the mind, we call this achievement or attainment. But this accomplishment is very different from the way we think of achievement in our ordinary lives. Through abandoning our negative karma and destructive emotions we can discover the very nature of our minds. Uncovering that wisdom is the extraordinary achievement that this third aspect describes.

The four noble truths are primarily taught in the Hinayana tradition of Buddhism. According to this tradition, nirvana is the ultimate accomplishment. However, the four noble truths have also been adopted by the Mahayana and the Vajrayana traditions of Buddhism, in which the ultimate goal is quite different.

The Mahayana tradition puts great emphasis on the bodhisattva path, in which we aim to free not only ourselves but all beings from suffering. We take the bodhisattva vow, by which we promise to continue to take rebirth in order to help others. The ultimate achievement in both Mahayana and Vajrayana is full enlightenment.

Full enlightenment is not the same as nirvana. Nirvana is the accomplishment of wisdom alone. But full enlightenment includes compassion. According to the Mahayana and Vajrayana traditions, enlightenment is the union of both wisdom and compassion.

The results of our practice will be determined by whatever vows we have taken. The Hinayana vow of *pratimoksha* emphasizes self-liberation as the ultimate state. If we take that vow we can achieve liberation in nirvana.

In the Mahayana tradition, we take the bodhisattva vow. We promise to practice for the sake of all sentient beings. Due to this vow we can achieve full enlightenment, the union of wisdom and compassion. But when we achieve full enlightenment, we effortlessly reincarnate in order to continue to help other beings.

Vajrayana practitioners take the samaya vow. But the samaya vow cannot be taken without the pratimoksha and the bodhisattva vows. Vajrayana encompasses all three vows. When we achieve the stage of a *yidam*, a fully enlightened being, then we have the same power to effortlessly manifest to help other sentient beings.

The only differences between the Mahayana and Vajrayana are the methods. Vajrayana offers us more elaborate and varied practice methods than Mahayana does. The resulting enlightenment, however, is basically the same. So this third aspect of the path, the aspect of achievement, will differ based on the Buddhist path we practice and the vows we take.

## LIBERATION OR DELIVERANCE

The fourth aspect of the path is *liberation* or *permanent deliverance*. Through our diligence and practice, the path has the power to deliver us to complete freedom from suffering and the causes of suffering.

The term deliverance in this context also means *cessation*. In this final stage, we go beyond all karma and emotions. The path has the power to free practitioners completely from suffering and the causes of suffering.

# 5

# The Noble Eightfold Path: Right View

WE HAVE ALREADY DISCUSSED the four aspects of the fourth noble truth. Now we will examine the path more closely. The fourth noble truth is the noble eightfold path leading us from suffering. This path has eight factors, which can guide us along the way.

## RIGHT VIEW

The first branch is right view, which is the most important part of the noble eightfold path. It is the most important because right view is related to wisdom which overcomes ignorance. In order to realize right view, however, we have to investigate the wrong view.

The Buddha taught that there are five wrong views. Wrong views are those misconceptions through which our defilements are increased. The first wrong view is seeing the five aggregates as the basis of the self. The first wrong view has a meaning of projecting ego onto the five aggregates. We project some inherent permanence of the self and ego onto these five aggregates of form, feeling, ideation, formation, and consciousness.

### The First Right View: Selflessness of Self and Phenomena

To counter the first wrong view of *satkayadrshti*—the view that there is a real self—the Buddha offered the first right view of the selflessness of oneself and phenomena.

We all cling very strongly to the self and the ego. The Madhyamaka masters emphasized that the source of suffering in samsara is this attachment. They observed that first we cling to the self, and then we cling to all the objects we possess, whatever we call *mine* in our universe. With these two wrong views of *self* and *mine*, we produce strong clinging, and all our destructive emotions increase.

Those who are on the path of seeing and have seen the aspect of emptiness for the first time will see that this clinging to the self and to the five aggregates is only relative. It is not an ultimate truth. We are born with an ego, and we spend much of our lives reinforcing that ego. But those yogis who are on the path of seeing realize that the ego is just a relative projection.

As we look deeper on the path of seeing, we begin to have a glimpse of emptiness for the first time. In this glimpse we realize that what we have projected is only relative; it is not inherently existent. Ultimately we cannot find any permanent self. That is why all these projections reflect wrong views. We begin to realize that ultimately we cannot find any inherent existence in the five aggregates.

If we look for a permanent self in each of the five aggregates, we cannot find any proof. When we study the great teachings of the *Heart Sutra*, we see the nature of the five aggregates. The sutra says, "Form is emptiness. Emptiness is form. Form is not other than emptiness, nor is emptiness other than form."

In this way the sutra breaks down all our assumptions about the five aggregates.

When we look closely at the first aggregate of *form*, from the gross level of the human body right down to the cellular or atomic level, we cannot find the self.

When we look into the second aggregate, that of *feeling*, we also cannot find a self. When we examine the third aggregate of *ideations*, we also cannot see any inherently existing self in all our thoughts.

If we continue on to the fourth aggregate of *formations*, we learn that there are over fifty different kinds of mental activities included in this aggregate. Even if we look into every single one of them, we cannot find any evidence of a self. Even if we look into the mind, into that fifth aggregate of *consciousness*, we cannot find the self or ego.

Now, due to our strong emotions, we become incredibly attached to our sense of self. If we look closely at our lives, we begin to see how much energy we invest in building up and protecting this ego. We are projecting a self, interdependently, based on the five aggregates.

Only through meditation, when we see the emptiness of all five of the aggregates, will we also see the empty nature of the self. Whenever we project a sense of self, it is actually a wrong view. Wrong view entails having emotional attachment to a sense of self in reference to the five aggregates. Buddhists would consider the Hindu belief in a permanent self or *atman* to be a wrong view.

Now, on the other hand, when we see selflessness for the first time, then we understand right view. In order to know what right view is, we need to fully recognize our wrong view. Wrong view includes not only belief in the self but also all our self-references. This includes the objects that we consider to be *ours*. We can only own something if we believe we exist in the first place!

This involvement with our possessions is also based on the five aggregates. This applies to all our attachments, material and mental, related to this idea of mine. We say "my car," "my child," or "my country," and we believe that these exist in relation to ourselves. Until we see the emptiness of all the phenomenal objects, as well as of ourselves, we will still be trapped by our wrong views.

For this reason the Buddha taught the selflessness of the person and

the selflessness of phenomena. Yogis and meditators on the path of seeing recognize the inherent selflessness and emptiness of all things. This
is the first right view.

### The Second Right View: Belief in Karma

To counter the second wrong view of *mithyadrshti*—the misunderstanding of how our world works—we must first examine our misunderstandings related with karma. We may talk about karma all the time,
but there are many misconceptions. We do not see the truth of cause
and result. We often overlook the interdependency between cause and
result on the relative level.

Of course, ultimately things are beyond interdependency. There are
two levels to everything: the relative level and the ultimate level. Every
object has relative interdependency and ultimate emptiness.

Take a bell, for example. A bell has relative interdependency. There
are causes and conditions that produced the bell. But the true nature of
the bell is emptiness. There are two aspects to each object. What we see
depends on how we look at that object and on the level of our meditation experience.

If we do not believe in interdependency on the relative level, then
we do not believe in karma. Not believing in karma cuts the roots of
our virtues and merits. If we do not believe in cause and effect, then we
have no motivation to increase our positive activities. It is vital to our
spiritual practice that we recognize the truth of interdependency in the
relative world.

Without belief in karma, there is a risk that we will become nihilists.
In the Buddha's time, in India, there were some non-Buddhist schools
that did not believe in karma. As a result, they also did not believe in
rebirth. The Buddha discussed karma to counter these misconceptions.

Failure to believe in karma is the second wrong view. We live in the
relative world. We live in interdependency. We must go through interdependency to see emptiness. If we do not believe in interdependency,
then it is unlikely we will realize emptiness. It is also unlikely that we

will cultivate the positive spiritual qualities and merit necessary to gain realization.

Belief in interdependency and karma relates to natural law. If we do not believe in natural law, then there is disharmony on a fundamental level. If we do not believe in karma, we will also not believe in rebirth. If we believe that we are only living for this one lifetime, then we will have very little incentive to accumulate merit or to do virtuous deeds that do not immediately benefit us.

As I have mentioned, the very reason the Charvaka philosophy was developed was to permit people to indulge their appetites and to become more narcissistic. According to that philosophy, then, even killing or stealing is permissible in the pursuit of pleasure. There is no belief in karma. Therefore, the Charvakas have no concern about the consequences of their actions. They believe only in momentary feelings, and in whatever actions will bring them pleasure. The Charvakas are known to be the most narcissistic philosophers. The Buddha taught the second right view to overcome such ignorance regarding karma.

### The Third Right View: Freedom from Extreme Views

To counter the third wrong view of *antagrahadrshti*, which refers to having an extreme outlook, we can use our understanding of the interdependency of the relative world to see the ultimate truth of emptiness. Using emptiness to understand that we live in interdependency in a relative world is also a right view. Only through truly understanding relativity can we see emptiness.

This is why we have to accumulate merit and perform the preliminary practices known as *ngöndro*. Ngöndro practices are focused on karma. We perform them to accumulate good karma and to purify negative karma. The ultimate aim of these practices is to go beyond karma altogether and see emptiness.

The third wrong view refers to having extreme views about our own conclusions. If we have concluded, through study and analysis, that our philosophical stance is superior, then we become attached to that conclusion. It is wrong to believe that our ideas are the best. This is the fundamental problem at the root of religious extremism and fanaticism. Terrible atrocities have been committed throughout history based on the belief that "My god is better than your god." Many wars have been fought to defend the belief that "My view is the best."

We can find these extremes in religion and within various philosophical schools. In Indian and Tibetan Buddhism, we find four main philosophies: Vaibhashika, Sautrantika, Mind-Only, and Madhyamaka. Each one of these philosophical stances can lead a philosopher to an extremist position. This is a danger within all Tibetan traditions. There are many debates among philosophers, and these philosophers often have decided that their conclusions are the best.

This is also a great danger for Buddhist scholars. This intellectual attachment to particular views can often be a huge impediment to meditation practice. This kind of extremism may help to spread knowledge and scholarship, but it can be counterproductive to spiritual practice. The purpose of Buddhist scholarship is threefold: first to study, next to reflect, and then to practice. Practice must free us from extremism and liberate us from clinging.

Now, if we are clinging to the very method that we are using to liberate ourselves, then that is one of the worst forms of attachment. It can prevent us from achieving any kind of true realization.

Sometimes the best scholars have the biggest egos. This is true in religion and in academia. If scholars have not used that knowledge to transform themselves, if they have not seen the wisdom within all the ideas they have collected, then there is very little growth and realization. They become trapped by their own intellects.

This is why we have so much fighting over "isms." We see this conflict between religions and between communism and capitalism. All these isms have something to do with coming to a particular conclusion.

If we become very attached to a particular conclusion, then there is the potential to become extreme. We can become extreme in our views based on either eternalism or nihilism.

Within theistic religion, eternalism can be a great danger. This is where we find views like "My god is the supreme god. My god is the best." We bring god into the realm of our own egos, projecting a sense of ownership over god.

As a result, we find any opposing view to be a direct threat. This is how we decide that "My god is the only god. Your god is the bad one." We are fighting over God. Would God really want it that way? We lower God to our level, and basically this becomes a fight of the ego.

The Buddha warned us against extreme views. Of course, even atheism can become an extreme. Recently, I saw a news story about humanists in New York who paid for a billboard in an Orthodox Jewish neighborhood and wrote on it in Hebrew saying something to the effect of "Your God is just a myth." These same humanists also bought a billboard in New Jersey and wrote a similar message in Arabic, insulting Muslims. So we see that even humanists can fall into extremes.

If we are attached to "our" God, we fail to realize that we do not know who God really is until we become enlightened. Until then our egos turn the notion of God into something fixed and rigid, and we may even fight with others over our understanding of God.

So eternalism is a wrong view. Nihilism is also a wrong view. This absence of belief in anything is equally extreme. Within any of the Buddhist philosophies, if someone thinks their view is the only *right* one, then in reality it is a wrong view. Tibetans think they have the highest and best Buddhist philosophy in the form of Madhyamaka. Within the highest forms of Madhyamaka, Tibetan scholars debate which conclusion is the best, arguing between *self-emptiness*, *other-emptiness*, and *emptiness free from the four extremes*. This argument has lasted for many centuries, and it still continues today.

Scholars cling to their own views. Those who believe in other-emptiness think they are the best. Those who explain emptiness according to freedom from the four extremes think they are the best. It is an ongoing argument. But the great yogis—the great meditators—are focused on their practice and do not worry about these arguments. Such yogis who are gaining realization on the path of seeing realize that ultimate reality is free from all the extremes.

The Buddha reiterated again and again that wisdom is inexpressible. Wisdom is beyond words, beyond expression. Most of the time we will fall into extremes the moment we try to express wisdom through words. If we read the sutras, we even find contradictions in the Buddha's teachings. This is a result of the Buddha teaching to a particular audience at a particular time. He would teach in a way that was most appropriate to those in attendance.

That is why there were said to be three turnings of the wheel. This was a graduated path, designed to lead people slowly toward some understanding. The Buddha knew that if he explained emptiness to people who had no other Buddhist foundation, then the truth of emptiness could be very shocking and terrifying. The Buddha realized that people might even become too frightened to practice.

That is why the Buddha's teachings lead us step by step. But when describing ultimate reality, the Buddha said that it is free from all extremes. We cannot express this ultimate reality, but it is something we can realize through great practice.

For those who have realized ultimate reality, that wisdom cannot be expressed. Understanding freedom from the four extremes is the best reference we can have for that experience. But that reference alone cannot give us direct experience of ultimate reality. Only meditation can offer us this realization of wisdom. Clinging to any of the four extremes of existence, nonexistence, both, or neither is the third wrong view.

### The Fourth Right View: Not Esteeming Our Own Spiritual Practices and Disciplines as Supreme

To counter the fourth wrong view of *shilavrataparamarsha*—esteeming one's own spiritual practices as superior to all others—we should be careful not to cling to any of our practices as being supreme. Whether we have taken pratimoksha vows, bodhisattva vows, or samaya vows, we must be very careful not to think that our approaches are the best.

Practice and discipline should be methods used to go beyond our emotions. But if we get too attached to our methods, then they will not liberate us. There are many cautionary stories about such attachments.

This is something for Buddhists who are doing a daily *sadhana* practice. When doing our sadhana, why do we do the generation stage practice? After reciting the mantra, why do we then do the completion stage practice and engage in meditation beyond thought? Why can't we just stay in that deity's form? We have to go beyond that subtle attachment to the divine and to the form of the deity we are practicing. That is why we must do the completion practice. If we get too attached to the method and to the deity, then that method can strengthen our ego. Instead of helping us to become liberated, our practice can bind us. That is how it can become a wrong view. We will never realize the path of seeing if we are too attached to our practices.

### The Fifth Right View: Not Esteeming Our Own Conclusions or Views as Supreme

To counter the fifth wrong view of *drshtiparamarsha*—esteeming our views as supreme—one should not think of one's own conclusions or views as being superior to all others. One Tibetan scholar said something interesting. He said, "In the end, we become extremists because we draw philosophical conclusions based on our extreme attachments, which are rooted in the ego." This implies that no matter how much we study and practice, until we are enlightened, we will only have limited understanding, and thus we will still fall into an extreme.

Knowledge is based on ego. That is why knowledge is not wisdom. We understand these philosophies at the level of our egos, and then we become attached to those views. Then we use the philosophies of Tibetan and Indian masters and of the Buddha himself to substantiate our views, but none of this is based on our own realization.

When scholars engage in academic research, they sometimes talk about uncovering "original" truths related to the Buddha's teachings. But how original are these truths? Their research is based on ego more than on enlightened wisdom.

Intellectual study is based on relative information and knowledge. We present some new findings, and then we believe that what we have done is authentic and original. But none of these academic findings is based on wisdom. They are based on research into the material, relative world and on synthesizing information from various places. So our own attachment to a conclusion can be a wrong view.

We have to recognize the five wrong views in order to correct them. Through our meditation practices we move beyond the paths of accumulation and application to reach that third path, the path of seeing. It is on this third path that we see these views are wrong, and for the first time we have a glimpse of the right view. This is called the noble view because for the first time we have achieved some realization on the path of seeing.

Until then, these five views may be very intellectual, and they may be very well researched; we may contemplate them rigorously, but they still are not noble because they are tainted with the ego, and they have the potential to increase our defilements.

Only after we reach the path of seeing do these views become noble. Now our seeing has the power to defy not only the active destructive emotions but also those latent or "sleeping" destructive emotions. For the first time we will truly understand this first and most important branch of the noble eightfold path, the branch of right view.

# 6

## The Noble Eightfold Path: Right Intention and Right Speech

RIGHT INTENTION IS the second branch of the noble eightfold path. Intention is very important. Intention in combination with volition is the beginning of all karma and all action. Intention starts in the mind, and then through volition that intention becomes connected with an object. This is how our intentions become active.

As long as we are in samsara, we have not seen the path of seeing or beyond it. We still struggle with the three root afflictive emotions of desire, anger, and ignorance. Even when we are feeling peaceful and content, those destructive emotions still remain as underlying emotions in our consciousness. The fact that we are not actively engaged in a destructive emotion does not imply that it is not present in our subconscious and capable of arising at the slightest provocation. Many of the views we hold in high esteem are still wrong views when we examine them in depth.

When we investigate this second branch of the noble eightfold path, we realize that underlying anger resides in us constantly, even when we are not actively experiencing it. Underlying anger is activated when our wrong intention becomes volition. We direct that anger toward our enemy or toward some object.

Intention has two potentialities. It can be wrong or right, depending on how it arises. Intention is related to mental karma or mental activities, which we call *semjung* in Tibetan.

If we look within the mind, we begin to see that the mind has many mental activities. Some scholars translate these activities as emotions. But the Sanskrit word is *chaitta*, stemming from the word *chitta*, which we translate as "mind."

Mind is a general word we use for what is actually a composite of many different activities. These activities can be divided into three categories of positive, negative, and neutral mental activities. In the higher Abhidharma teachings there are fifty-one mental activities described. In the lower Abhidharma there are forty-six mental activities.

Mind is not just one single independent entity. It is composed of many factors. Due to volition, mental activities are activated. Through volition our anger becomes directed to an object that we consider to be an enemy. When this occurs, we may feel like our entire mind is anger. But that anger is also closely related to desire.

Anger arises because there is also an element of desire operating. Maybe the person we do not like, who has now become our enemy, is somehow obstructing our desire and depriving us of what we want. Ignorance is also present in anger. But when the dominant afflictive emotion is anger, we may only recognize that one emotion.

Overcoming anger is one of the primary right intentions. There are many spiritual practices designed to help us overcome anger. Developing bodhichitta and loving-kindness can be a great antidote to anger. An angry mind is always activated to harm someone or something through speech or physical actions. Meditations on love and compassion, and especially cultivating bodhichitta, can help us to generate positive emotions toward others.

*Harming* refers to the physical or mental suffering we create. *Helping* is defined by how much happiness and pleasure we can bring to another being. The Buddhist understanding is that as long as we have love, compassion, and bodhichitta, then we are helping others to feel more happiness and to develop the causes of happiness.

On the other hand, when we do not develop these positive qualities, we continue to experience hate instead of love. We will feel passion instead of compassion. Without the cultivation of bodhichitta, we experience self clinging. These negative emotions of hate, passion, and self-clinging create tremendous conflict between ourselves and others.

As long as our egos are not fulfilled, we will want to harm others because they are not letting us have what we want. This is why taking the bodhisattva vow is so important to our spiritual transformation. The bodhisattva vow helps us to correct our intention and motivation.

If we do not make a strong resolution like taking the bodhisattva vow, then our intention remains harmful. We may not recognize this because it is so subtle. But if we are attached to ourselves, we will continue to be competitive and to place our own desires above others.

That attachment to the self will extend the territory of the ego further and further into the universe. In some sense, everything becomes a threat to our sense of self. When this egotistical attitude reaches an extreme, we see people in power willing to kill thousands and destroy whole countries in order to extend their territory. This is a magnification of the ego and anger. The Buddha gave us practices like bodhichitta to counter these wrong intentions.

Whatever practice we undertake has to start with the mind and mental activities. This is especially true about right intention. When we can overcome our anger in the mind, we can generate right intention. Right intention is the beginning of all wholesome karma. Wrong intention, based on anger, is the root of all harmful activities.

## The Importance of Taking Precepts and Vows

Taking resolutions and honoring precepts is a vital antidote to wrong intention. The term *path* has a meaning of practice and transformation.

Transformation must take place at the very core. Making resolutions helps us to correct our motivation on the deepest level.

Most of the time we are not aware of our underlying emotions. If we are not actively experiencing anger, we may deny that we have any anger at all. But anger still exists silently in our minds. If we take the precept of overcoming any negative actions, this helps us to counteract the roots of anger in the mind.

The physical and mental precepts we take are disciplines. How quickly these disciplines serve as antidotes to negative emotions depends on the strength of our habitual patterns.

If we are people who are used to expressing anger and being violent, then when we take a precept not to kill, it may be very challenging at first. These habitual patterns of anger are as strong as any other addiction in the mind. If we are addicted to alcohol or drugs, then when we make resolutions to quit those addictions, it will be extremely challenging in the beginning.

In the case of alcohol, repeated intoxication has created a systemic dependency. When we first deprive the body of this substance, it may be very uncomfortable. Even if we try to detox from caffeine, the withdrawal may give us a terrible headache and make us exhausted.

The discomfort of detox is a result of how these substances have become part of our entire physical bodies. In a similar way, when we first try to overcome the destructive emotion of anger, we may be surprised by the strength of that habitual pattern. It is very difficult to begin cleansing our minds of that addiction.

## OVERCOMING ANGER, DESIRE, AND IGNORANCE

When we operate in certain ways for years and years, our habitual patterns become so strong that we mistake them for our personalities. We may start to believe that we are wired to have a short temper. We may claim that we are just emotional and passionate by nature.

If we do anything with enough repetition, we begin to believe it is a fixed personality trait. These negative habitual patterns become mental addictions very easily. We begin to believe that this is naturally who we are and that it is not in our control to change.

Most of the Buddhist precepts we take are to counteract these patterns of thought and action. In the beginning this may feel like an artificial repression of emotion, but eventually these antidotes will begin to break down the roots of our underlying emotions.

Although our experience of active anger may seem like the most challenging emotion to overcome, it is actually the subtle, underlying anger that is hardest to uproot. Active anger exists because we have underlying aggression deep down in our minds. When we can begin to access these more subtle levels of emotion, we can break down the root causes of this anger.

It is vital that we honor our precepts and vows. This discipline is essential to the work of deep transformation. Overcoming anger is a vital component of right intention.

The other important aspect of cultivating right intention is overcoming desire. As we have discussed, anger and desire depend on each other. We become angry when our desire is not fulfilled. When we do not get something we want, or when something threatens our egos, we have pain and anger. These emotions are all mixed together.

As long as we have underlying ignorance, we also will be subject to all five of the wrong views discussed in the previous chapter. Although ignorance is the most difficult sleeping emotion to recognize because it is so subtle, it is still considered a primary cause.

Overcoming ignorance is also included in right intention. When we take precepts, we are correcting three unwholesome or nonvirtuous mental actions. The first is coveting, which is related to desire. The second is possessing a harmful mind, which is related to anger. The third is holding a wrong view, which is related to ignorance. These are the three fundamental wrong intentions that the precepts aim to correct.

This second branch of the noble eightfold path is primarily concerned with ways to overcome the harmful mind of anger and its corresponding emotion of desire. Overcoming desire is central, especially because we humans are living in the desire realm, and everything we consume is based on attachment.

If we examine our feelings of happiness and pleasure, we realize we are often operating with a very conflicting message here in the desire realm. We may say that we act virtuously in order to experience happiness and pleasure, but even that intention is not pure. It is still relative. That happiness and pleasure seeking is rooted in feelings of desire and self-clinging.

## The Importance of Renunciation

If our virtuous activities are focused on attaining happiness and pleasure, then that result is not perfect. When we look closely, we see that pleasure always becomes the cause of future desire. Since that pleasure is not permanent, the minute it fades we have a strong desire to experience it again.

Momentary happiness becomes the cause and condition of more desire. The more we consume, the more our appetite grows here in the desire realm. This is the reason why the resolution of renunciation is so strongly emphasized in Buddhist practice. Renunciation is key to overcoming our desires.

In the graduated path, whether it is in Hinayana, Mahayana, or Vajrayana Buddhist practices, renunciation is essential. Why is renunciation so important? Because renunciation is our first step toward gaining some freedom from desire.

If we examine the vows, from the first precept we take of not killing right up to full ordination vows, which include some two hundred and fifty precepts, we can understand why the Buddha developed such complex ethics of renunciation. Renunciation is the essential method to counteract desire.

Desire creates many challenges in our meditation practice. As soon as we want to focus on one object of meditation, a desirable object immediately shows up in our minds instead.

When our desire is not fulfilled, we become angry or irritable. Desire obscures our ability to see reality clearly. As long as we have desire, we never see the true nature of an object. We will romanticize one object; we will reject another object. We will bring all these conflicting emotions into our meditation practices, and they will obscure our vision.

Cultivating renunciation is essential in our practice. This is the reason why we take all these precepts. The precepts are presented in terms of renunciation: no killing, no stealing, and so on. We are trying to stay away from those activities. We are trying to refrain from those actions and those emotions. Once we have taken the precepts, then each time we refrain from a negative activity, we are actually cultivating positive qualities.

If we are used to doing something all the time, like drinking or smoking, then abstaining from it will be very difficult. Right intention begins with renunciation. If we are on the Mahayana path, then we also take the bodhisattva vow and cultivate love and compassion for the sake of all sentient beings.

## Right Intention and Karma

Right intention is important because it is the beginning of all karma. Karma is multidimensional and very complex. Karma starts with our intention and volition. If we change our intention, then we begin to transform our karma.

For a yogi who has reached the path of seeing, the intention is noble because it is free from both anger and desire. At this point the yogi has experienced real wisdom. Once we have experienced wisdom, we have overcome ignorance, and most of our actions will become noble.

Right now, our actions cannot be called noble because our intentions are shaded by ignorance. If we examine the five wrong views closely and reflect on our own personal views, we will begin to see that what we thought were right views actually still arose from ignorance.

Right view and right intention, as a practice, help us to overcome the root mental negativities of ignorance, anger, and desire. Ignorance by itself, anger by itself, and desire by itself are not karma. But when they are drawn toward an object by intention and volition in the mind, they become action. This action is harmful when it is rooted in the afflictive emotions and then it becomes part of our karma.

We need to make the distinction between emotions and actions. It is important to examine them separately, as well as to look at what happens when they are combined. The Buddha's teachings help us to better understand how and why we are acting and feeling in certain ways.

Often, when we do things, we limit our actions only to verbal and physical levels of expression. We usually do not look deeper to see the roots of our intentions. Intentions are often overwhelming and blinding to us. Intention is the root of action. When defilements and emotions are directed toward objects by volition, then they become karma.

These first two branches of the noble eightfold path are related to mental actions. They describe right mental actions and offer insight into overcoming wrong mental actions. Buddhist practice involves taking vows and precepts to counteract destructive emotions and their causes.

## RIGHT SPEECH

The third branch of the noble eightfold path is right speech. In order to understand right speech, we have to learn how to overcome wrong speech. The Buddha taught four categories of wrong speech.

### Idle Chatter

The first category is idle chatter. This means useless trivial talk that is devoid of meaning. This chatter arises from unfiltered thoughts and concepts. If we have a lot of inner chatter inside our own minds, we may feel the need to express it verbally. This expression may give us some relief.

Some psychologists at Harvard conducted a study. They determined that talking on the phone makes people happier. Maybe this happiness is due to the fact that when we are talking, we forget about ourselves. Maybe this distraction makes us feel better.

But trivial conversations do not do anything fundamentally transformative. Useless chatter is like watching an entertaining movie. It is just another way of trying to forget or deny other feelings by distracting ourselves. So while it may be temporarily enjoyable, idle conversation is actually a waste of our energy.

The Buddha preferred to practice meditation. He maintained a noble silence. That is why his name was Shakyamuni. *Muni* means "silent one."

Generally we meditate in silence because it helps to quiet the chattering inside us. Talking activates certain parts of the brain that may not be conducive to meditation. Even if we talk a lot during times when we are not practicing, this could still have a lasting effect on the quality of our mind.

Idle talk is considered wrong speech because it is just a waste of our effort. Useless chatter becomes the source of lots of emotions and concepts. Often we speak before we think, and this can be harmful to others. Talking gets us into a lot of trouble! Talking also includes so much affirming and negating that we are led into extreme ways of thinking.

There is a story about the Buddha that illustrates this point. Once some hunters were chasing a deer, and they came upon the Buddha. They asked him where the deer went. He maintained his noble silence. If he mentioned the truth of where the deer went, then the hunters would kill the deer. But he also could not lie. By maintaining silence, he avoided creating any negative karma.

Another example is the famous fourteen questions that the Buddha didn't answer. This was not necessarily because he didn't know the answers. It had more to do with the fact that he knew that regardless of whether he answered "yes" or "no," he might somehow lead the questioner toward wrong conclusions.

Talking gives rise to many emotions in ourselves and in others. If we can try to talk less and maintain that noble silence, we will experience more peace.

In order to counteract this form of wrong speech, we can strive to have meaningful conversations and to only speak when it is necessary and useful. We can choose silence instead of trivial chatter.

### Lying

Lying is another form of wrong speech. The obvious antidote to lying is to always tell the truth. But karma is still in the realm of relativity. It is not a perfection. For this reason there are exceptions where telling the truth can be too harmful.

Only when we are like the Buddha will we know what is truly helpful. If lying brings pain and suffering, then we must counteract that by telling the truth.

### Harsh Speech and Deceptive Speech

A third action we must avoid is harsh speech. The Buddha always emphasized speaking gently. Speaking harshly actually increases anger, and it can be very harmful to others. Speaking gently is very important to maintaining right speech.

The fourth action to avoid is speaking deceptively. Deception here has a meaning of misleading others. We may inflate some story to benefit ourselves. Saying things with the intention of personal gain, whether it is fame, power, attention, or wealth, is all considered deceptive speech.

### Right Speech and the Ten Nonvirtues

The path of right speech helps us overcome negative karma that is motivated by destructive emotions. Right speech means avoiding all four types of wrong speech. The four types of wrong speech are included in the natural law of the ten nonvirtues.

The ten nonvirtues include three mental nonvirtues, three physical nonvirtues, and the four verbal nonvirtues we have just discussed. The fact that speech has the greatest number of nonvirtues attached to it is a reflection of how much karma is produced by our verbal actions. Our karma is primarily created through our speech.

The extent to which physical actions affect others is fairly limited. This is because the target of those physical actions must be close by to feel the effects. Speech can reach much further than physical actions, and as a result it can create more karma.

We can call someone who lives in India on the telephone, and we can yell at them or lie. We can be deceptive or speak harshly. But it is hard for us to hit someone in India from here! Speech, however, is very powerful. So that is why there are four nonvirtues that involve speech.

We need to maintain right speech for as long as we can. The more meditation we do, and the more we maintain a noble silence, the better chance there is that all four negative aspects of speech can be overcome. Most of our social interactions are based on speech. The more we can pray or chant or meditate, the more we can counteract these four aspects of wrong speech.

We have now discussed the first three branches of the noble eightfold path. These include right view, right intention, and right speech. We have covered all the wrong actions related with the mind and all the wrong actions related with speech.

# 7

# The Noble Eightfold Path: Right Action and Right Livelihood

## RIGHT ACTION

THE FOURTH BRANCH of the noble eightfold path is right action. When we refer to an action, such as killing, this includes not only the killing of humans but also the killing of any other sentient beings, even the smallest insect.

As a society we presume killing always has to do with anger. But the fact is we probably kill more from desire and ignorance. We have created an entire meat industry out of our desire for certain foods. In prehistoric times, we would hunt for just enough food to feed ourselves, but the modern world is very different.

Once I met someone who worked at a chicken slaughterhouse. He told me that every day the company kills millions of chickens. When the market was opened to China, the killing greatly intensified. The company exported massive amounts of chicken meat to China. When we watch documentaries about the food industry, we understand that this era's killing has extended far beyond what it once was. Today we have the corporate, industrialized killing of great numbers of sentient beings.

One of my lama friends from New York sent me a video of how pigs are raised and traded. It would be hard to eat pork again after watching that suffering. When we sit down to eat at our tables, we rarely think of where the meat comes from and of how inhumane the conditions were for those poor, abused animals.

Right action is not just about action related to humans. Right action is also about how we treat animals and other beings. We kill many beings through our desire and ignorance.

Right action has to do with overcoming our wrong actions toward humans and all sentient beings. These wrong actions, such as killing, can arise from any or all of the three destructive emotions of desire, anger, and ignorance. But regardless of which destructive emotions are involved, killing is wrong as far as karmic law is concerned. Karmic law has nothing to do with the laws of a particular country.

Even within Buddhism, depending on our practice and on how many precepts we have taken, there are different consequences. But as far as natural law is concerned, any actions we do based on destructive emotions are considered wrong actions.

Wrong action is not just related with other sentient beings. Wrong actions can also be related to things. For example, a wrong action would be to misuse something that is not ours. It is also possible to commit wrong actions with objects that we possess.

Right action involves finding some kind of middle path. The Buddha's life is a good example of finding a middle path. For six years the Buddha lived as an ascetic. He starved himself and meditated. But this strict discipline and deprivation did not allow for very high levels of realization. At the end of his sixth year, a girl from the nearby village offered him some rice pudding. When the Buddha tasted the rice pudding his meditation experience became stronger. In this moment he recognized that it is better to maintain a middle way on the spiritual path.

We cannot become too extreme in our actions. Even if we own something, we should be careful not to misuse it. Most actions are expressions of emotion. If our expressions serve to increase our destructive emotions, we need to change how we relate to an object. If we deprive ourselves of something, and if our minds are not strong, then this can increase our pain and generate more anger.

Deprivation can create many emotions for people who are poor. If you do not have many material things, if your basic needs are not being met, then deep down you can carry resentment toward those who are wealthy. We see these class struggles throughout history.

On the other hand, if we are indulging too much, then that indulgence can make us more narcissistic. Our appetites can become insatiable. We are always craving more. Neither extreme will bring us to the middle way.

This fourth branch of the noble eightfold path shows us that whatever action increases our destructive emotions is potentially a wrong action. And whatever actions help us to overcome our destructive emotions will have the potential to increase positive things.

How we own things and what we own are also part of right action. This is very controversial. As a developed society, we have developed a sense of entitlement based on artificial systems. These systems do not have any intrinsic value. The value is only projected.

The only intrinsic value is what is directly related to sustaining our lives. We place a great deal of importance on money, as if that alone were keeping us alive. But without air, earth, water, energy, or soil, money would be worthless. Money does not actually keep us alive. If we cannot breathe, then no matter how much money we have, we cannot live. But our entire society is based on artificial projections of value. Society has convinced us that we need many things.

The former prime minister of Malaysia, Dr. Mohamad Mahathir, is a great economist. Recently I watched an interview with him on the BBC. He said that our present economic system is just high-stakes gambling. The stock market deals with billions of dollars every day, but nothing is really being produced through the stock exchange. Traders are buying and selling, but there is nothing tangible to show for this. It is all just numbers and projected values.

Dr. Mahathir said that as long as we keep on doing this, our economy will be at risk. It is all just legalized gambling. He suggested that everyone who is trading like that needs to produce something instead. Then, according to what is produced, they should get a return. They can live on such a return. Otherwise, if we try to live based on gambling, then someday we may lose everything. We have already seen Wall Street suffer major losses in the past.

This leads us to the topic of stealing. If we look into it more deeply, we come to understand that we are stealing whenever we use something that we do not own. Even if we own something but misuse it and waste it, then in some sense we are depriving others of these resources. With every liter of gas we use, we are essentially taking the earth's energy.

If we look closely at our consumption of food or our use of material things or resources, it is important to connect that consumption with cultivating positive emotions. Every time we eat, we should bring some purpose to why we are eating.

A Buddhist food offering prayer says very clearly, "I'm not eating this food out of desire, anger, ego, or pride. I'm eating just to sustain my physical body with the essence and nutrients my body requires so that I can practice and perform positive deeds."

We should learn to approach everything we do in our lives with this clarity of purpose. If we have altruistic goals, then there is more justification for our use of resources. Otherwise, if we are living just to eat, then what is the difference between humans and animals?

Sakya Pandita states in his *Elegant Sayings* that wild animals spend their whole day looking for something to eat. They are just focused on basic survival. So what is the difference between animals and humans? There is no difference if we too are living only to consume. But if we live so that we can do something beneficial for ourselves and others, then we are engaging in right action. Right action includes our attitude toward all the things we consume.

Another important aspect of right action is how we act in our interpersonal relationships. How we conduct ourselves with regard to others is incredibly important. If our relationships are based on strong destructive emotions like anger and desire, then we can become obsessed or aggressive. Good relationships depend on how many positive qualities of mind we bring to one another. Qualities such as love, compassion, and forgiveness have far more potential to create and sustain positive relationships.

Right action includes all physical actions. We try to bring positive emotions and awareness into everything we engage with through our senses. Whether it is what we look at, what we hear, what we smell, or what we eat, we try to bring positive qualities to this experience. In essence, right action has to do with how we conduct ourselves physically in relation to all sentient beings and to all objects.

## RIGHT LIVELIHOOD

The fifth branch of the noble eightfold path is right livelihood. The Buddha specifically described four wrong livelihoods.

The first wrong livelihood is selling intoxicants like alcohol or drugs because these increase our ignorance. Intoxication can deprive people of their mindfulness, their attention, and their conscious discrimination of what is right and wrong. For this reason, selling intoxicants is actually one of the most dangerous livelihoods.

I am not sure why people drink so much. Sometimes when people are depressed they drink. Sometimes it seems like a cultural thing. Cultures can promote drinking as a part of their social fabric. In Tibet they drink this home-brewed drink called *chang*. For many, chang is a source of enjoyment and festivity. It helps people celebrate together or forget their pain and suffering. But slowly it becomes the cause of many other problems, and we see an increase in addiction.

Drugs are also very harmful. Engaging in selling drugs is a wrong livelihood because drugs completely cloud a person's mind. Drug users lose the ability to discriminate between what is right and what is wrong. There are many drug-induced crimes.

The second wrong livelihood that the Buddha described is that of being a butcher. Any worker in a modern slaughterhouse could be said to have wrong livelihood. The more meat eaters there are, the greater the demand for meat will be. We essentially create more killers.

Killing is taking another life forcefully. Due to that unnatural death, there is so much pain. Why does someone become a butcher? And why does that person kill? There is desire involved, even if it is just for material gain—just for a paycheck. The killing of animals or any sentient beings produces very heavy karma.

The third wrong livelihood that the Buddha described is dealing in the manufacture and sale of weapons. In the Buddha's time that likely just pertained to bows and arrows and cruder weapons. These days weapons have become massively destructive. Nuclear bombs have the potential to destroy the planet, so dealing in weapons is very destructive. It creates lethal karma by inflicting so much pain and suffering.

The fourth wrong livelihood that the Buddha described was the trafficking of humans, whether in the slave trade, or for prostitution, or for any kind of abuse of human rights. This produces incredibly heavy karma as well.

Right livelihood should be something that is ethical, humane, and that cultivates positive qualities within us and within others. Any livelihood that cultivates more destructive emotions in ourselves and others is considered wrong.

Now there are also more subtle types of wrong livelihood. Teachers, for example, have to be very careful. My teacher used to say, "If you become a teacher and an object of faith, then people will make offerings to you. If you misuse those offerings, then that produces very heavy karma."

The Buddha said in a sutra, "If people offer something to you out of faith, and you misuse that offering, that is such heavy karma to digest that you will need steel teeth to chew those offerings!"

Any livelihood we have that is beneficial for us and beneficial for others is right livelihood. Whenever a livelihood becomes harmful to oneself and others, then that is a wrong livelihood. These are the aspects that those on the spiritual path have to attend to.

Generally, in the Buddhist understanding, being more harmonious with the natural law of karma will bring more harmony with nature, and as a result there will be more peace.

Many of these aspects, even in the way we live, are regulated by government statutes. These statutes are not necessarily ethical, but most of the time ethics are incorporated into the state and federal laws. So generally we need to follow these laws unless they openly oppose our spiritual ethical vows and precepts.

Taking precepts does not necessarily force us to do something good. Taking precepts is a way of creating good ethical protection through natural laws. As a byproduct, these can offer us protection from legal laws. For example, drinking may be legal, but driving drunk is highly illegal. Through our precepts of refraining from drinking, we automatically protect ourselves from breaking the laws against drunk driving.

Even though we take the precepts, we are still human, and sometimes we make mistakes. However, we have many confessional and purificatory practices to correct our motivation and renew our vows.

There are general confession practices, and in the higher teachings we have Vajrasattva purification practices. It is always better to take the precepts, even if we sometimes make mistakes. It is better that we make the resolution to become stronger, even if we sometimes fail along the way and need to recommit ourselves.

Taking precepts is important and beneficial. Taking the precepts helps us to act better. All the pratimoksha vows are designed as antidotes and guidelines. Right view and right intention are related to mental actions. Right speech is related with verbal action. Right action and right livelihood are related with physical action.

The noble eightfold path has been perfected by those yogis who have seen the path of seeing. We are not at that level yet. We still need to admit that we have many wrong views, wrong intentions, wrong actions, and wrong habits of speech. And then we have to apply the antidotes for how to correct them. Taking the vows and making positive resolutions are fundamental to creating this transformation.

8

# The Noble Eightfold Path: Right Effort

Right effort is the sixth branch of the noble eightfold path. Right effort can also be translated as right diligence. To know this noble path, we have to reflect upon the previous five elements of the eightfold path. Right effort is about integrating those elements into our lives.

This was also true of right view. We have to know what the wrong views are in order to understand what right view means. In a similar way, it is important to understand all the other elements of the eightfold path in order to practice right effort.

As we have discussed, right view and right intention are related with mental actions and mental karma. Right view is connected to right intention because our view affects our thoughts. Intention starts in the mind.

## The Three Forms of Wrong Mental Karma

There are three forms of wrong mental karma: wrong views, the harmful mind, and coveting. Those are related to the three fundamental destructive emotions of ignorance, desire, and anger.

Ignorance is related to wrong views. Even if we have cultivated a lot of intellectual ideas, if our conclusions are wrong, they are still part of ignorance. Desire and anger are related to wrong intentions. A state of mind that is desirous, harmful, or coveting arises from wrong thoughts or mental actions. When we are free from these destructive emotions, we will have right view and right intention.

## RIGHT EFFORT

In contemplating right effort, it is important to remember all the aspects of wrong speech: lying, idle chatter, and harsh words. We must also remember all the wrong actions and wrong livelihoods.

Right effort means increasing our right activities on all three levels: mentally, verbally, and physically. We increase our right effort at the mental level when we cultivate the right thoughts. We increase our right effort at the verbal level when we strive to cultivate right speech. Finally, we act with right effort at the physical level when we perform the right deeds.

The Sanskrit word for right effort is *virya*. Virya is part of the practice of the six perfections, and it has a deeper meaning. It implies that enthusiasm for wholesome activities is considered to be right effort. Whenever we engage diligently in positive activities, we help to free ourselves at the mental, verbal, and physical levels.

Right effort is essential to the process of transformation. This happens at an individual level. Whether we will enjoy wholesome activities depends on our habitual patterns. If we have been enjoying all the wrong activities, then we have created habits that are hard to break.

For example, if someone has become a pathological liar, it will be very difficult for that person to avoid lying. Or when people have engaged in killing for long periods of time, they can become very cold hearted. They may not even feel anything when they kill.

These negative patterns become entrenched in us. How long have we been thinking certain thoughts? How are we accustomed to speaking, and what are our physical tendencies? According to these habitual patterns, our personalities will be formed. At a certain point we may even believe that these personalities are our true nature. When we first try to counteract these tendencies, it may be very challenging and stressful.

For example, the first time we meditate can be physically and mentally painful! Our minds are not used to a meditative state. We are met with a waterfall of feelings and inner chattering. Our bodies may be restless and uncomfortable when we first try to sit still. In order to transform ourselves, we need to begin with right effort.

How do we cultivate the energy to meditate? Most of our enthusiasm is cultivated based on what we enjoy doing. If we like doing something, we will sacrifice everything to pursue it. We may even risk our lives to get to the top of the Himalayas or to travel deep into the oceans, and yet it may be difficult to cultivate an interest in meditation.

How do we create the energy to do wholesome things? This is our challenge. If we are used to engaging in unwholesome activities— engaging in wrong speech and negative deeds—then how can we make that shift?

Meeting a teacher is critical to beginning that transformation. We have to meet a guru or mentor with whom we feel a strong connection. Or perhaps we will feel drawn to a temple or be deeply inspired by a teaching. Something has to happen to activate our effort. Buddhists call this a *karmic connection*. That is where our spiritual journey begins.

## THE POWER OF FAITH

The Buddha said there are five powers, and the first power is faith. When we have faith, it can generate more effort. Effort is the second power.

We can see this among yogis and meditators. Those who have strong faith can recite mantras all day long, or even meditate in a small cave for years. In the beginning, faith might not be based on any knowledge or wisdom. It may just be blind faith similar to when we fall in love with someone. But it has the power to increase our effort.

When we first fall in love with someone, we may think about that person constantly. Our feelings are very powerful, and we may even lose ourselves in that love. That feeling of falling in love is similar to that first feeling of blind faith. The only difference is that on the spiritual path, the object of our love is pure. For this reason, it becomes faith, rather than worldly romantic love or attachment. When we fall in love with the Dharma, when we fall in love with the Buddha, and when we become devoted to our gurus, then that love becomes faith.

That karmic connection to the teacher or to the Dharma is very important. In the beginning we might not know who the Buddha is or what the teachings are about. Maybe we do not have any meditation experience. But if we feel a strong connection to a teacher, it will generate effort.

If we have not made such a connection, then how will we be inspired to pursue the teachings? Karmic connection, or whatever term we prefer to use for that feeling of inspiration, is the beginning of cultivating our effort. Only when we meet a spiritual person, or when we go through a life-changing event, will we pay attention and pursue the teachings. Otherwise it is difficult to break out of our habitual patterns.

The more we pursue the teachings, the more interest and attention we will have. As we cultivate a relationship to a spiritual teacher, we will study that teacher's actions, and we will investigate the truths of the teachings.

If the truth resonates in us, and if we trust that we have met a true teacher, then we will begin to emulate these spiritual qualities. However, as our blind faith wears off, if we discover that we do not trust this path or this teacher, we will break away from this relationship.

If our faith remains strong, it deepens our effort. Through meditation and study, we will begin to know more about the Buddha, the Dharma, and the Sangha. The more we learn about these truths and qualities, the more we aspire to find these qualities in ourselves.

This is the stage where our *blind faith* becomes *unshakeable faith*. At this stage we have tested the methods. We have observed the teacher for a period of time. We have used our brains as well as our hearts. Now our emotions of faith and our intellectual reasoning have come together to give us real conviction.

When faith and reason are combined, they produce unshakeable faith. Unshakeable faith helps us maintain right effort. We begin to completely devote our lives to wholesome activities of body, speech, and mind.

Now, having unshakeable faith does not mean we are perfect. We may still have many imperfections, but the strength of our faith begins to transform our lives on every level. At this stage, no matter what happens, nothing will turn us away from our faith in the Buddhist teachings.

Until our faith is unshakeable, we are operating on blind faith that is based on feelings. Our feelings and circumstances are changing constantly. That is why we are so fickle in so many environments and relationships. We keep on changing things in our lives in the pursuit of something better. We move from one house to another, one relationship to the next, but still we are carrying our same emotions, and we are restless.

When we have developed unshakeable faith, we naturally want to cultivate more wholesome actions. Whether it is wholesome thoughts, wholesome speech, or wholesome deeds, we want to focus on these positive efforts. We especially want to cultivate those good qualities which have not yet arisen in us.

As we begin to feel the benefits of wholesome activities, our enthusiasm increases, and we continue to break negative habitual patterns. These positive efforts will also prevent future unwholesome actions from arising.

If we look honestly into our minds, into our thoughts, our speech, and our physical actions, we see how conflicted we really are. Maybe sometimes we tell lies even though we want to be honest. For whatever reason, there is a habitual pattern to tell the lies we have come to repeat. If we look closely at our relationships, we also see that it is possible to love and hate the very same person or object. Love and hate go together. Why is this conflict there?

Since the day we were conceived, and throughout our entire lives, we will experience these dualistic feelings of pain and pleasure, love and hate, attachment and aversion. That is why we are never at peace.

Although all we truly want is peace, we remain very restless because we are always moving between extremes. We are never in the center. That is why faith is one of the most important energies we need in order to cultivate right effort.

Through our spiritual practice, our blind faith becomes clear faith. Our clear faith can then become unshakeable faith. And ultimately we have to develop faith based on wisdom. When faith is based on wisdom, it is incredibly powerful.

The Buddha taught in the sutras that as long as we are here in samsara, so conflicted with attachment and aversion, the universe will not seem perfect to us.

If we are always looking for perfection outside ourselves, we will not find it. Although faith cannot find perfection, it can help us to connect to the positive side of any one object. That is why some masters say "faith is like a magnet that attracts all positive things."

As we develop more faith, it has the power to transform our minds. For this reason, faith is one of the mental factors that has the greatest power to cultivate right effort.

## THE FOUR PRACTICES OF RIGHT EFFORT

Traditionally we are taught that there are four different practices related to right effort. First we develop faith, and we try to abandon our negative habitual patterns at the mental, verbal, and physical levels. This is the reason why the preliminary Buddhist practices emphasize accumulating so many repetitions of mantras. We have to repeat our practices over and over again in order to break unwholesome habitual patterns.

The second aspect of right effort is about strengthening ourselves to prevent future unwholesome actions from arising. After abandoning unwholesome patterns in our mental continuums, we then have more power to avoid future negative actions.

The third aspect of right effort is about increasing any positive actions we are performing at the mental, verbal, and physical levels. We try to cultivate these positive activities until we achieve some perfection.

The fourth aspect of right effort is about locating the positive qualities that we have not yet begun to cultivate and then nurturing those qualities as well.

So these are the four practices emphasized under right effort. As we have discussed, right effort is important because it integrates the other branches of the noble eightfold path.

The noble eightfold path can be divided into three categories: training in wisdom, training in discipline, and training in meditation.

Right view and right intention are part of training in wisdom. As we have established, wrong view is ignorance. So to counteract that ignorance we need to train in wisdom. Right view is an antidote to ignorance, which is the most basic destructive emotion we have.

Right speech, right action, right livelihood, and right effort are all part of the training of discipline, which involves mental, verbal, and physical discipline. In other words, discipline means having the resolve to not commit negative actions of body, speech, and mind.

There are many discussions about the human tendency to engage in negative activities and about how to develop ways to stop such tendencies. The training of discipline is about refraining from those activities. Discipline is an antidote to the destructive emotion of desire.

Right mindfulness and right concentration, which we will discuss in the following chapters, are considered to be part of our training in meditation and are antidotes to the third destructive emotion of anger.

9

# The Noble Eightfold Path: Right Mindfulness

THE SEVENTH BRANCH of the noble eightfold path is right mind-fulness. Right mindfulness is divided into the four foundations of mindfulness. These four foundations are mindfulness of the body, mindfulness of feeling, mindfulness of mental consciousness, and mindfulness of mental phenomena. To understand right mindfulness, we need to understand the nature of all conditioned things. The Bud-dha categorized conditioned things into the five aggregates: form, feel-ing, ideation, formation, and consciousness.

## MINDFULNESS OF THE BODY

The first foundation of mindfulness is mindfulness of the body. Mind-fulness of the body corresponds with the first aggregate of form or matter. According to Buddhist philosophy, all material things are com-posed of the elemental atoms of earth, water, fire, and air. Whatever is created from these atoms is called *matter*. Our physical bodies are also composed of these elements. We interact with the world around us through our six sense organs.

These are called *sense* organs because through them we can perceive the material world. Because we have an eye organ, we can see visual objects. Whatever we see is matter. Because we have an ear organ, we can hear sounds. Sound, according to Buddhist philosophy, is also matter. Everything we can smell, taste, and touch with our bodies is matter. The sixth sense organ of the mind or mental consciousness also perceives phenomena in the material world.

There are many ways to study matter. Biologists and chemists examine the components of matter. Physicists study matter and its motion through space and time. The Buddhist way of studying matter is to study its properties intellectually and then to use meditation to overcome the emotions related with it.

Whatever sensory objects we experience through our sense organs and through our mind become the causes and conditions for different emotions. When we see something agreeable, we are attracted to it, and we become attached. When we see something repulsive, it gives us pain and suffering, and we may become angry in response.

Every sense organ has its corresponding sense object. For example, the sense organ of the eye has visual objects. The sense organ of the ear has the sense object of sound. Each sense organ, when interacting with the sense objects, has the power to elicit different emotions in us.

Buddhists do not wish to manipulate atoms for some ordinary worldly incentive, such as seeking monetary gain. The main purpose of studying the material world through Buddhism is to learn how to overcome the causes and conditions of destructive emotions.

There are some schools of Buddhism that conduct rigorous studies of phenomena. Their main purpose, however, is to overcome afflictive emotions. For this reason, they practice meditation.

When we speak of this aspect of mindfulness called mindfulness of the body, we include not only our own physical bodies but also all other physical bodies and the material world.

Intellectual study of phenomena cannot free us from destructive emotions. To overcome emotions, we have to look deeper through meditation. Mindfulness gives us insight into the material components of our bodies as well as into the outside material world. But this insight also extends well beyond the scope of what is apparent.

Apparent things are objects perceived through our first five sense organs. Yet the insight we gain through mindfulness is more profound. It has more to do with the sixth sense organ of mental consciousness.

Insight is gained through a meditative state of mind. In Buddhism this is considered a sixth sense organ, which is known as mind or consciousness. When that mind is sharpened through meditation and our insight grows deeper, we may see something that we have never seen before.

Ordinarily our perceptions remain at a very gross level. Through mindfulness, though, we are able to see something far more subtle. With this meditative insight, all material objects are recognized as being a part of mindfulness of the body. As our insight becomes more refined, we see a greater truth or reality. Reality will appear very different from how we had previously seen the phenomenal world.

There is a big difference between how we see a material object and how the noble ones, the enlightened masters, see the same object. I think enlightened beings see purity in all things. They have reached the third level of seeing, which is the level of pure vision.

Without that pure vision, what we see in the world is based on our karma. How we perceive the outer world is based on our inner conditions. For example, when we see something visually alluring, some color or shape that we are attracted to, that beauty is not necessarily inherent to that object. As the saying goes, "Beauty lies in the eye of the beholder."

In the Buddhist understanding, attraction and aversion are a result of our emotions and karma. This karma is based on our past habitual patterns. When something generates an agreeable condition within us, when we feel very drawn to something, it is considered a *karmic link*. Based on our past experiences, we have developed an affinity for certain objects, places, or people.

All of these experiences of outer objects are based on what yogis call *karmic vision*. These perceptions are all based on our individual karma. That is why what we experience is not a universal truth.

For example, while humans can see a certain color or shape, cats and dogs may have a very different relationship to these same visual objects. And even among humans, our perception of each object, and our resulting emotions, are as individual as our respective karma.

How we perceive reality, at our level, is based entirely on our inner conditions. That is why it is called karmic vision. Karmic visions are personal as well as collective. When we speak of collective karma, it refers to the fact that certain groups of beings perceive things in a similar way. For example, humans have certain shared visions of reality. But within humanity, each person still has his or her own personal karma, which is unique.

As humans, we experience some things in an agreeable way. Within such collectively agreeable experiences, we can still have personally disagreeable responses. This has more to do with our karma than with the object itself.

This is why the Buddha said that personal karmic experiences are relative. Such experiences are not independent or universal. We often try to project a collective karmic experience as being something that is universally true. When we conduct a thorough investigation, however, it becomes clear that this is not the case.

We have to start from where we are. All the great Buddhist philosophers agree that we must use relative truth in order to see ultimate truth.

Through meditative experience, we have to go deeper and deeper into our exploration of the nature of reality. Are all our material experiences now only relative truths? If so, then what is ultimate truth? These are the questions that yogis are trying to answer through meditation.

This mindfulness of the body includes mindfulness of all material things. As long as we are in the desire realm or in the form realm, we will remain in a physical body. We have to use our personal experiences of our own physical bodies to understand outer phenomena. Since all material objects are composed of these same elemental atoms, we can know outer objects through mindfulness of our own bodies.

The only difference between us and outer inanimate objects is that we are psychosomatic beings, operating from this interaction of mind and body. It is only consciousness that separates all sentient beings from other physical matter.

As sentient beings, we are capable of awareness, which leads to exploration. But the mind and body also create great obstacles. When we possess all these emotions and karmic propensities, everything becomes a very complex puzzle.

In order to better understand this, the Buddha taught the five aggregates, the twelve *ayatanas* or sense sources, and the eighteen *dhatus* or elements. He taught these aspects in order to help us look deeper into the nature of things. Mindfulness of the body allows us to examine the nature of the material world.

## Mindfulness of Feelings

The second foundation of mindfulness is mindfulness of feelings, which corresponds with the second aggregate of feeling. Feelings are experienced through the mind and body. The Buddha taught that there are five kinds of feelings. There are physical feelings of pain and pleasure. There are mental feelings of happiness and unhappiness. And there are neutral feelings, which can be physical, mental, or both.

Feeling is one of the most important aspects of our lives and personalities. Feeling plays such a big role in our experience because it is based directly on our egos and on our sense of self. Most of the things we do in our lives are motivated by our wish to feel more pleasure and happiness and to avoid pain and suffering. Most of the major decisions we make in our lives are based on our feelings rather than our intellects.

When we practice mindfulness of feelings, we examine where a sensation or a feeling is coming from. Through meditative insight we question the nature and properties of that feeling. Mindfulness of feelings allows us to know the basis of a particular reaction.

We treasure and cherish feelings of pleasure and happiness. As a result, we get very attached to these rewarding experiences. This drives us to try harder to attain more of these positive feelings.

Feeling is crucial to our human experience. As a result of our attachment to ourselves, we are easily subject to hurt feelings. The minute someone says or does something that threatens our egos, we respond with pain, sadness, or anger.

Everything we do in our lives is based on our desire for happiness and pleasure. The whole entertainment industry is built on our wish to feel good and our need to be distracted from ourselves and our uncomfortable feelings. We find pleasure in watching movies about other people's emotional dramas. It allows us to forget ourselves and feel less alone in our human experience.

Through meditative insight we can come to see the true nature of our feelings. We can understand the source of these feelings and the ways in which they impact our reality. This is the second foundation—mindfulness of feeling.

## MINDFULNESS OF THE MIND

The third foundation of mindfulness is mindfulness of the mind or mental consciousness. This corresponds with the fifth aggregate that the Buddha taught, which is the aggregate of consciousness.

Consciousness arises in the mind. Each of the six sense organs have corresponding sense objects, which we have described. For example, the sense organ of the eye has visual objects as its sense objects.

Each of these six sense objects also has a corresponding sense consciousness. When we see, when we hear, when we taste, and when we experience any of the six sense objects, basic consciousness arises in the mind.

Take, for example, the eyes. When we see a visual object, then mind arises as eye consciousness. Eye consciousness is the part of the mind that becomes present when a healthy eye organ and a visual object come together.

It takes all three of these factors—the eye organ, the visual object, and the eye consciousness—for visual perception to arise in the present moment. If one of these three factors is missing, then we will not be able to see.

The Buddha taught that these six consciousnesses are present. But the fact that they are present does not entail that they are not based on emotions and defilements. Although we perceive these apparent objects with our present consciousness, our projections are still based on the inner conditions of the basic mind. This basic mind is always traveling with us from moment to moment, from life to life, filled with emotions and karma that then determine how these sense organs experience the world around us.

This foundation of mindfulness of the mind or mental consciousness is to see the true nature of these six sense consciousnesses. Where do they come from? Are they present all the time? What are their properties? Through meditation we will begin to see the nature of consciousness more clearly.

## Mindfulness of Dharmas or Phenomena

The fourth foundation of mindfulness is called the foundation of *dharmas*. Here the term dharmas does not refer to the Buddhist teachings. In this context dharmas refers to all phenomena. This fourth foundation corresponds with the aggregates of ideation and formation. That fourth aggregate of formation is very complex and includes the entire Buddhist understanding of psychology. This is outlined thoroughly in the texts of the Abhidharma.

The aggregates of ideation and formation are included in the fourth foundation, which is mindfulness of dharmas or mental phenomena. As long as we have all these thoughts inside our minds, we create karma. Karma is the origin of all our experiences in our lives. As we have discussed, our entire experience of reality is based on our individual and collective karmic vision.

As long as we have karmic vision, then nothing is universal. Here the term dharmas does not include those first three foundations—our physical bodies, our feelings or sensations, and our sense consciousnesses. But everything else we experience is included in this fourth foundation of mindfulness of dharmas. Here we find insight into Buddhist psychology and into all the different kinds of mental actions.

When I use the term *psychology*, I am referring to all the root positive and negative emotions and to all our mental activities. We usually say that desire, anger, and ignorance are the three fundamental destructive emotions. However, this fourth foundation of mindfulness of dharmas includes all destructive emotions, as well as all the positive emotions like faith, concentration, and memory. It also includes all the neutral emotions. We have many mental activities.

Our minds are constantly filled with these mental activities. Our mental actions respond to what occurs circumstantially, to our interactions with an apparent object. At any given moment, anger, jealousy, or attachment might take over the mind based on some internal or external event.

Whenever the mind interacts with an object, through the sense organs or through mental projections, a strong emotion is activated. Although we may feel that the whole mind is suddenly experiencing anger, we must remember that our underlying emotions still exist in us. We may think that when we have strong anger, we do not have any love. But love is still there inside us as an underlying emotion. We tend to only focus on the emotions that are actively present.

All conflicting emotions exist in our minds, but whenever one emotion overtakes all the others, we forget our underlying emotions. We also forget the true nature of the mind.

This is the reason why the higher tantric teachings reveal that all destructive emotions by nature are in fact wisdom. In tantra, we have all these wrathful deities, and we say that they arise out of wisdom. This profound practice is based on an understanding of this basic composition of our minds.

This fourth foundation of mindfulness of dharmas is the most complex and includes more of the aggregates. The first foundation of mind-fulness relates simply to matter. The second foundation of mindfulness refers only to feeling or sensation. The third foundation of mindfulness is related solely to the fifth aggregate of consciousness. But this fourth foundation of mindfulness includes the aggregates of ideations and for-mations. This fourth foundation includes a person's mental activities, emotions, and psychology.

## INSIGHT INTO IMPERMANENCE

When we investigate our experiences through these four foundations of mindfulness, we see the nature of outside objects as well as the nature of our internal projections of objects. We attempt to understand this in order to overcome the ego and to gain a more noble understanding of ourselves and of the world.

The more we examine these four foundations of mindfulness, the more we realize that they are all impermanent. Our physical bodies and matter are impermanent. Our feelings, our consciousness, and all the core emotions are impermanent. They are changing every moment.

When we see something beautiful, or when we feel something plea-surable, it brings us happiness, and we become attached to those objects or that experience. When we grow attached to an object or an experi-ence, we try to make it permanent. This creates so much conflict and unhappiness because it is impossible to make that experience last.

Only through meditation will we learn to see the true nature of things. The more we meditate, the more we will see that our physical bodies are constantly changing. Every moment our feelings are chang-ing. Every moment our minds are changing. Every moment our emo-tions are changing. So we come to accept impermanence.

Impermanence is the opposite of our wishes and desires. We all want to have a permanently healthy body. So when our bodies begin to age and to decay, they become a great source of mental and physical pain.

This pain is not only a result of these changes in our bodies. This suffering is based largely on the ego. Our ego believes that our body should be young and beautiful forever. Our ego strongly resists the conditioned nature of things.

We believe that having these wonderful young bodies and all these fresh material things will bring us more pleasure. But the truth is that even when these things bring us happiness in our youth, they are sowing seeds of future suffering. Inevitably we will lose these strong agile bodies and these wonderful possessions, and that loss will bring us pain.

## INSIGHT INTO SUFFERING

As long as we have feelings, they are based on ego. And as long as anything is based on ego, it is based on the root destructive emotions. Due to this fact, even pleasure and happiness are part of our destructive emotions.

Eventually we will come to see that all feelings and pleasures based on our bodies and sensations—or based on ideas and emotions—are actually a form of suffering.

The more deeply we look, the more we will recognize the reality of the second noble truth, the origin of suffering. Whatever is impermanent, changing, and aging creates suffering.

The origin of suffering is hard to accept because it goes against the wishes of our ego. Our ego wishes for pleasure and happiness all the time. Our natural condition of suffering is the opposite of how we want to feel.

If we return to our discussion of the first noble truth of suffering, we see that the Buddha taught that suffering includes all feelings—even pleasurable and neutral feelings. This is because all feelings are based on the destructive emotions of the ego.

The Buddha didn't teach the noble truth of suffering and mindfulness of suffering in order to make us more miserable! Students sometimes ask me, "We already have so much pain and suffering in our lives, so why does the Buddha have to tell us that even our pleasure is suffering?" The reason that the Buddha taught this was to help us achieve complete freedom from suffering. In order to achieve this, we have to be realistic and pragmatic. Insight related to suffering is critical for understanding the path to freedom.

## Insight into Insubstantiality

When we delve deeper, breaking down matter to the atomic level, or examining the causes of emotions, we come to see that everything is insubstantial. We cannot find any permanence. There is no inherent existence of even a subatomic particle.

Even physicists and psychologists have reached the same conclusions. The more they investigate, the more they agree that there is no permanent basis for form, feelings, ideas, or any phenomena.

## Insight into Emptiness

The fourth insight is that not only are these things insubstantial, their very nature is emptiness. Form is empty. Feeling is empty. Mind is empty. All of the emotions are empty. Those who are enlightened and who have achieved nirvana realize this empty nature through the mindfulness of these four foundations. That is how they achieve enlightenment. Then they are finally free from pain and suffering.

The more we investigate, the more there is to see. From impermanence we see emptiness. From emptiness we see ultimate truth or the ultimate nature of things. This realization is the purpose of the four foundations of mindfulness, which are taught primarily in the Theravada or Hinayana Buddhist tradition. This is the main practice in countries including Burma, Thailand, and Sri Lanka.

In the Mahayana tradition, in texts like the *Heart Sutra*, we read, "Form is emptiness. Emptiness is form. Form is not other than emptiness, nor is emptiness other than form." In the Vajrayana Buddhist tradition we have profound sadhana meditation practices, which provide the deepest insight into emptiness.

All these traditions are complimentary. The purpose of the four foundations of mindfulness is to reveal the empty nature of our five aggregates. When we see that the nature of form, feeling, ideation, formation, and consciousness is emptiness, then we have the realization of selflessness.

Here, for the first time, we see the true face of our egos, which is egolessness. We see the true nature of the self, which is selflessness. At this point we begin to free ourselves from ignorance.

When we're free from ignorance, we're free from attachment and aversion. At that point we no longer create any karma. We experience the whole universe, including our personal experiences, as pure vision.

As long as we have egos, we will continue to have karmic experiences. Right mindfulness is based on the four foundations of mindfulness, which will ultimately lead us to pure vision and to the ultimate truth of selflessness. This is the purpose of all insight meditation.

# 10

# The Noble Eightfold Path: Right Concentration

THE FINAL BRANCH of the noble eightfold path is *right concentration*. As we know, the main obstacle to good meditation is distraction. The more distracting our lives become, the more difficult it is to focus our attention. Not only are we missing these important elements of attention and concentration, distraction also brings additional negativities into our lives.

If we investigate the sources of these constant distractions, we will see that they are all rooted in destructive emotions. The more ignorance we have, the more anger and attachment we have in our mental continuum. This means that our attention will diminish.

This constant state of distractibility produces more negative karma. Without attention, we are much less aware of our physical actions, our speech, and our thoughts. When we act without true awareness, we create causes and conditions for future suffering.

At a worldly level, constant mental distraction prevents us from performing well at our jobs. It interferes with our ability to communicate well with the people around us and to achieve success because we simply cannot focus our attention on the task in front of us. Instead, we are always daydreaming. We are thinking about the past or the future. We are wondering what we'll eat for lunch, or wishing we were doing something else. Often we obsess about something someone said that hurt our feelings.

Mental distraction impacts all facets of our lives. If you are a student, and your mind is constantly wandering, it can be extremely challenging to study properly or to write a term paper. If you are working at a stressful job, then your inability to concentrate on the task at hand can impact your performance. If you are in a relationship, and you cannot be present to your children or to your partner because you are always thinking about other things, then you will experience conflict and disappointment within your family.

If we look closely in this way, we see that distraction is not just an issue when it comes time to meditate. Distraction impacts our lives on every level, and meditation is the first step in beginning to examine those habitual patterns.

If we do not begin to break down those habitual patterns through meditation while we are alive, then even when we die that distracted mind will continue. After death, we will experience the bardo stage as a series of rushing, distracted dreams, and we will take rebirth with that same disoriented mind.

When the mind is plagued with distractions, it is said to resemble a waterfall. All the emotions and karma come rushing over us, pushing us further and further down, which produces additional negativities.

The main cause of distraction is our unexamined destructive emotions. This is especially true for us humans living here in the desire realm. This realm is filled with craving and attachment. We are driven by our need for desirable objects to consume.

Out of all these objects of attachment, our strongest desire is for other humans. Our other greatest attachment is toward the objects that we wish to possess. Our need for human relationships and our desire to have many possessions are driving forces in our lives.

The most direct method to overcome distraction is through meditation. At the highest level, we reach a state of concentration or *samadhi*.

There are four levels of concentration in the form realm and four levels in the formless realm. These eight levels are all considered worldly concentrations. These meditations in the form and formless realms can help us to calm our emotions and achieve deep states of peace, but they do not necessarily help us to transcend all three realms of samsara in order to achieve complete liberation.

In the Theravada or Hinayana tradition of meditation, the aim of meditation is to achieve nirvana and to go beyond samsara entirely. The method of practice in the Theravada tradition is based entirely on renunciation. Renunciation means seeing that the nature of our lives is pain and suffering. Due to this realization we then wish to renounce the whole cycle of suffering and to achieve cessation—nirvana.

## Shamatha Meditation

Based on this focus on renunciation, we then practice shamatha meditation. Shamatha is also known as *calm abiding* meditation. According to the texts of the Abhidharma, there are two methods for practicing shamatha meditation.

The first method is to use shamatha practice as an antidote to desire. Since we live in the desire realm, desire is our strongest destructive emotion. In order to overcome this strong, active desire and attachment, we need to know why we have these emotions.

## The Four Objects of Attachment

Shamatha meditation can help us to overcome the four objects of attachment. These objects are color, shape, touch, and attention. When we examine desire more closely, we will see that our desire for visual objects is especially strong. We are drawn to objects because of their color, shape, design, and all their appealing visual characteristics.

Our sense of touch is also a strong source of attachment. We want something to feel good to us. Whether it is the touch of another person, the feel of something soft under our hands, or even the feel of warm sunlight on our skin, touch is something we crave. Anything tangible that we find pleasurable can become a source of attachment.

The fourth object of attachment is attention. We crave the attention of others. We crave recognition and appreciation and love. We want to do well in our lives and achieve some level of success.

Shamatha meditation can help us to overcome these four objects of attachment by giving us antidotes. In order to overcome our attachment to color, we have to do shamatha practice based on undesirable color. In order to overcome our desire for shape, we have to do shamatha meditation on an undesirable shape.

For example, if we are attached to the beautiful body of someone we desire, then we can meditate on that shape becoming very unattractive. If we are attached to the feel of something being smooth or soft, then we have to do shamatha meditation on an undesirable texture. If we are attached to recognition, then we can meditate on the negative side effects of that attention.

## Shamatha Meditation on a Corpse or Skeleton

Meditation on a human corpse is a very effective method for counteracting these objects of attachment. The Abhidharma texts describe nine meditations on a corpse to work through these four different attachments.

The Buddha said that if we cannot meditate on the specific color or shape of the corpse, if that is too gruesome or challenging at first, then we can also just meditate on the skeleton. The skeleton has the antidotal power to overcome all of the four objects of attachment. So this is how, through our practice, we can overcome strong, active desire and attachment so that our shamatha meditation will be effective.

## Shamatha Meditation on the Breath

The second method of shamatha meditation is designed for those people who have lots of thoughts and inner chatter. This chatter is not necessarily related to attachment and desire. It can include anger, neutral thoughts, and all intellectual distractions.

When the mind is very busy in this way, it is very good to do shamatha meditation focused on the breath. The Abhidharma texts describe six different ways to use breathing as an object of meditation.

The first breathing meditation is called *counting*. You can count to ten over and over again. Beginning on the inhalation you count "one," and on the exhalation you count "two." Each time you get distracted, you return again to the beginning. It is emphasized that you should not count higher than ten, or it could make you more active and distracted. It is also advised that you do not count fewer than ten, or you may become lazy in your practice.

The second breathing meditation is called *following*. In this exercise you follow the movement of the inhalation, the circulation of the air inside you, and then the exhalation. In this way, you try to follow the movement of the air in your body.

The third breathing meditation is called *placing*. Here you pay complete attention to the movement of the breath in your body. You focus on the circulation of the breath from the nostrils down to the feet and back up again, like a rope of air. When you concentrate in this manner, you see that the air is continuously circulating. You notice the temperature of the air. When you can focus your concentration on the complete process of the circulation of air , then that is the third shamatha practice called *placing*.

The fourth practice is called *more placing*. By observing the movement of the air inside you, you begin to realize that air is not just composed of the air element. As your shamatha practice strengthens, you begin to see that air contains all four elements. You also begin to realize that air supports the mind and the emotions. Through this you begin to see that air is integral to all five aggregates. So this fourth practice of *more placing* deepens your concentration on the breath.

The fifth practice is called *modification*. With modification, you use whatever concentration you have achieved based on the previous breathing meditations in order to cultivate the spirituality inside you.

This in turn allows you to achieve higher levels of realization. This concentration is applied to increase positive spiritual qualities and decrease negative destructive emotions.

The sixth practice is called *complete purification*. You use the modification practice to continue cultivating positive spiritual qualities and completely purify destructive emotions and negativities. Eventually this cultivation will help you to go beyond negative emotions and negative karma.

We can choose the object of our shamatha meditation depending on our temperaments. If we have a lot of clinging and desire, we can perform shamatha meditation on the corpse or skeleton. And if we are filled with many ideas and concepts, we can quiet the mind by engaging in shamatha meditation on the breath.

Both of these objects of meditation include the nine stages of shamatha. The first three stages are placement, continual placement, and repair and placement, which allow us to overcome distractions so that we can pay attention to the object of our meditation. The next three stages are perfect placement, the state of being subdued, and calmness, which strengthen that attention. Finally, the last three stages of shamatha are perfect calmness, one-pointedness, and placement in equanimity, which build on the attention you have achieved and apply it to the result, which is concentration.

After gaining some experience with shamatha meditation, you can proceed to the next meditation, which is mindfulness practice or insight meditation. Mindfulness practice is based on the seventh branch of the noble eightfold path. Only when you have established a good shamatha practice and a good level of concentration will you be able to use that attention to be successful in your practice of insight meditation.

In insight meditation you start with the four foundations of mindfulness, which we have already discussed. Through cultivating mindfulness of the body, you have the realization that the physical body is the base of all suffering, and that helps you to accept the first noble truth of suffering.

As a result of our physical bodies, we are subjected to three kinds of suffering. Because we have a physical body, we experience the suffering of suffering, and we are unable to avoid sickness and pain. Because of our physical bodies, we also have the suffering of change, since nothing pleasurable can last. Furthermore, as a result of our physical bodies, we will be subjected to old age and death, and we will have to experience the suffering of conditioned existence.

Through practicing mindfulness of the body, we come to recognize that this physical body is the base of all three kinds of suffering. This leads us to a profound understanding of the first noble truth of suffering.

The second mindfulness practice is mindfulness of feelings. When we look more closely, we realize that feelings are the cause of all our craving. This craving creates all the causes and conditions for our afflictive emotions and suffering. By practicing mindfulness of feelings, we will come to the realization that feeling is the origin of all our suffering. This will deepen our understanding of the second noble truth of the origin of suffering.

The third mindfulness practice is mindfulness of the mind. Through this practice we come to the realization that the mind is impermanent—the mind can cease. At present, our minds are the basis for the self. But through the practice of mindfulness of the mind, we can develop insight into the third noble truth of cessation.

The fourth mindfulness practice is mindfulness of dharmas, which in this context means phenomena. Through this practice we come to see that within dharmas there are things to abandon and things to accept. Based on learning what to accept and what to reject, we will come to know the fourth noble truth of the path.

Including the four foundations of mindfulness, there are thirty-seven noble practices in the Theravada tradition that instruct us on how to achieve nirvana.

The Mahayana tradition takes this concentration to another level. After taking the bodhisattva vow, we cultivate loving-kindness and compassion. In the Mahayana tradition we use the six paramitas, also known as the six perfections, to achieve complete enlightenment.

# PART II

The Wisdom Gone Beyond

# प्रज्ञापारमिताहृदयसूत्रम् ।
## prajñāpāramitāhṛdayasūtram |

‖ नमः सर्वज्ञाय ‖
|| namaḥ sarvajñāya ||

एवं मया श्रुतम् । एकस्मिन् समये भगवान् राजगृहे विहरति स्म गृध्रकूटे पर्वते महता भिक्षुसंघेन सार्धं महता च बोधिसत्त्वसंघेन । तेन खलु समयेन भगवान् गम्भीरावसंबोधं नाम समाधिं समापन्नः । तेन च समयेन आर्यावलोकितेश्वरो बोधिसत्त्वो महासत्त्वो गम्भीरायां प्रज्ञापारमितायां चर्यां चरमाणः एवं व्यवलोकयति स्म । पञ्च स्कन्धांस्तांश्च स्वभावशून्यं व्यवलोकयति ‖

evaṃ mayā śrutam | ekasmin samaye bhagavān rājagṛhe viharati
sma gṛdhrakūṭe parvate mahatā bhikṣusaṃghena sārdhaṃ
mahatā ca bodhisattvasaṃghena | tena khalu samayena bhagavān
gambhīrāvasaṃbodhaṃ nāma samādhiṃ samāpannaḥ | tena ca
samayena āryāvalokiteśvaro bodhisattvo mahāsattvo gambhīrāyāṃ
prajñāpāramitāyāṃ caryāṃ caramāṇaḥ evaṃ vyavalokayati sma | pañca
skandhāṃstāṃśca svabhāvaśūnyaṃ vyavalokayati ||

अथायुष्मान् शारिपुत्रो बुद्धानुभावेन आर्यावलोकितेश्वरं बोधिसत्त्वमेतदवोचत् यः कश्चित् कुलपुत्रो वा कुलदुहिता वा अस्यां गम्भीरायां प्रज्ञापारमितायां चर्यां चर्तुकामः कथं शिक्षितव्यः । एवमुक्ते आर्यावलोकितेश्वरो बोधिसत्त्वो महासत्त्वः आयुष्मन्तं शारिपुत्रमेतदवोचत् यः

# The *Heart Sutra*

Salutations to the Omniscient One.

This is what I once heard at the time the Blessed One was seated on Vulture's Peak in Rajagriha with a huge congregation of the exalted community of bhikshus and bodhisattvas. At that time, the Blessed One was dwelling in the meditation called Profound Vision.

Also at that time, the great being and bodhisattva Arya Avalokiteshvara was reviewing the profound characteristics of the Prajnaparamita and saw the natural emptiness of the five aggregates.

Then the elder Shariputra, moved by the power of the Buddha, addressed Arya Avalokiteshvara with these words: "Noble son! How should someone who wishes to perform the profound practice of the Prajnaparamita train himself?"

The great being, the bodhisattva Arya Avalokiteshvara replied, "Shariputra! That son or daughter of a good family who wishes to perform the profound practice of the Prajnaparamita should first rightly see that all the aggregates, by their very nature, are empty.

"Form (matter) is emptiness. Emptiness is form. Form is not other than emptiness, nor is emptiness other than form.

कश्चिच्छारिपुत्र कुलपुत्रो व कुलदुहिता वा अस्यां गम्भीरायां प्रज्ञापारमितायां चर्यां चर्तुकामः तेनैवं व्यवलोकितव्यम् पञ्च स्कन्धांस्तांश्च स्वभावशून्यान् समनुपश्यति स्म । रूपं शून्यता शून्यतैव रूपम् । रूपान्न पृथक् शून्यता शून्यताया न पृथग् रूपम् । यद्रूपं सा शून्यता या शून्यता तद्रूपम् । एवं वेदनासंज्ञासंस्कारविज्ञानानि च शून्यता । एवं शारिपुत्र सर्वधर्माः शून्यतालक्षणा अनुत्पन्ना अनिरुद्धा अमला विमला अनूना असंपूर्णाः । तस्मात्तर्हि शारिपुत्र शून्यतायां न रूपम् न वेदना न संज्ञा न संस्काराः न विज्ञानम् न चक्षुर्न श्रोत्रं न घ्राणं न जिह्वा न कायो न मनो न रूपं न शब्दो न गन्धो न रसो न स्प्रष्टव्यं न धर्मः । न चक्षुर्धातुर्यावन्न मनोधातुर्न धर्मधातुर्न मनोविज्ञानधातुः । न विद्या नाविद्या न क्षयो यावन्न जरामरणं न जरामरणक्षयः न दुःखसमुदयनिरोधमार्गा न ज्ञानं न प्राप्तिर्नाप्राप्तिः । तस्माच्छारिपुत्र अप्राप्तित्वेन बोधिसत्त्वानां प्रज्ञापारमितामाश्रित्य विहरति चित्तावरणः । चित्तावरणनास्तित्वादत्रस्तो विपर्यासातिक्रान्तो निष्ठनिर्वाणः । त्र्यध्वव्यवस्थिताः सर्वबुद्धाः प्रज्ञापारमितामाश्रित्य अनुत्तरां सम्यक्संबोधिमभिसंबुद्धाः । तस्माद् ज्ञातव्यः प्रज्ञापारमितामहामन्त्रः अनुत्तरमन्त्रः असमसममन्त्रः सर्वदुःखप्रशमनमन्त्रः सत्यमिथ्यत्वात् प्रज्ञापारमितायामुक्तो मन्त्रः । तद्यथा गते गते पारगते पारसंगते बोधि स्वाहा । एवं शारिपुत्र गम्भीरायां प्रज्ञापारमितायां चर्यायां शिक्षितव्यं बोधिसत्त्वेन ॥

athāyuṣmān śāriputro buddhānubhāvena āryāvalokiteśvaraṃ bodhisattvametadavocat yaḥ kaścit kulaputro vā kuladuhitā vā asyāṃ gambhīrāyāṃ prajñāpāramitāyāṃ caryāṃ cartukāmaḥ kathaṃ śikṣitavyaḥ | evamukte āryāvalokiteśvaro bodhisattvo mahāsattvaḥ āyuṣmantaṃ śāriputrametadavocat yaḥ kaścicchāriputra kulaputro va kuladuhitā vā asyāṃ gambhīrāyāṃ prajñāpāramitāyāṃ caryāṃ cartukāmaḥ tenaivaṃ vyavalokitavyam pañca skandhāṃstāṃśca svabhāvaśūnyān samanupaśyati sma | rūpaṃ śūnyatā śūnyataiva rūpam | rūpānna pṛthak śūnyatā śūnyatāyā na pṛthag rūpam | yadrūpaṃ sā śūnyatā yā śūnyatā tadrūpam | evaṃ vedanāsaṃjñāsaṃskāravijñānāni ca śūnyatā | evaṃ śāriputra sarvadharmāḥ śūnyatālakṣaṇā anutpannā aniruddhā amalā vimalā anūnā asampūrṇāḥ | tasmāttarhi śāriputra śūnyatāyāṃ na rūpam na vedanā na saṃjñā na saṃskārāḥ na vijñānam na cakṣurna śrotraṃ na ghrāṇaṃ na jihvā na kāyo na mano na rūpaṃ na śabdo na gandho na raso na spraṣṭavyaṃ na dharmaḥ | na cakṣurdhāturyāvanna manodhāturna dharmadhāturna manovijñānadhātuḥ | na vidyā nāvidyā na kṣayo yāvanna jarāmaraṇaṃ

"So too all feeling, ideation, formation, and consciousness are empty.

"Shariputra! In the same way, all dharmas are devoid of characteristics, unborn, unstopped, unsullied, unpurified, undecreased, unfilled.

"Therefore, Shariputra, in emptiness there is no form, no feeling, no ideation, no formation, no consciousness, no eye, no ear, no nose, no tongue, no body, no mind; no form, no sound, no smell, no taste, no touch, no dharmas. There is no element of eye and so on through the element of mind and the element of mental consciousness. There is no ignorance, no elimination of ignorance; no death and decay, and no elimination of death and decay.

"So too there is no pain, no origin, no cessation, no path; no wisdom, no attainment, no nonattainment.

"Shariputra, because nothing is really obtained, all bodhisattvas who have no fear rely on and dwell in the Prajnaparamita, for they have no mental obscurations. They are perfectly liberated and have gone completely beyond deception. Relying on the Prajnaparamita, all the buddhas of the three times are completely enlightened to that unsurpassable, noble, and perfect enlightenment.

"Therefore, the mantra of the Prajnaparamita, the mantra of great wisdom, the unsurpassable mantra, the mantra equal to the unequalled, the mantra that fully allays all pains, because it is not false, should be known as truth. The mantra of Prajnaparamita is spoken thus:

*Tadyatha om gate gate paragate parasamgate bodhi svaha!*

"Shariputra! In this way, bodhisattvas should train in the profound Prajnaparamita."

Then the Blessed One arose from that meditation called Profound Vision and spoke to the bodhisattva Arya Avalokiteshvara: "Well

na jarāmaraṇakṣayaḥ na duḥkhasamudayanirodhamārgā na
jñānaṃ na prāptirnāprāptiḥ | tasmācchāriputra aprāptitvena
bodhisattvānāṃ prajñāpāramitāmāśritya viharati cittāvaraṇaḥ
| cittāvaraṇanāstitvādatrasto viparyāsātikrānto niṣṭhanirvāṇaḥ
| tryadhvavyavasthitāḥ sarvabuddhāḥ prajñāpāramitāmāśritya
anuttarāṃ samyaksambodhimabhisambuddhāḥ | tasmād jñātavyaḥ
prajñāpāramitāmahāmantraḥ anuttaramantraḥ asamasamamantraḥ
sarvaduḥkhapraśamanamantraḥ satyamamithyatvāt
prajñāpāramitāyāmukto mantraḥ | tadyathā gate gate pāragate
pārasaṃgate bodhi svāhā | evaṃ śāriputra gambhīrāyāṃ
prajñāpāramitāyāṃ caryāyāṃ śikṣitavyaṃ bodhisattvena ||


अथ खलु भगवान् तस्मात्समाधेर्व्युत्थाय आर्यावलोकितेश्वरस्य बोधिसत्त्वस्य साधुकारमदात् साधु
साधु कुलपुत्र । एवमेतत् कुलपुत्र एवमेतद् गम्भीरायां प्रज्ञापारमितायां चर्यं चर्तव्यं यथा त्वया
निर्दिष्टम् । अनुमोद्यते तथागतैरर्हद्भिः ॥
atha khalu bhagavān tasmātsamādhervyutthāya āryāvalokiteśvarasya
bodhisattvasya sādhukāramadāt sādhu sādhu kulaputra | evametat
kulaputra evametad gambhīrāyāṃ prajñāpāramitāyāṃ caryaṃ
cartavyaṃ yathā tvayā nirdiṣṭam | anumodyate tathāgatairarhadbhiḥ ||


इदमवोचद्भगवान् । आनन्दमना आयुष्मान् शारिपुत्रः आर्यावलोकितेश्वरश्च बोधिसत्त्वः सा च
सर्वावती परिषत् सदेवमानुषासुरगन्धर्वश्च लोको भगवतो भाषितमभ्यनन्दन् ॥
idamavocadbhagavān| ānandamanā āyuṣmān śāriputraḥ
āryāvalokiteśvaraśca bodhisattvaḥ sā ca sarvāvatī
pariṣat sadevamānuṣāsuragandharvaśca loko bhagavato
bhāṣitamabhyanandan ||


इति प्रज्ञापारमिताहृदयसूत्रं समाप्तम् ।
iti prajñāpāramitāhṛdayasūtraṃ samāptam |

said, noble son, well said! It is just so. One should practice the Prajna-paramita as you have taught, and all the tathagatas will rejoice."

When the buddhas had spoken thus, the elder Shariputra and the bodhisattva Arya Avalokiteshvara, together with that assembly, as well as gods, humans, demigods, and gandharvas, joyfully praised the words of the Blessed One.

This concludes the *Heart Sutra*.

# 11

# The *Heart Sutra* and the Three Trainings

THE CONCISE TEACHINGS of the *Heart Sutra* are among the most influential and profound in the Mahayana. The teachings of this sutra pertain primarily to right view. All of the Buddha's teachings are divided into three trainings: wisdom, discipline, and meditation. Right view is part of training in wisdom. Put simply, it teaches us how to start seeing things in the right way.

Right view in this context does not necessarily mean seeing something visual with our eyes. When we first see something with our eyes, before any conceptual thoughts arise, we may have some glimpse of its real nature. In the next moment, however, we begin to respond to that object based on our emotions and inner conditions.

Training in *darshana* or "seeing" has more to do with right view, which is cultivated through training in wisdom. The more we study and practice, the more we begin to see with our inner wisdom eye.

All the buddhas have a wisdom eye, which is also called the third eye. Often in sacred Buddhist thangka paintings we can see that the deities are depicted with a third eye on their foreheads. The third eye is located between the other two eyes and symbolizes that the wisdom eye is open. The buddhas can see so much through their wisdom eye that we are not yet aware of.

Our wisdom eye is not open. What we have instead are two ordinary physical eyes that we have inherited from our father and mother. These physical eyes are part of our physical *pain body* constituted by our emotions.

We are all familiar with the phrase, "Beauty is in the eye of the beholder." This reminds us that there is no ultimate truth in our visual perceptions. Without a wisdom eye, everything that we see will be mere relative truth. How we measure beauty will be a direct result of our individual karma and emotions. According to these emotions, the same object can have different value to different people.

Through the training of wisdom, we can begin to see clearly and completely, in a way that we have never seen before. Through the wisdom eye we can begin to see a more universal or ultimate truth. The essence of Buddhism is this darshana wisdom training, and the *Heart Sutra* is the most profound teaching through which we can cultivate right view.

Cultivating right view cannot happen through study alone. We must also take these teachings into our meditation and cultivate them through repeated practice and contemplation. This is why the Buddha included meditation as one of the three most important trainings along with wisdom and discipline.

Training in discipline, however, is the most important training of all. Through discipline we learn to bring the training of wisdom and meditation into our daily lives. This discipline or ethical conduct is paramount to the proper integration of wisdom and meditation into every aspect of our lives.

Darshana is right view. *Bhavana* means meditation, and *charya* means conduct or discipline. When we are not formally studying or meditating, we must use ethical conduct to bring our awareness and understanding into every facet of ordinary life. Conduct is the most important because it has the power to create the most profound transformation.

If you have proper conduct, then that conduct can even begin to transform you while you are sleeping! If you have taken a resolution not to kill, then even in your sleep you may find you no longer have violent dreams. Your conduct becomes so integrated into your mind that your discipline continues even in your sleep. When we are not actively studying or meditating, it is conduct that can steadily transform us. Wisdom, meditation, and discipline are the three essential parts of any complete practice.

If your meditation is not guided by right view, then your practice will not help you go beyond. Without right view, your meditation is essentially blind because it is not guided by your wisdom eye.

Furthermore, if you have right conduct but do not have wisdom, then even though you may accumulate merit, you still will not transcend the suffering of ordinary existence. Without the wisdom eye, your conduct will be blind. Wisdom is the most important guide of conduct, and conduct is essential to inner transformation. Wisdom determines where your meditation will lead you. This is why we are focusing on the wisdom gone beyond that is addressed explicitly in the *Heart Sutra*. In this sutra, meditation and conduct are addressed implicitly.

It is important to know more about the origins of this sutra. The Buddha gave many different teachings. His series of wisdom teachings is one of the largest collections. The extensive teachings of the Prajnaparamita, which means "wisdom gone beyond," fill 100,000 stanzas when translated into Tibetan from the original Sanskrit.

The second-longest version of the sutra is contained in 25,000 stanzas. The next version is condensed to 18,000, then 10,000, then 8,000, then 2,500, then 700, then 500, 300, 150, 25, and then ultimately the sutra can be distilled into the single syllable *ah*. These different versions are also classified into mother and son Prajnaparamitas depending on whether all or partial practices are mentioned.

I received the *Abhisamayalamkara* teachings of eight sections and seventy topics, starting with twenty-two bodhichittas from Khen Rinpoche Rinchen. This is a shastra based on the 8,000-stanza and other *Prajnaparamita Sutras*. Occasionally I have read the 8,000-stanza

*Prajnaparamita Sutra* while giving teachings on the *Heart Sutra* to provide more detail.

The version of the *Heart Sutra* that we are studying here is the twenty-five-stanza version. Although it is abbreviated, it contains the essence of these wisdom teachings. It is considered complete because it is an accurate distillation of the heart of these teachings and allows us to go deeper and deeper the more we study.

To understand the *Heart Sutra*, we must study it and integrate it fully into our meditation practice. The training of wisdom cannot be accomplished through scholarly study alone but must be incorporated into our practice.

This sutra is considered a vital Buddhist teaching in countries where the Mahayana is practiced. This includes China, Japan, Korea, and Vietnam. It is also important for Vajrayana Buddhists in the Himalayan regions. It is not considered as important for Theravada Buddhists. I have met Theravada monks who do not even accept this sutra as the Buddha's words.

Theravada Buddhists follow the Pali Tripitaka. They do not accept the *Heart Sutra* as the Buddha's teachings because it is not found in their Tripitaka. The study of this sutra, however, is very complementary to the teachings of the *Abhidharmakosha*. Each word of the *Heart Sutra* is embedded with so much profound meaning that can be deepened by studying the *Abhidharmakosha*.

For the purposes of this study, we are using the English translation of the *Heart Sutra* given above. We can find subtle differences between the Sanskrit version and the resulting translations into various languages.

Salutations to the Omniscient One.

With this first line, we are paying homage to wisdom. In Sanskrit, wisdom is called *prajna*. Wisdom is characterized as feminine because it is considered to be the mother of all the buddhas of the past, present, and future. For this reason, wisdom is portrayed as a female energy.

What is the wisdom we are referring to? We are referring to the

Prajnaparamita or the Perfection of Wisdom—the *wisdom gone beyond*. It is very important that we understand the various meanings of the wisdom gone beyond.

One meaning is that such wisdom has gone beyond the cycle of our existence—it has gone beyond the cycle of birth, life, death, and rebirth.

Buddhists describe our life cycle based on the wheel of life. If our present lives were full of peace, joy, and bliss, then there would be nothing to go beyond. When we look honestly at our lives, however, we see that there is an underlying dissatisfaction and restlessness here in samsara.

Due to this discomfort, the Buddha said that the nature of life is *dukkha*, which means "suffering" or "dissatisfaction." Everything that we do in our lives has both a positive and a negative side, but nothing is perfect, and nothing can last. As a result, there is always a level of discontentment. There is no static perfection in our lives. It is all constantly changing. Along with that impermanence, we have so much intense emotional involvement, which creates so much suffering.

The wisdom we are describing is called the wisdom gone beyond because it has the power to help us go beyond the wheel of life. This wisdom can help us go beyond birth and death.

If we look at the very foundations of our suffering here in samsara, we see that suffering is based on the fact that we are dying. Every moment we are moving closer to our own deaths, but we are in denial of this basic truth.

No matter what we accomplish, no matter what we achieve or what wealth we gain in our lives, we will all die. Death is the greatest source of suffering because we do not want to die. We do so much in our lives to try to avoid this truth. Yet it is this denial of death that creates a deep source of pain and restlessness in our lives. We spend so much effort trying to distract ourselves from this inevitable death.

By karma we are forced to die, unwillingly; and by karma we will be forced to take rebirth repeatedly. You can think of birth and death and the intermediate stage of the bardo as a cycle of waking and sleeping.

Death is like going to sleep at night. The bardo is like a dream state. Rebirth is like getting up again in the morning.

Just as we repeat this cycle over and over in our lives, we also repeat this cycle of death and rebirth endlessly from one life to the next. The duration is longer in the cycle of death and rebirth, but the actual experience is very similar.

Wisdom has the power to go beyond this cycle and to free us from samsara. Going beyond that cycle of birth and death is the state of cessation or nirvana. According to the Theravada tradition of Buddhism, when death and birth have ceased, then you are in a state of nirvana or liberation.

The wisdom of the Prajnaparamita is even greater than nirvana. The wisdom described in the *Heart Sutra* is beyond nirvana. The wisdom gone beyond has a double meaning in this sutra that we always need to remember.

According to the Theravada tradition, wisdom that leads us beyond the cycle of life and death is sufficient. When we understand this sutra as a training in the Perfection of Wisdom, however, then this wisdom can even lead us beyond nirvana.

This wisdom has the power to go beyond both samsara and nirvana. It has this power because it is wisdom combined with compassion. Wisdom that has limitless compassion has the power to go beyond even nirvana; that is the complete meaning of the wisdom gone beyond.

We cannot understand this wisdom through study and discussion alone. To actualize that wisdom, we must engage in meditation practice. Here we are using words as a reference point, but words alone cannot give us wisdom.

Masters who have actualized the wisdom gone beyond through deep meditation have achieved a meditative state that is inconceivable to us. It is impossible to convey that experience through language or to approximate it through conceptual thought.

Our lives are filled with concepts. We are thinkers because we have not uncovered the purity of things. We are caught in the *three circles* that the Buddha described.

First, we do not have the purity of oneself. We think we know who we are, but we are blind to our true nature. We may spend much of our lives creating elaborate identities for ourselves through our culture, education, and our outer accomplishments. We may go through our entire lives without having a complete realization of our true nature.

To better understand the three circles, let's examine the perfection of giving, which is one of the six paramitas or six perfections. The three circles here would be the giver, the gift, and the receiver.

When the giver has the realization of his or her own true nature, then that is the first purity. Considering that first purity, the giver then has the realization of the true nature of the gift. The third purity is that the giver then has the realization of the true nature of the receiver.

Only when you have gained wisdom concerning the true nature of the three circles will you begin to be free of concepts. If you do not have any insight into the three circles, then you will remain trapped in a dualistic view. You will remain attached to your idea of your own self. As a result, you will continue to have attraction and aversion to objects in the world. You will also continue to extend these judgements to the receivers.

The perfection of giving can only become a perfection when it is integrated with wisdom. Wisdom involves knowing the ultimate nature of the giver, the gift, and the receiver. Only then will you be free from all ideas—from both the thought and the thinker.

The wisdom gone beyond is inconceivable in that it is impossible to comprehend conceptually and can only be realized through deep meditation. Through meditation you can become free from all ideas related to subject, object, and all other phenomena.

Here *inconceivable* means going beyond all concepts related with the three circles. These three circles can also be understood as subject, object, and all other phenomena. When you see the true nature of wisdom in all three circles, then you are free from ideas. That liberation is inexpressible. Once you have realized that wisdom, no words can describe it. Language cannot explain that state.

In the wisdom teachings, there is great emphasis on the letter *ah*. It is said that all the vowels and consonants can be included in the letter *ah*. *Ah* is the source of all sound, of all letters, of all language.

According to the Buddhist teachings, the letter *ah* is formed when you are first conceived inside the mother's womb. At the moment of your conception, your consciousness becomes trapped between the father's sperm and the mother's egg, between their white and red elements.

The very first thing that develops after conception is a very fine line, like a thin hair, or a tiny brushstroke on the mother's womb. That line carries all potentialities. Your consciousness is residing there in that tiny line.

Although the line is very thin, it is still hollow like a reed instrument. When there is volition, air, and energy moving through that tube, it makes the sound *ah*. That primordial sound is the source of all letters and all language.

For those great meditation masters who have experienced wisdom, that sound *ah* is recognized as emptiness. Any expression the masters make arises from that emptiness; it is devoid of emotion and karma.

The actions of the masters are almost like the wind and the rain, like great storms blowing in the sky. Those weather systems do not create any karma. Storms are just the movement of energy. If storms destroy things, it is not because they are acting out of anger. They are just a natural movement of energy.

It is our human minds that are filled with anger, desire, and ignorance. As a result of these afflictive emotions, all our words and inner chattering are only an expression of our feelings. This expression does not arise from the empty sound of that inner space. It arises from our destructive emotions, which force the mind to express itself.

You may be wondering what that personal experience of wisdom is like. This is a challenging question to answer since the experience itself involves the dissolution of the person. An individual must experience it to understand it, yet the individual vanishes in the experience.

In deep meditation there is great silence. All thoughts dissolve. All emotions dissolve. Once you have a glimpse of that inner space, then whatever you produce will no longer be an expression of emotions. It will all be emptiness.

There is no expression in that inner space. That is why it is so peaceful. That is why there is no karma driving our actions or being produced. There is no emotion in that inner space, which is why it is so restful.

The wisdom gone beyond is also *inexpressible*. Such wisdom is connected to the inner space between our thoughts. In deep meditation, when you experience wisdom, it is inexpressible.

During a tantric empowerment ritual, when you are introduced to a mantra by your teacher, you are also introduced to the nature of sound, which is emptiness. As you recite the mantra thousands of times, you become increasingly familiar with that emptiness of sound.

Now if you do not have that realization of emptiness, then sound will continue to be a method of expression. Sound will continue to be a vehicle for all the emotions. If we attempt to express this experience of wisdom through emotional language, it will be misunderstood. For this reason, wisdom cannot be transferred or transmitted through study alone. We can be introduced to it through tantric empowerment rituals, but we can only truly realize it through practice.

You may be wondering how you can certify the realization of authentic wisdom. How can you measure it? How can you determine if it is true? Only through your meditation, when you have higher and higher realizations, will you know without a doubt that you have realized wisdom.

After meditating for six years, the Buddha attained enlightenment. Once he was enlightened, others requested that he share his experience. At first he chose not to teach. He said, "I have realized this great wisdom, but you are not ready yet. Even if I give you teachings, you will not receive anything." He remained in silence for another forty-nine days. He knew that he had gained realization, but he recognized that there was no true way to communicate his experience to others. Only the earth, sky, and space were his witnesses.

True self-awareness occurs for the first time when you see that inner space. That inner space is not just a state of nothingness. Along with emptiness there is clarity and awareness. It is empty of all emotions and thoughts. At the same time there is a deep awareness of that emptiness. That empty nature is the first moment of true self-awareness.

Self-awareness can only unfold when your mind is purified of destructive emotions. In the resulting mind of *clear light*, there is the first opportunity to see the true nature of the self, which is emptiness.

We see the term *clear light* very often in Buddhist texts. Clear light is like candlelight. Candlelight is self-illuminating. If a candle sees anything, it is because of its own light. Likewise, the mind can only see its true nature when it has become its own clear light.

Our wisdom nature can only be revealed through the purification of negativities. When all negativities are gone, when all obscurations are removed, then the light of wisdom will shine. That is the first moment of true self-awareness.

According to the Buddha, we all have buddha nature. Our buddha nature is concealed by negative karma and defilements. If properly practiced, meditation and skillful methods can purify our karma and our destructive emotions.

Once our defilements are purified, we can uncover the clear light within us. That is the buddha nature. Buddhists believe that our true nature is pure—it is good. Due to our karma and emotions, that innate purity is temporarily obscured.

For something to be created, it needs to have causes and conditions. For a plant to grow, it must have a seed, sunlight, water, and soil.

Wisdom does not need a cause or condition. That is why it is unborn. Wisdom is there from beginningless time. Wisdom will be there without stopping even when you have become a buddha. Just like outer space, wisdom will always remain.

Space does not have any beginning. Space is not created by any causes and conditions. Regardless of what unfolds within that space, no matter how many stars and planets come and go, space will remain unconditioned.

We all have that inherent wisdom. Right now, that wisdom is buried under all our emotions and karma. We do not see our true natures yet. The practice of meditation and discipline can purify our karma and emotions. Then, for the first time, we will see the clear light inside us.

Outer space is a great mirror for inner space. At present, our minds are filled with a continuous series of thoughts. Those thoughts are like drops of water rushing so quickly one after another that they appear to be a continuous stream. Through meditation, we can slowly begin to see the space between our thoughts. Whenever we can see a gap between those drops, then we are catching a glimpse of the true nature of the mind.

Some wisdom teachings say, "In the nature of the mind, mind does not exist." Mind exists with thoughts and a thinker, with desire, anger, and ignorance. Once we have seen the true nature of the mind, then even the mind does not exist.

We can say that mind was born, and mind may cease, but our wisdom nature is never born and will never cease. That nature of the mind is just like outer space. It is infinite and unconditioned. For yogis who have seen the inner space between thoughts, inner space and outer space are the same. They are unified, and those yogis are no longer separate from the universe.

In this inner space, there is no idea of a *self.* Without the self there is also no concept of other. Without self and other, all conflicts that arise between subject, object, and phenomena dissolve. Everything is unified in that inner space, and there is profound peace.

Outer space can become a great mirror to see the inner space within us. Most of the time we do not see that inner space, and we choose to not even contemplate the vastness of outer space. We are caught up in this cycle of birth and death. We are distracted by all the conflicts that arise in this interdependency. We are struggling constantly with change, with illness, with the conditioned nature of our existence. If we go beyond all these interdependencies, then we see the wisdom of space and can achieve liberation.

It is this wisdom that we can study and reflect on in the *Heart Sutra.* This sutra is very interesting. Most sutras consist of the Buddha's own teachings, but the Buddha speaks only a few words in the *Heart Sutra*. The rest of the sutra is a discussion between Shariputra and Avalokiteshvara. Shariputra is an arhat who represents Theravada Buddhism, and Avalokiteshvara is a bodhisattva who represents Mahayana Buddhism.

For Theravada Buddhist practitioners, Shariputra is an arhat—a highly realized meditator who has achieved enlightenment. In the Mahayana tradition, however, an arhat is not considered completely enlightened. For this reason, Shariputra is still trying to learn from Avalokiteshvara. Throughout the dialogue, the Buddha is in a profound state of meditation and does not speak. Shariputra is inspired by the Buddha to ask Avalokiteshvara questions.

The terms arhat, bodhisattva, and buddha reflect three different levels of realization. A buddha is fully enlightened and has attained complete wisdom. Shariputra and Avalokiteshvara are not yet fully enlightened. They are attempting to discuss the wisdom that they do not yet have. All the while, the Buddha is just meditating quietly without saying a word!

The Buddha already knows that wisdom is inconceivable and inexpressible, so he remains silent. Those of us who do not have this wisdom yet need to discuss the teachings in order to reach a greater understanding.

It is important that all that study and reflection and discussion are moving in the right direction. That is why it is essential to learn this through right view. If we discuss this without right view, it will take much longer to understand.

Even though we are only studying the concise version of this sutra, we will still see how profound these teachings are. Studying and reflecting on this sutra will help us to learn about our true nature and will inspire our meditation.

# 12

# The Five Aggregates

This is what I once heard at the time the Blessed One was seated on Vulture's Peak in Rajagriha with a huge congregation of the exalted community of bhikshus and bodhisattvas. At that time, the Blessed One was dwelling in the meditation called Profound Vision.

Also at that time, the great being and bodhisattva Arya Avalokiteshvara was reviewing the profound characteristics of the Prajnaparamita and saw the natural emptiness of the five aggregates.

THIS PASSAGE FROM THE *Heart Sutra* is certifying that it reflects the teachings of the Buddha. The main narrator here is the Buddha's attendant Ananda, who was traveling everywhere with him. It was Ananda who compiled the sutra. It is said that Ananda had a photographic memory and that whatever he heard he remembered verbatim. As a result, he is a reliable witness and narrator.

As noted earlier, the Buddha is in a very deep state of meditation called Profound Vision throughout most of the sutra. "Profound" refers to emptiness and ultimate truth, while "Vision" refers to inter-dependent origination and relative truth. It is only at the very end that the Buddha speaks. Even while maintaining his noble silence, he could communicate in different ways. He was always teaching, although not necessarily through spoken words. Since the wisdom gone beyond contained in the *Heart Sutra* is inexpressible, the Buddha's meditative silence here is perhaps a more effective teaching.

Words are useless and ineffective when it comes to expressing ulti-mate truth. Through deep meditation, however, the Buddha can com-municate in different ways through light and energy.

It is said that there are five right conditions needed for a proper teaching. An authentic teacher is essential. Since the Buddha was a fully enlightened teacher, he is a very reliable source. Teachers can only become teachers when they have students. Students are the second right condition.

It is interesting that if you visit Vulture's Peak today, you will see that the actual summit is quite a small area. The sutra describes a huge congregation gathered there. This congregation included all of the Buddha's disciples who are represented by Shariputra. Meanwhile, Avalokiteshvara, who is speaking with Shariputra in the sutra, rep-resents all the bodhisattvas of Mahayana Buddhism.

The sutra also states that there were humans, gods, demigods, and gandharvas present on Vulture's Peak. In Buddhism, there are twenty-seven classes of gods from the desire, form, and formless realms. These gods are still caught in the wheel of life and are not liberated from sam-sara. The formless gods are immaterial, so they do not need much space to attend the gathering!

Gandharvas are like spirits that are formed in the intermediate state of the bardo, after we die but before we take rebirth. Gandharva means "smell eater" because these spirits cannot eat real food in the bardo, but they can still experience smell.

A huge congregation can fit on this small mountain peak because many of them are formless. Shariputra and Avalokiteshvara were joined by the Sangha of bhikshus and all the bodhisattvas. All these beings are the Buddha's students.

The teaching is the third right condition. At the core of the *Heart Sutra* is the Prajnaparamita, the Perfection of Wisdom. This is the most profound wisdom that the Buddha has shared with his students.

The fourth right condition is the right time. Timing is very important if the teachings are to successfully take root in the student. As we know, after the Buddha first attained enlightenment, he refused to teach. His disciples were requesting that he share his wisdom, but he did not feel the students were ready. He remained silent for forty-nine days before teaching the four noble truths at Sarnath. It was only after delivering the four noble truths that the Buddha felt his students were ready for the profound Prajnaparamita.

The Prajnaparamita is a Mahayana teaching based on emptiness. Correct timing is pivotal to properly receiving the emptiness teachings. The teachings say that if the timing is not perfect, then even if students listen to a profound emptiness teaching, they will misunderstand its essence. The students may even become overwhelmed and frightened, and this could be harmful to them.

Recently I saw a new commentary on the *Heart Sutra* titled *The Heart Attack Sutra*! This is a reference to many incidents where disciples were not ready for the Prajnaparamita teachings. When these students heard the *Heart Sutra*, they were completely shocked! Some students even panicked and experienced symptoms like heart attacks. Other students became very spaced out in order to cope. We can learn from this experience that timing is very important to delivering teachings correctly.

The fifth right condition is location. For this reason, the Buddha chose Vulture's Peak, which is a very special place. I believe that it is the highest peak in that region. The higher you go, the more the energies are affected. Place can make a big difference.

I heard a story once about the famous violinist Joshua Bell. One day he performed an experiment by bringing his violin to a busy metro station in Washington, DC, during rush hour. He stood on the platform and played his three-million-dollar violin for forty-five minutes while thousands of commuters rushed past him. He played some of the most intricate Bach pieces ever written.

Only six people stopped to listen during those forty-five minutes. He made only thirty-two dollars in change that people threw into his violin case. When he stopped playing everyone ignored him and no one clapped.

This is a great example of the importance we give to location. When Bell played that same music in concert halls all over the world, he sold out every show. Tickets were very expensive, and his skill was deeply valued.

We can see from this story how venue, popularity, promotion, and showmanship all factor into an attraction. He was the same musician, playing the same intricate music on the same violin, but barely anyone stopped to listen in that busy metro station.

Often in the Buddhist tradition these five conditions are also called the *five auspicious conditions*. When all five conditions come together, then the teachings can be fully transmitted.

We see here in the sutra that all five conditions have come together: right teacher, right teaching, right disciples, right place, and right time. Even if one of these conditions is missing, if one condition is wrong, then the teaching will not be transmitted. Even if the teacher is right, but the students are not ready, then the teachings will not be understood. Even if the teacher and students are right, but the teaching is not authentic or appropriate at that time, then the wisdom will not be conveyed.

For example, if the Buddha had taught the *Heart Sutra* to Theravada practitioners without any foundational teachings, most of these Buddhists would have been completely shocked. The teaching has to occur at the right time and in the right place.

The five auspicious conditions were present at Vulture's Peak in Rajagriha. The Buddha and Avalokiteshvara were both in a profound state of meditation on emptiness. The student Shariputra was curious about emptiness and was ready to receive the wisdom teachings.

Although the Buddha was in a meditative state and remained silent, his powerful presence inspired this dialogue between Avalokiteshvara and Shariputra. The Buddha had the power to communicate to others through many different forms.

> Also at that time, the heroic being and bodhisattva Arya Avalokiteshvara was reviewing the profound characteristics of the Prajnaparamita and saw the natural emptiness of the five aggregates.

As discussed above, the five aggregates are the Buddhist presentation and categorization of all conditioned things. The first aggregate is the aggregate of form. Form includes all objects in the material world. It refers to something that is composed of atoms. According to Buddhist philosophy, atoms are made up of the four elements of earth, air, fire, and water. These elemental atoms are the foundation of the material world.

Form refers to outer objects as well as to our own physical bodies. It is only due to our physical organs that we are even able to relate to outer objects. If we were blind, then we could not perceive visual objects. This aggregate of form includes the outer sense objects and all sense organs. Here the eye organ is the sense organ, and whatever it perceives is considered the sense object. There are sense objects corresponding to all other sense organs. These sense organs include the ear, nose, tongue, and body.

Due to the sense organ of our ears, we experience all kinds of sounds in the material world. Some are natural sounds, like falling rain or the murmur of a stream. Some sounds are produced by other beings, such as a dog barking or a rooster crowing. There are so many different types of sound, but they are all considered to be a kind of form.

The same is true with smell. Smell is considered part of the material world and is perceived by the sense organ of the nose. There are also many different tastes, which the sense organ of the tongue can experience. Due to our physical bodies, we also have tangibles. This includes all objects that our physical bodies can touch.

In addition to the sense organs and sense objects, the Buddha also said that there are mental materials. When we get angry, that anger can generate chemicals in our physical bodies. Scientists are now saying that if you have more negative emotions, then you generate more toxins. If you have more positive emotions, then you produce a healthier physical body.

According to the Buddhist understanding, whenever we make a resolution—not to kill, for example—then that resolution to avoid killing has the power to transform us and even to generate positive forms inside us. These mental resolutions have the power to change us even on a material level. Neuroscientists are now able to prove that meditation alters the physical structure of the brain.

The sense objects are like food for their corresponding sense organs. All the visual objects that we perceive are like food for our eye organs. When those visual objects are agreeable to us, they will give us pleasure. When they are disagreeable, they will generate aversion in us. In this way we can see that when sense organ, sense object, and consciousness come together, they generate feelings. For this reason, the second aggregate is the aggregate of feeling.

Feelings arise within us because of our interactions with the objects of the universe. When we see something very beautiful, it will generate feelings of attraction, desire, and happiness. When we smell something delightful, it may generate positive memories. The same is true with hearing. When we experience beautiful sounds, like music, they may inspire many pleasurable feelings in us. When we taste delicious foods, we may have a rush of positive sensations. When we touch something soft like silk, or when we warm our hands by a fire, we may feel real comfort in these tangible sensations.

When the sense organs interact with material objects, they create conditions for all kinds of feelings to arise. When we eat our favorite foods, we experience pleasure at the physical level and happiness at the mental level. When we consume something disagreeable, then at the physical level we may experience pain, and at the mental level this may generate unhappiness inside us.

The Buddha said that along with feelings of pain and pleasure, happiness and unhappiness, there is a fifth category of neutral feelings. Neutral feelings mean that there is neither pain nor pleasure, neither happiness nor unhappiness.

Although there are five feelings, the Buddha said that by nature these five feelings can be categorized into three root emotions. He taught that all feelings are the result of interactions based on the three afflictive emotions of desire, anger, and ignorance.

Whenever we have attachment and desire for an object, if our desire is fulfilled, we will experience pleasure and happiness. When we interact with objects based on anger, this will generate more pain and suffering. When we interact with them based on ignorance, this will generate neutral feelings.

In this way, all five feelings can be condensed into three core afflictive emotions. We tend to be most aware of happiness and unhappiness, pain and pleasure, in our daily lives. Neutral feelings dominate our lives, but we tend to ignore them because they are not experienced as strong feelings. We often do not even realize that neutral reactions are feelings at all. When we do not feel tangible pain and pleasure, happiness or unhappiness, then the resulting feeling is a neutral one, but we do not register it as a feeling.

Even when we think we are not feeling anything, we are still operating on underlying neutral feelings. Even when we are sleeping, we experience neutral feelings. Neutral feelings are dominant because ignorance is our dominant emotion.

Desire and anger are both based on ignorance, which means that happiness, unhappiness, pain, pleasure, and neutral feelings are all rooted in ignorance. This basic ignorance is the ignorance of not knowing one's true self. As long as we are driven by our egos and are ignorant of our true natures, the resulting ignorance will be the base of all our feelings.

This second aggregate of feeling is experienced by all beings in samsara. In Buddhism we describe six different classes of beings. There are hell beings, hungry ghosts, animals, humans, demigods, and gods. Beings in the lower realms experience more physical feelings. Beings in the higher realms, like the demigods and gods, primarily experience strong mental feelings.

Here in the human realm, when we are starving, when we are thirsty or have physical pain, those physical sensations overtake our mental feelings. When we have more physical comfort in the human realm, if we live in more developed countries, our suffering is often greater at the mental level.

You can see this if you visit poorer countries. People who have to physically work hard all day just to get enough food to eat are often more mentally satisfied. When the meal is attained, there is a feeling of contentment.

On the other hand, in areas where people do not need to worry about food and material comforts, we often find much higher levels of mental dissatisfaction. Mental feelings have much less to do with the consumption of objects. When all our basic needs are easily met, then it is the emotions in the mind that can generate all kinds of feelings.

The more thoughts we have, the more miserable we often become. Mental feelings of happiness and unhappiness depend on our ideas and our perceptions. These feelings have more to do with our concepts and ideas. These feelings arise from all our mental projections. The mental feelings are not dependent on material objects. They are all based on our thoughts and emotions.

Physical feelings depend on consumption or interaction with an object. This is one important distinction we need to make between physical and mental feelings. Pleasure is a physical experience. Happiness is a mental experience. Although they are both related to fulfilling desire, they work in different ways. The teachings say that mental feelings are actually stronger. Mental feelings have the ability to remain with us even if the physical object is not present. In fact, mental feelings can remain in our mindstreams even after we lose our physical bodies.

Even in the bardo state after death we can continue to experience mental feelings.

The third aggregate is ideation. Ideation means forming ideas based on the characteristics of objects and names. Everything has general characteristics. Within those general characteristics, we identify an individual or an object based on their unique characteristics. Unique characteristics include broad categories as well as very specific characteristics.

For example, we can tell the difference between a human and an animal based on a series of unique characteristics. Within that broader category we can then tell the difference between a man and a woman based on the characteristics of their genders. Between people of the same gender, we have another level of unique characteristics to identify each individual on the planet.

Along with unique and the general characteristics, we also use our own karma and emotions to form all kinds of ideas and reactions to everything we perceive. Due to our inner conditions, we project different values onto the objects around us, which then influences our perceptions.

In this way, ideation includes the characteristics and inner conditions with which we perceive the world. Ideation refers to our concepts: all knowledge, all opinions, all schools of thought. As discussed earlier, all the isms are included in the third aggregate of ideation.

The fourth aggregate is called formation. Formation includes all mental activities as well as fourteen formations that are neither mental nor material. When we look closely, we see that all activities of the mind are rooted in our emotions. When we examine our inner psychology, we can see that there are three categories of emotion: positive, negative, and neutral emotions.

This fourth aggregate of formation includes the foundations of all Buddhist psychology. This is a very profound subject. Through closer examination we can see how our emotions are the creators of our karma.

All karmic actions are based on our emotions. However, the same action may have different causes. We may kill an animal out of desire for meat, we may kill an enemy out of anger, or we may accidentally kill another living being through ignorance. In all of these cases, the activity is still rooted in one of the afflictive emotions.

This fourth aggregate of formation is really a study of Buddhist psychology. If you wish to explore this in depth, you can study the *Abhidharmakosha*, which enumerates the emotions and their characteristics in great detail. The *Abhidharmakosha* examines how the emotions are formed and all of the actions related to these emotions.

The fifth aggregate is consciousness. When we are first conceived between the father's and mother's elements, we only have our basic mind. Once the egg and sperm and our basic mind come together, the fetus can begin to develop. As our organs are formed, the six consciousnesses related to the six sense organs will arise.

Through our sense organs the basic mind has vehicles for the six consciousnesses. When the eye organ perceives visual objects, eye consciousness arises. When the ear organ hears sounds, ear consciousness occurs. In this way, there are six consciousnesses corresponding to the six sense organs of eye, ear, nose, tongue, body, and mind. The fifth aggregate includes all of these consciousnesses.

Only through proper understanding of the five aggregates will the words of the *Heart Sutra* be comprehensible. If we have studied the first aggregate of form, then when the sutra says "form is emptiness," we will have some idea of what this means.

Avalokiteshvara has attained a very high level of realization. He is a bodhisattva who has realized the empty nature of the five aggregates. He has not only realized the empty nature of oneself but also the empty nature of all beings and the entire universe.

> Then the elder Shariputra, moved by the power of the Buddha, addressed Arya Avalokiteshvara with these words: "Noble son! How should someone who wishes to perform the profound practice of the Prajnaparamita train himself?"

Here Shariputra is inspired by the Buddha to ask Avalokiteshvara how to train in the Prajnaparamita or the Perfection of Wisdom. He wants to understand how one can train to realize the empty nature of the five aggregates.

The term we are translating as *aggregate*—*skandha* in Sanskrit— can also mean "collection." By understanding the aggregate of form in the present moment, we simultaneously reach a realization about the nature of all form, past, present, and future. That is why it is called an "aggregate." Through gaining insight into the aggregates, we come to an understanding of all conditioned things regardless of time or place.

The present aggregate is what you will see and experience. We recognize something as material because it has a form; it is tangible, and we can see it in front of us. This object could have existed in the past and may exist in the future. Aggregates are a collective realization that extends through all three times. The same is true of the aggregates of feeling, ideation, formation, and consciousness.

These five aggregates are vital to our experiences. Our physical bodies are composed of the first aggregate of form. We experience the second and third aggregates when we have so many feelings and ideas in our lives. All our karma and mental activities are related to the fourth aggregate of formation. The fifth aggregate of mind is the foundation for all six sense consciousnesses to experience the universe.

The five aggregates are the basis for all our projections of self and ego. The aggregates create a sense of an individual self, an "I" that we cling to. As a result of this sense of "I," we are able to project ownership onto the outer objects of the five aggregates, and we cling to them as well.

All of your five aggregates and all of the five aggregates of the universe can become the domain of "I" and "my." When this happens, we are making them the properties of our emotions.

For this reason, whenever we have a strong sense of "I" and "my" in our lives, there are generally very strong emotions related to our experiences. These intense projections of self and property are rooted in the three destructive emotions of attachment, anger, and ignorance.

We have these destructive emotions to begin with because we do not recognize the empty nature of the aggregates. As long as we are identifying with a substantial self, we will also have attachment to other things in the universe. If something happens to threaten any of these attachments, then we will have pain and anger.

# 13

# Feeling and Ideation

AVALOKITESHVARA IS a bodhisattva who represents limitless compassion. *Bodhi* in Sanskrit means "awakened." Bodhisattvas are courageous because they have realized selflessness, and they have generated a strong resolution to achieve buddhahood for the benefit of all sentient beings. Based on that resolution, they have done years of meditation practice and have become awakened.

According to legend, Avalokiteshvara was known to have postponed his own enlightenment for the benefit of other sentient beings. It is said that he was about to become a fully enlightened buddha but chose to delay his complete enlightenment so that he could help others.

There are different ways to take the bodhisattva vow. One approach is called the *shepherd-like vow*, which is probably what Avalokiteshvara had taken. It is the duty of the shepherd to follow and protect the sheep. When you take the bodhisattva vow as a shepherd, you are essentially vowing to help all sentient beings to achieve buddhahood. You are promising that you will not accept complete enlightenment until all other beings have become enlightened.

For this reason, Avalokiteshvara will remain a bodhisattva forever because sentient beings are limitless. There will never be a time when all the sentient beings will be simultaneously enlightened. For this reason, in keeping with his resolution, Avalokiteshvara will remain a bodhisattva.

Although Avalokiteshvara is a bodhisattva, his realization of the wisdom gone beyond—of the Prajnaparamita—is at a very high level. He has seen the natural emptiness of the five aggregates.

If we look deeper, we find that all five aggregates are insubstantial. We cannot find any independently existing aggregates. They are constantly changing. The five aggregates are based on our afflictive emotions and negative karma. As a result, we are subject to continual pain and suffering.

We cannot find any static existence in the five aggregates. Not only are they void of inherent existence, but their very nature is emptiness. This empty nature is not something that has been theorized or created. It is a truth that is revealed to those who gain some level of realization.

Although their nature is emptiness, the five aggregates are interdependent and can be created by our emotions—by our karma. They are still in the domain of karma. They have causes and results.

Karma can be created by volition in the mind. The fourth-century Indian Buddhist scholar Vasubandu said, "The universe is created by karma, and karma is created by volition in the mind." So these five aggregates are interdependent. They arise as a result of volition and karma, but their true nature is emptiness.

Avalokiteshvara had this realization of the natural emptiness of the five aggregates, so he was highly qualified to train Shariputra. We have not seen the natural emptiness of the five aggregates yet. That is why we are still here in samsara.

I think there is an order to how we experience the reality of the five aggregates. For example, right now in our lives we do not have much doubt about our material objects or our physical bodies. We can see form. We can touch it. We have some common agreement as far as form and as far as our physical bodies are concerned.

Due to our physical sense organs, we can perceive all of these physical objects. We can see, hear, touch, smell, and taste. Our inner conditions and emotions will project very different experiences onto the same objects. Two people may see the same object in very different ways, based on their emotions and karma.

This first aggregate of form provides our physical experiences of the outer material world. Our sense organs gather all this information around us. Through this aggregate of form we then have a basis for the aggregate of feeling to arise.

The second aggregate of feeling is a little more subtle than the first aggregate of form. Whether you will feel pleasure, pain, happiness, unhappiness, or neutral feelings in response to an experience is unique to your present circumstances. Form is operating on a grosser level. Feeling is more subtle, which is why the Buddha made feeling the second aggregate.

The third aggregate of ideation can be even more subtle than feeling. The Buddha organized the aggregates from gross to subtle. The aggregate of formation is even more subtle than ideation. The fifth aggregate of consciousness is the most subtle of all. It is subtle enough to exist even after death and does not depend on a gross material body.

When we are steeped in education based on the science of matter, it can be very difficult to accept mind or consciousness as something immaterial. If you speak to scientists or doctors about mind or consciousness, they rarely describe it as something immaterial. Instead, they will often say that consciousness is just a product of the brain's functions. Since consciousness is too subtle to locate in any tangible way, there is confusion about it.

From our current experience as humans, we understand these aggregates in the order that the Buddha taught them—from gross to subtle. We have a physical experience, we respond with feeling, we develop ideas, we create mental activities, and we gain consciousness.

This order of experience is different when we are first conceived. When we are first in utero, we do not have any of these sense organs yet. These organs grow in the later stages of fetal development.

In that first moment of conception, our consciousness becomes imprisoned or sandwiched between the egg and sperm. At that level, all we have is consciousness. Then, from this consciousness, our emotions arise.

Due to the ignorance of not knowing one's true self, when our father and mother are in union, we have this attachment to one of them. That attraction is what draws us to the moment of conception.

The process begins with the ignorance of not knowing our true nature. Then, due to our attraction to one of the parents, our mind is drawn to conception. When we have attraction, we also naturally have aversion. We will experience a subtle aversion to the other parent.

Formation, as I mentioned, refers to all mental activities. This includes all the emotions detailed in Buddhist psychology. There are so many emotions you can study, but the root afflictive emotions are always ignorance, attachment, and anger.

We bring those core afflictive emotions to the moment of our conception. Based on these formations, we develop ideation and feeling, and then slowly the physical organs develop in the fetus. Our fetal development moves in reverse through the five aggregates, relative to how we experience them now. Currently we experience the aggregates from gross to subtle. However, we evolved in the opposite order, from subtle consciousness to gross matter.

Since we have not seen the natural emptiness of the five aggregates, we become attached to these aggregates. Due to our emotions and karma, we have formed a strong sense of ego based on these five aggregates.

This strong sense of self that we carry is based entirely on these five aggregates. We have very deep attachments to "my body," "my feelings," "my ideas," "my emotions," and "my mind." We have the strongest emotional involvement with ourselves. This attachment to the self is what creates attachment to all our possessions.

This notion of ownership is really an extension of our attachment to ourselves. We say, "my house," "my car," "my town," "my country," and really we are just expanding our attachment to ourselves into the universe.

In the teachings it is said that the root cause of samsara is attachment to "I" and "my." When you have these strong attachments, you cannot experience wisdom. Instead, these attachments create more obscurations and karma. Samsara is an endless cycle of birth, death, and rebirth. We are trapped in this cyclic existence unless we gain some realization of the empty nature of things.

The Buddha said that the second aggregate of feeling and the third aggregate of ideation could both be included under the fourth aggregate of formation. This is because they are mental activities. The Buddha kept them separate because feelings and ideations are the primary causes of conflicts in the world.

## FEELINGS

Let's examine the role of feelings in our lives. Everything we pursue and consume in our lives is an attempt to gain more pleasure and happiness. The wish to attain happiness and pleasure are a driving force in our lives.

If we look closer, we see that this hunger for external happiness and pleasure is due to the fact that we have not cultivated inner contentment and balance. If we are not at peace within ourselves, then we will search everywhere for happiness. We will even create conflict with others, blaming our unhappiness on those around us.

Arguments between couples are often related to one person feeling the other person is not making them happy or meeting their needs anymore. So many conflicts are based on the expectation that something external can make us happier. This is true of nations fighting over resources or religion. As long as we have not cultivated inner peace and happiness, we will look to our external lives to fulfill us.

Feeling is one of the main causes of samsara. As we study the twelve interdependent links in the coming chapters, we may be surprised to learn that the link of feeling is the key to whether we will circle back into samsara or whether we will reach enlightenment.

This must be the reason why the Buddha chose the first noble truth, the truth of suffering, as his very first teaching. After reaching enlightenment he could have chosen some loftier idea as his first teaching. He realized in his infinite wisdom, however, that acknowledging the truth of suffering was the first step to liberation.

We are constantly pursuing happiness and pleasure. We have been doing this for many, many lifetimes. Yet still we have not found genuine happiness. Instead, the harder we search for happiness, the more miserable we seem to become! We are looking in the wrong place and in the wrong way. The word *dukkha* means "suffering" or "dissatisfaction." Since we do not know where to look for genuine happiness, no matter what we do in our lives we remain dissatisfied.

Relationships in samsara often start in a good mode and end in a bad mode. We are conceived through desire. We come into this life looking for pleasure, but the end is always pain and suffering. The end is always death!

Buddha was an expert on the truth of feelings. Since he had freed himself from all feelings, he was able to observe how they cause us to suffer. Feelings blind us. We do not see feelings in an objective way. We should never underestimate the power of feelings in our lives. The more we study them and gain some awareness, the more we will begin to free ourselves.

One time a student asked me, "If we are already miserable, and we want to become happier, then why did the Buddha focus on this noble truth of suffering in his first teaching?" The Buddha taught the truth of suffering so that we can achieve freedom from that suffering.

The Buddha did not teach the noble truth of suffering to make us suffer more! He was trying to show us all aspects of suffering so that we could achieve liberation. Just as we need to become aware of the root causes of an illness before we can find the proper treatment, we have to find the root causes of our suffering before we can achieve freedom.

Suffering is part of the aggregate of feeling. As we have discussed, there are five kinds of feelings: happiness, unhappiness, pain, pleasure, and neutral feelings. Suffering is very much a product of these feelings.

Our feelings are the cause of the suffering in our lives. They create karma and cause us to be reborn repeatedly. Feelings are also the basis for our fights and arguments. Even though feelings can be included under the fourth aggregate of formation, the Buddha made them the second aggregate to emphasize their importance.

Feelings may play an even more vital role for those who are less intellectual. I imagine that in the animal world, feelings may be more important than they are to humans. Generally animals' IQs are lower than the IQs of humans, but perhaps animals are more sensitive. It is possible that animals are driven predominantly by feelings.

Unlike animals, humans have the potential to refine their intelligence through education and meditation. The more we meditate, the more awareness we gain about our feelings, and the more we may be able to overcome them.

There is a risk with humans, though, that the more intelligent they are, and the more educated they become, the more attachment they will have to ideas. Their intellectual reasoning may help them gain some control over their feelings, but in the process they may come to over identify with their ideas.

## IDEATION

This is why the Buddha kept ideation as a third aggregate even though it could also be included under the fourth aggregate of formation. He did this to emphasize the power that ideas also have in our lives. Intellectuals can become very attached to their ideas and isms. They can sacrifice feelings in order to protect their ideas.

Throughout history, people have been willing to endure all kinds of pain and suffering in the name of religion. They have also been willing to let their isms become so extreme that they commit violence to defend their belief systems. In this way, we see that ideation is also a great obstacle on the path to liberation.

Feeling and ideation have great power over us. The Buddha chose to give them each their own category even though they can be considered part of the fourth aggregate of formation. He did this to emphasize what a critical role they play in our lives.

Due to our five aggregates, we develop strong attachment to ourselves.

When there is a "self," then everything else becomes "other." Once there is "self" and "other" there is the potential for conflict to arise. All of this dualism is the result of us not realizing the natural emptiness of the five aggregates.

Avalokiteshvara has seen the emptiness of the five aggregates, which includes the emptiness of all conditioned things. Emptiness is often misunderstood to be equivalent to nothingness. The original word for emptiness in Sanskrit is *shunyata*. It is impossible to truly describe emptiness through language. If emptiness is not realized through meditation, then no matter how much we try to express it in words, there may still be some misconception.

It is for this reason that at the beginning of the *Heart Sutra* it says that the wisdom gone beyond is inexpressible. The sutra is merely a reference point. It cannot give us an experience of emptiness. Only meditation can give us that inner experience.

Emptiness must not be misunderstood to be a state of nothingness. Furthermore, emptiness is not eternal, independent, or inherently existent. When we refer to emptiness it is something that has gone beyond the four extremes of existence, nonexistence, both, and neither.

The purpose of this emptiness is to free the mind from its own emotions. Right now, our minds are imprisoned in our emotions and mental activities. Due to these conditions our minds create more karma, and we remain trapped in this cycle of samsara. Emptiness is the realization that can free us from the extremes. Emptiness is vital to our liberation.

Even within Buddhism we have four different philosophical conclusions about emptiness. The higher you go philosophically, the more you realize the lower philosophies are inconclusive. The emptiness we speak of here in the sutra is the emptiness that goes beyond all four philosophical schools of reasoning.

The four schools of Buddhist philosophy I am referring to are the Vaibhashika, Sautrantika, Mind-Only, and Madhyamika. As a student you can spend many years studying these philosophies. They are very complex. Such an undertaking is difficult because it involves studying the emptiness of the limitless universe, including the emptiness of ourselves!

For our own practical purposes, though, we are studying emptiness so that we can go beyond the personal self. We are studying emptiness so that we can go beyond our clinging to the self and to phenomena. Self-clinging—to the ego and to our possessions—is the cause of all our afflictive emotions and karma. That is why we cycle again and again through samsara.

Philosophical study can give us a very good reference point, but merely studying philosophical conclusions will not make emptiness a personal experience. These conclusions are coming from great teachers, both Tibetan and Indian. It is valuable to study their profound texts as a guide, but those texts cannot give you the experience of emptiness. The realization of emptiness can only happen through meditation.

Scholars may spend many years studying emptiness. It will remain a kind of intellectual accumulation unless they actualize that experience. Intellectual accumulations can never become wisdom. Regardless of how much information we gather, we will only experience transformation through our own experience of emptiness.

Scholars may develop stronger and stronger attachment to their ideas the more they study. It is essential to understand this third aggregate of ideation to counteract these attachments. Scholars can become very opinionated and attached to their beliefs. There is no wisdom if you cannot go beyond grasping at knowledge.

Seeing the natural emptiness of the five aggregates is a method to free us from samsara and even from nirvana. This may be confusing at first to those who see nirvana as an end result. The wisdom of the Prajnaparamita is profound and even goes beyond nirvana. It goes beyond all four philosophical schools of Buddhism. It is the realization of complete wisdom through meditation.

Only through such realization will you become a bodhisattva like Avalokiteshvara. Only then will you be qualified to discuss something based on your inner experience. Until that personal realization is achieved, you are just repeating the words of others. You are merely redistributing information you have gathered.

In the *Heart Sutra*, Avalokiteshvara shares his personal realization of wisdom with Shariputra. This does not reflect an intellectual experience of emptiness. It is coming directly from meditative realization. These are not mere words. They are rich with meaning and blessings.

At our level of understanding, the *Heart Sutra* may seem very paradoxical. This is because we cannot understand this highest level of wisdom from where we are now. The bodhisattvas have seen the wisdom of emptiness. They see with wisdom eyes, and we see only with our emotional human eyes. What we see is always shaded by our inner conditions, emotions, and karma. We must keep this distinction in mind. When the sutra feels confusing to us, we can remember that it comes from an enlightened source.

# 14

# Formation and Consciousness

## MENTAL FORMATION

THERE ARE TWO KINDS of formation. The first is mental formation. The Abhidharma lists fifty-one different mental activities, which include many emotions, and it can teach us about ourselves and about human psychology.

There are some emotions or mental activities that are neutral, which are there with us all the time. For example, memory is neutral by its own nature. It is neither negative nor positive. It can easily become negative if it is filled with anger, and if memory becomes a part of that anger. It can also become positive, as with memories that are filled with compassion. Memory by itself is a neutral function, but it can easily be connected with either positive or negative emotions.

Anger is a good example of a negative mental activity. Anger is negative because it is destructive. Anger is negative because it is harming you and has the potential to harm others. There are many emotions and mental activities that are destructive and negative.

Compassion is a good example of a positive mental activity. Compassion is positive because it can bring more happiness to oneself and others.

There is another category of mental activity that is considered "indefinite." Regret is an example of an indefinite mental activity because it has the potential to go either toward the positive or the negative. If we regret doing something good, then that regret can become negative. If we regret doing something negative, then that regret can become positive.

It is essential to understand mental activities. We can study them objectively, but the most important thing is to look within ourselves to deepen our understanding of our own mental activities.

We have all these emotions that are fluctuating. They are never static. They are changing all the time. One moment you are in love with someone. The next moment, due to some hurt or betrayal, you may feel hatred for that same person.

It can be so confusing to be human because all these emotions are changing. It makes our inner experience so complex. The Buddha said that the mind and mental activities are like food with so many different spices. All the flavors exist simultaneously, but we tend to only taste the strongest one. Likewise, we tend to only experience the strongest emotion at any given time, even though all the other emotions are still present underneath. If we feel anger, it will take over our minds. This does not mean that anger is without memory or other emotions. It is just the strongest emotion at that given moment.

This study of mental activities is complex because our mental functioning is so complicated. Emotions and ideas are running through our minds, and they have the potential to drive us crazy. They have tremendous power, especially when they are unexamined.

Understanding the mind is essential on the path to liberation. That is why we have to study this fourth aggregate in greater detail. All karma is created in the mind as a result of these mental formations. Karma can be translated as "action." Action starts from the mental activities.

When we are angry, that anger can become action through the volition created in the mind. Volition is another neutral mental activity. Like memory, volition has the potential to support either positive or negative emotions.

We feel anger when we are confronted with some disagreeable object or action. There is a connection formed between the anger and that enemy. The connection is formed through that volition in the mind. This is why the Buddha taught that karma starts with volition.

Whether anger will become karma or not has to do with whether the anger has volition in the mind. In this way, all mental activities, whether they are positive, negative, or indefinite, have the potential to become karma when they are fueled by volition.

You will often hear this fourth aggregate being referred to as karma or action rather than formation. What philosophers are implying is that these mental activities are the source of our physical and verbal actions. By knowing our minds and the nature of our mental activities, we can understand how karma is created. This is vital on the path to liberation.

## Neither Mind nor Material Formation

The second category of formation is called *neither mind nor material formation*. Everything that is not included in the other aggregates will fall into this category of formation.

There are fourteen classifications in the Abhidharma teachings that fall under this second category of formation. This includes things like time, which are never included in the other aggregates. Whenever you encounter something that does not belong to the other aggregates, it falls under this category of neither mind nor material formation.

It is important to clarify that not all formations are necessarily karma. Those mental activities are only the source of the action. The formations that are neither mind nor material are not necessarily related to karma.

One could argue that since these fourteen categories of formation are part of conditioned things, then they must be the result of karma. Time includes the past, present, and future. Everything is happening within this timeline. Due to the past, we have the present. Due to the present, we will have the future. Karma is dependent on a timeline. Cause and result happen in the past, present, and future. We can see that time is related with karma, but it is not necessarily a creator of karma. It is more like a vehicle for karma, a stage upon which the karma can unfold.

In the *Heart Sutra* we are studying darshana, the training of wisdom. This is training us to see things in the highest way, in a universal way, in a complete way. It is training in ultimate truth.

If we wanted to understand each and every thing in the universe, we could keep on pursuing knowledge for the rest of our lives. We could become great scientists. Here instead we are studying ourselves as well as all conditioned things. There is a greater potential for wisdom in this approach.

We need to look within ourselves in our study of the mental activities. We need to learn from our own emotions. Whenever we have some emotional outburst, we should try to see whether these emotions were harmful to us or to others, or whether they were good for us.

The Abhidharma is often called "the mother of all Dharma" because it allows us to understand the higher teachings so much better. Transforming the five aggregates into the five wisdoms is only possible when we have been introduced to the potentialities of ultimate truth in these aggregates. These teachings on the five aggregates are a vital foundation. They give us much deeper insight into the workings of the mind.

## Consciousness

Let's move on to the fifth aggregate, which is consciousness. As we have discussed, there are six consciousnesses related to the six sense organs. These sense organs are eye, ear, nose, tongue, body, and mind. It is through these six consciousnesses that we experience the world.

When you have a healthy eye organ and you see a visual object, then there is eye consciousness. When you have a healthy ear organ and you hear a sound, then ear consciousness arises. When you taste something, your tongue consciousness perceives that flavor.

There are three different names used for mental consciousness that correspond with past, present, and future. In Sanskrit, our present consciousness is called *vijnana*. According to Buddhist psychology, vijnana refers to our awareness of an object in the present moment.

Since present consciousness cannot happen without the past, there is also a name for the past mind, which is called *manas*. Present consciousness will create future consciousness, which is called *chitta* in Sanskrit.

These three different names are given so that we can make a distinction between the three times—past, present, and future. Basic mind is a continuum; it is like a river. Other sense consciousnesses are expressed from that continuum of the mind. These names for past, present, and future consciousness can help us understand this continuum better.

Our consciousness always begins in the present. In the first moment when you become aware of an object, your sense organs are perceiving it without any concepts. That first consciousness is nonconceptual.

The five aggregates are the Buddhist way of categorizing natural phenomena. These aggregates are not something that the Buddha made up. The Buddha merely organized and simplified how we study natural phenomena so that it would be easier for us to learn.

I was recently speaking with a theoretical physicist. He travels the world giving presentations. He relies on mathematics to explore the physical world. Physicists, scientists, and Buddhist philosophers explore the same things, but they use different terminology and different approaches. Buddhist texts are deeply rooted in Sanskrit, which is sometimes called the divine language. Sanskrit is rich in spiritual meaning, and as a result, it is a good vehicle for Buddhist philosophy.

Scientists develop a theory, and they experiment, test, and try to discover something new. Buddhists study and then reflect and meditate in order to gain wisdom. There is a science to both of these approaches to understanding the universe; they are just using different methods.

There are a number of leading scientists who also have become meditators. It is very powerful to see what happens when compassion and wisdom are combined with science. It is also fascinating to see the commonalities between advanced scientific thought and Buddhist philosophy. At the far reaches of physics we see theories that are in accord with

Buddhist philosophy. We are studying the same phenomena through different methods.

Conclusions in science and Buddhism have varied over time. We can see how scientific understanding has progressed. Old theories are continuously being disproven. New experiments are revealing new breakthroughs. Buddhism has also reached various conclusions according to different philosophers. As mentioned earlier, this has given rise to four main schools of Buddhist thought.

Scientists and Buddhists agree that causes and conditions allow phenomena to arise. When scientists discover something, they are always looking at its relationship with other things. Science shares this Buddhist view of interdependency.

Whatever is happening in the universe, even if it is considered a natural phenomenon, is happening due to causes. Rain or fire are considered natural, but they are dependent on causes and conditions. They are natural, but they do not just happen by chance.

Rain is falling because of temperatures lifting moisture from the oceans and creating clouds. Without the moisture or the oceans or the clouds, there could be no rain.

The term natural does not imply that something is happening by accident. It is natural because it is interdependent. If we think that nature is happening by chance, then we are breaking from the natural law of relativity. It is only through interdependency that we can learn to see emptiness. We must work within the relative world to see ultimate truth.

All sensory information is completely reliant on interdependency. To see something, we need a healthy eye organ, we need a visual object, and we need mental consciousness. If one of those three factors is missing, we will not see the object. If we are blind, how can we see anything? If the object is too far away, then even if our eyes are healthy, we will not see it. Even if the object is visible, and the eye is healthy, if the mind is distracted with something else, we will not see what is right in front of us.

It takes all three components happening together for the experience to occur. That is a good example of interdependency. Everything happens when causes and conditions come together.

When you look more closely, you cannot find any independent existence in the eye, in the object, or in your mind. If you cannot find any independent existence, then it is proof that there is no inherent existence. The more you investigate interdependency, the more clearly you understand natural emptiness.

Avalokiteshvara has seen the natural emptiness of the five aggregates. He has seen emptiness with his wisdom eye through meditation. Through profound meditation, Avalokiteshvara has seen emptiness related with form, feeling, ideation, formation, and consciousness.

Avalokiteshvara is offering this wisdom to Shariputra. Avalokiteshvara has reached such a high level of realization that he can respond to whatever questions Shariputra asks.

> Then the elder Shariputra, moved by the power of the Buddha, addressed Arya Avalokiteshvara with these words: "Noble son! How should someone who wishes to perform the profound practice of the Prajnaparamita train himself?"

To paraphrase, Shariputra is asking Avalokiteshvara, "How can one train in the wisdom gone beyond through study, reflection, and meditation?" He is wondering if he can actualize the wisdom that Avalokiteshvara has realized.

> The great being, the bodhisattva Arya Avalokiteshvara replied, "Shariputra! That son or daughter of a good family who wishes to perform the profound practice of the Prajnaparamita should first rightly see that all the aggregates, by their very nature, are empty."

This is how Avalokiteshvara responds in his effort to train Shariputra. We can really identify with Shariputra because we are also learning. "A good family" refers to those who are on the spiritual path and have taken refuge and bodhisattva vows.

When we are discussing these lines of the *Heart Sutra*, there is no Avalokiteshvara, there is no Shariputra, there is no Buddha! It is just us trying to train in wisdom. At the same time, we can become Shariputra, we can become Avalokiteshvara, and we can also become the Buddha. We all have the same buddha nature as these three beings. We should not feel that they are separate from us. We all share the same buddha nature.

The sutra is merely offering us a map, a guide. If we were to train in wisdom without the help of this discourse, it would take a much longer time.

There do exist *pratyekabuddhas*—solitary buddhas who gain realization without having any teachers. They gain enlightenment through their own meditation and discovery, but this generally takes a very long time because these individuals have no other foundation, no guidelines.

For practitioners like us, this sutra can give us confidence in the path. It is very reassuring to be guided by someone who has already gone this way before. It encourages us to have faith that if we walk the same path, according to their training, we too could reach enlightenment.

This does not mean that anyone else can walk the path for us. There are no shortcuts. We have to take every step on our own. These sutras, these maps, cannot transfer wisdom automatically. They can only inspire us to be travelers.

Realization has to be experienced by the individual. We cannot make a carbon copy of someone else's awakening and use it for ourselves. We can only follow their directions. We can study the path they took, but then we have to actually begin walking! This is why the Buddha said, "I have shown you the path to liberation, but you are the one who has to walk."

The *Heart Sutra* focuses on three main figures: the Buddha, Avalokiteshvara, and Shariputra. All three can become our heroes. All three can be reminders of our inner potential. All three can guide us on the path until we too become like them.

# 15

# Form Is Emptiness

Form is emptiness. Emptiness is form. Form is not other
than emptiness, nor is emptiness other than form. So too all
feeling, ideation, formation, and consciousness are empty.

THIS IS HOW the bodhisattva Avalokiteshvara trains Shariputra to
see in the correct way. First we should use right view to understand the aggregate of form. The sutra says, "Form is emptiness." There
are four kinds of form and emptiness. This is very important. In order to
go beyond extreme views, you have to go beyond the four kinds of form
and emptiness.

We have to start where we are. Right now, we see all these material
objects through the experience of our own physical bodies. We can
hear, taste, smell, touch, and so on, and we believe that the objects we
experience really exist.

If these sensory experiences give us pleasure and happiness, then we
get very attached. Through our strong attachment we have many feelings and ideas. This generates actions and reactions due to our emotions
and the conditions in our mind. All of these processes convince us that

these material objects inherently exist. It is important that we examine this assumption more closely.

Objects exist only in relation to our sense organs. We have eyes, and we have a mind. Due to our eye organ and eye consciousness, a visual object can exist. If the sense organ, the sense object, or the sense consciousness are missing, then it is hard to prove that the object exists.

In this way, our entire experience of the universe is based on this interdependency between the sense organs, sense objects, and sense consciousnesses. When I see a cup, for example, it is proof to me that the cup exists. I am also able to tell others, "I have seen the cup, so it must exist."

We all agree that the cup exists because the majority of us can see and touch it. We also share a name for this object within our own country and language. We have a shared understanding among the majority of humans of what the cup can be used for.

If we investigate more deeply, we realize that if this cup exists independently, then it should exist universally for every living being.

Most adult humans see a cup as something that can be used to hold a liquid. There is a utility value. In addition, there is often a monetary value that adds to the meaning of the cup. If the cup has been in our family for a while, then we may attach some sentimental value to it.

This same cup may be a very different object from a baby's perspective. A baby may see the cup as a toy or something to chew on. This cup may be something else to your cat or to your dog. If it inherently existed, then every living being should perceive it as a cup. If it existed independently, it should appear as the same object to cows and horses and even to fish!

Do animals see the same value in the cup? Do they see the same utility? Do they project the same emotional attachments? Not necessarily. There is no universal agreement on what a cup is. There is only projected value and truth.

Buddhist philosophers have taken this investigation to the next level. They have asked the question, "If we break the cup down into pieces, down to the smallest particles, to mere ashes, is it still a cup?"

If the cup is reduced to atoms, to mere dust, can anyone recognize it as a cup? All the material objects that we are attached to, all the objects we project value onto, do not inherently exist once we examine them objectively.

One of the ways in which we can prove this lack of inherent existence is by observing that all objects are constantly changing. Although we cannot always perceive the changes because they are so subtle, we still know that by nature everything is changing. Whatever is created is subject to aging and decay. There is no denying this natural fact.

Any object that is created is immediately subject to decay. Although we may not like to think about this, right now we are moving closer to our own deaths. Every moment our bodies are decaying.

When our emotions are involved with an object, we become convinced that the object should last forever. If I paid a lot of money for a cup, I want it to be permanent. If it belonged to my grandmother and is very special to my family, then I want it to last a lifetime.

Whenever we project value onto something, our attachment tries to make that object eternal. Not only do we create this unrealistic projection on the object, but we project an eternalism onto ourselves. We want the object to last as long as we are attached to it. We develop elaborate ways to avoid the truth of impermanence.

Pain arises because there is a conflict between the reality of the object and our emotional attachment to that object. We experience suffering because we want desirable things to remain the same. To transcend that suffering, we have to realize that all the objects, including ourselves, are impermanent. None of us exist independently. When we are reduced to mere atoms, to mere ash or dust, then where is the person? Where is the object?

All that remains stable is the empty nature of the person and the empty nature of the object. Sometimes, even if we break the cup down to mere atoms, although we cannot recognize it, we remain emotionally attached to the idea of that cup.

I have been thinking about my mother who passed away recently. We cremated her at Mount Auburn Cemetery in Cambridge, Massachusetts.

After only a few hours her whole body was reduced to just a few pounds of ashes. After a few days someone from the funeral home came with a box wrapped in plastic. It weighed only two or three pounds. "This is your mother," they said. Even though I knew it was only filled with ashes, I still carried an attachment to the contents of that box.

We built a stupa for my mother there at Mount Auburn Cemetery, and that is where her ashes are now. She is not in the stupa. She is not in the ashes. But due to love and attachment, my whole family feels very close to her when we are there. According to Buddhism, my mother has already taken rebirth. Her mind is no longer with us. Our love and attachment have projected her onto this stupa.

This is just an example of how, even after the object is gone, we will carry the object in our minds and in our hearts. Although the object is gone, we have not given up our emotional connections to it. We have not gone beyond. We have not let go of that person. We are still attached to that loved one in our minds.

Our attachment makes that loved one exist for us mentally. This mental existence, due to our attachment, is what we really need to focus on as practitioners. This is why we need to meditate on impermanence and the empty nature of all conditioned things. This is the only way we can go beyond attachment to that object.

Buddhists use meditation to examine objects and try to come to some philosophical conclusion about emptiness. As we discussed earlier, scientists also examine the nature of conditioned things. Scientists use theories and conduct experiments to try to reduce matter to the smallest measurement. Objectively, scientists have been making incredible discoveries about the universe for a while. Their work has only recently begun to transcend matter.

Recently a physicist was telling me about a scientific principle called the quantum vacuum. He was explaining that this theory holds that all material objects are just composed of energy. Physicists are coming to conclusions that are very similar to what Buddhists have come to through meditation.

Furthermore, scientists have discovered that even though matter is just energy, this energy can be changed by the observer. That is also very similar to Buddhist ideas. Between mind and matter, who is the creator? If we do not have a mind, if we are dead, how can we experience the material world? If we are blind, how can we see visual objects? If we are deaf, how can we prove the existence of sound?

If we reduce material objects to mere atoms, then our sense organs will not find any object to become attached to. Buddhist philosophy says that even a single atom does not exist independently. There is no independent atom. There is no atom that is not composed of other elements. What that is saying is that even the smallest atom is empty by nature. It has no inherent existence.

When the sutra says, "Form is emptiness," it means that form is impermanent. All the material things of the universe are insubstantial. They are constantly changing. For us living beings, those changes can be a huge source of pain and suffering because we are so emotionally attached. This is why understanding the empty nature of form is essential for us as practitioners.

Ultimately everything is decaying and dying. This may sound like an overly negative way to view our lives until we begin to see the freedom that we gain by accepting impermanence.

Suffering primarily relates to the conflict in us between what is happening and what we wish would happen. When something changes, we experience sadness because we want things to stay the same.

If we meditate on emptiness and impermanence, this conflict between our projected reality and the nature of reality begins to disappear. There is real freedom in that acceptance. Recognizing the suffering of conditioned existence is an essential step in gaining liberation from that suffering.

As practitioners, we not only have to work through our attachment to objects but also our emotional involvement with them. As I mentioned with the example of my mother, it is the attachment that we carry in our own minds that has the greatest power of all. That attachment remains long after the object is gone. The Buddha taught the doctrine of emptiness to cut through our attachments. He knew that freedom from attachment was critical for our transformation.

When our possessions are gone, when our loved ones are gone, we still remain mentally and emotionally involved with them. We have so much longing for those objects and experiences. As long as we carry those emotions in our mind, we will not be free. This realization of the emptiness of form is vital to our inner transformation. We must become more than just philosophers. We must become practitioners if we are to experience change.

When I was a student in India studying philosophy, we had to study five non-Buddhist philosophies of the Hindu tradition. We also had to study four different levels of Buddhist philosophy. Students of philosophy are also taught logical and dialectical methods. We can try to prove the truth of certain claims using these methods. But what academia often ignores is that if knowledge does not help you transform, then the truth you are pursuing is limited to the objective level of inquiry. It does not benefit your transformation.

Philosophers may be highly successful in their academic lives, but on a personal level they may not be at peace if their work does not help them transform. In Buddhist teachings we are told that the reason to study philosophy is to transform the philosopher.

Without that inner transformation, knowledge will remain purely intellectual. This is true of so much of academia. Philosophy is just intellectual information you accumulate. Often you are just parroting information you have read and gathered. You can study what the great Indian masters have said. You can learn about what Western philosophers such as Aristotle or Socrates said. You can repeat this knowledge in books and papers, and you can theorize forever. If it remains merely intellectual, though, nothing inside you will have been transformed in the process.

The Buddha's way of studying philosophy combines knowledge with wisdom. The greater purpose of this study is to transform the philosopher. The Buddha provided us with all the methods we need. There are four kinds of emptiness. There are four levels of philosophy. There are four levels of seeing: impermanence, dissatisfaction, emptiness, and selflessness. There are four tantric methods to integrate these aspects into our sadhana meditation practices.

The Buddha did not limit emptiness to form. He extended his discussion of emptiness to include the emptiness of all five aggregates. Even feelings are empty. Even ideas are empty. Even formations and mind have empty natures.

As we have discussed, there are five kinds of feelings: happiness, unhappiness, pain, pleasure, and neutral feelings. These feelings operate interdependently. That is why the aggregate of feeling is so critically important for us. Independently, you cannot find feeling. Feeling is just like matter in the sense that it is always changing, it is never permanent.

As we can observe, our feelings toward objects are changing constantly. When we look deeper, we see that the very nature of feeling is suffering. Even happiness and pleasure are a form of suffering because we cannot have happiness and pleasure without desire. Desire is a destructive emotion. Whatever is arising from a poison cannot be wholesome. That is why every pleasurable and desirable feeling is the seed for pain and unhappiness.

The Buddha taught that all feelings by their very nature are dukkha. They are a form of suffering. Feelings are always in flux, such that you cannot find stable and independent feelings. Only in your deepest meditation will feelings finally dissolve. At that point you will finally realize their empty nature.

The same is true with the aggregate of ideation. Ideas are empty. They are always changing. Ideation is also a source of great pain and suffering. We can see this play out on a global level as the isms remain a major source of conflict. These isms include capitalism, socialism, communism, and all the religions of the world. One of the founders of the Sakya tradition said, "If one has grasping, one does not have right view."

We are fighting all the time because of our beliefs and our ideas. Two major denominations of Islam are fighting amongst themselves in conflicts between the Shiites and the Sunnis. Christians are fighting with

Muslims. Christians are also fighting amongst themselves due to long-lasting tensions between Protestants and Catholics. Even within Buddhism there are disagreements between the Theravada, Mahayana, and Vajrayana schools.

We can see on a global scale how ideas are causing terrible pain and suffering. If we look more closely, we cannot find any independent existence in any of the isms. They exist only because of our attachment to our own egos and to whatever we project our faith and beliefs onto. We cannot find any independent existence in any of these ideations.

The same is true for the aggregate of formation. Karma is reliant on a timeline. Cause and result, action and reaction, all play out in the past, present, and future. They are interdependent. They are changing constantly. These mental activities, these karmas, are sources of deep pain and suffering.

We cannot find any independently existent karma. The nature of karma is emptiness and selflessness. As we've discussed, formation refers to the mental activities and volitions that are the source of action. Action comes from the emotions and thoughts inside the mind. When we bring volition to these mental activities, we express them verbally or physically.

The mind and mental consciousness are also empty by nature. Mind and consciousness are changing all the time. Their nature is impermanence, suffering, and ultimately emptiness.

The more you investigate, the more you see how all five aggregates are impermanent. By nature they are constantly changing, moment to moment. Until their natural emptiness is recognized and brought into our meditation practice, they will remain a source of pain and suffering. Their nature is emptiness. Their nature is selflessness. When we understand this, we realize that they are not worthy of attachment.

When we become attached to things, we try to make them eternal. We try to carry them with us forever, but all things are conditioned. All things are created. All things will change. All things will age and decay. All living things will die. That is how nature is. That is why all these things are understood to be conditioned.

Through knowing the natural truth of these five aggregates, we will come to the realization of emptiness and selflessness. As practitioners we will then have all the methods we need for inner transformation.

Right now, our strongest attachment is to ourselves. If we look deeper, though, how do we identify the self? Where is the ego? Some people may think, "I am my physical body." Other people may define themselves based on their feelings. Some people may identify themselves most strongly through their attachment to their ideas and opinions. Some people may identify themselves most strongly through their activities and actions in the world. Others may be very attached to their *atman* or "soul" or to some form of mind or consciousness.

These five aggregates are the objects upon which we base our strongest clinging, which is the clinging to the self. The ego is based on these five aggregates. Understanding the emptiness of these aggregates can help to unseat the ego. If the aggregates by their very nature are empty, then what is left to cling to? This truth is very important for the practitioner to experience. There is a huge distinction between how we currently see the world through our emotional attachments and how we can learn to see the world through this wisdom training.

As I explained earlier, the wisdom eye of the buddhas is open because they have seen something that we have never seen. We have only seen the five aggregates through our emotional involvement and our clinging. We have tried to solidify our image of ourselves by believing that these aggregates are fixed and permanent.

When buddhas see with that wisdom eye, they see that all the aggregates are empty. This view is the only way we can cut our attachment to ourselves and to all conditioned things in the universe. This is how we can begin to dissolve that solidified "self," which our attachment has worked so hard to create.

Dissolving the five aggregates into emptiness transforms us as meditators. It cuts our attachment to existence. With this first statement "form is emptiness," Avalokiteshvara is training Shariputra to go beyond existence.

All things that exist in our minds can be included within the five aggregates. Our five aggregates have so much power. It is through our aggregates that the whole universe exists for us. That is why we have such strong attachment to ourselves and to our possessions. The whole purpose of seeing emptiness is to go beyond this attachment.

We have three more kinds of emptiness yet to discuss. There are three more freedoms to liberate us from the other three extremes. Until we go beyond all four extremes, we will not have a full understanding of emptiness.

# 16

# Emptiness Is Form

Form is emptiness. Emptiness is form. Form is not other than emptiness, nor is emptiness other than form. So too all feeling, ideation, formation, and consciousness are empty.

THIS WISDOM TRAINING in the *Heart Sutra* is profoundly important because it is training us to go beyond samsara and nirvana to achieve full enlightenment.

To reach complete enlightenment, we need to go beyond the four extremes. When the sutra says "form is emptiness," this goes beyond the first extreme, which is existence. When the sutra says "emptiness is form," that goes beyond the second extreme, which is nonexistence. When the sutra says "form is not other than emptiness," that goes beyond the third extreme, which includes both existence and nonexistence. When the sutra says "nor is emptiness other than form," that goes beyond the fourth extreme, which is neither existence nor nonexistence.

Existence, nonexistence, both, and neither are called the *four extremes* by Buddhist philosophers. Contemplating these has tremendous potential to awaken us to reality. Ordinary people do not care much about these realities. Most of us are far more interested in our feelings. We are motivated by the wish to achieve happiness and pleasure, and we are not eager to contemplate these four aspects.

When you enter into Buddhist practice, you become part of a nontheistic religion. When you turn toward a spiritual life, it is often an indication that you want to pursue a deeper truth. In the search for these truths, Buddhists have developed elaborate philosophical schools.

Before the Buddha's time in India, many non-Buddhist schools of philosophy already existed. In our education as monks and nuns in India, we were required to study some of these other conclusions as well.

In ancient Buddhist times in India, there were six philosophical schools. Many of these philosophies were pursued in an intellectual and academic way. As we have discussed, this approach to philosophy does very little to transform the philosopher. When you merely study the philosophy without any meditation or wisdom, then there is a great danger you will fall into one of these four extremes.

Those philosophers who were not transformed became attached to the subtleties of the various isms. They became too identified with their ideas. Whenever you are limited by your attachment to an idea, the study of that philosophy does not lead to wisdom. You are merely accumulating knowledge, and it will not help you go beyond the four extremes and achieve liberation.

We can see how attachment to ideas creates conflict among philosophers and scholars. We engage in intellectual arguments when our ideas become fixed and when we believe our conclusions are superior. These arguments do not occur between practitioners who have unbiased minds and who have been transformed by their practice.

If we study the six philosophies that existed in India, both Buddhist and non-Buddhist, we see many limitations. With those philosophies there is so much risk of falling into the extremes of eternalism, nihilism, both, or neither.

If we want to engage in a more extensive study of the four kinds of emptiness, it is beneficial to study all of the philosophies. We can also study the major theistic religions of the world such as Judaism, Christianity, and Islam. We can investigate whether these philosophies and religions cultivate transformation. We can see the potential extremism within religions, and we can also see the purity of their deeper message. Faith has the potential either to breed extremism or cultivate profound inner transformation.

How can we transform knowledge into wisdom? We need training in meditation, and we also need training in discipline. This is why Buddhism introduces us to the three trainings. For complete practice we need the trainings of wisdom, discipline, and meditation.

If our training in meditation is not guided by wisdom, then it can be blind! This is also true of training in discipline. If you become attached to your precepts, then those precepts may help you accumulate some merit for attaining a higher rebirth, but they will not help you achieve complete enlightenment.

If you become attached to your precepts, you may become an extremist. This is also true of meditation. If you have extensive experience in shamatha meditation, you may fall into a deep absorption, a state of samadhi. Due to this, you may be reborn in the form or formless realms. Yet this shamatha will not help you go beyond samsara. This is because you have become too attached to your experiences in meditation.

The purpose of training in wisdom, meditation, and discipline is to go beyond the four extremes. Only then will these become methods for profound transformation leading to enlightenment.

Wisdom training based on the Prajnaparamita shows us how the four emptinesses can counteract the four extremes. The purpose is to go beyond the personal self as well as phenomena. The goal is to achieve complete enlightenment. Moving beyond the four extremes is critical to this process.

We need to integrate this at the personal level. We need to study each of the different kinds of emptiness, integrating that awareness into our lives. When we say "form is emptiness," we should practice seeing the emptiness of the material world and the emptiness of our sense organs. We should practice mentally reducing our material possessions to dust.

If we reduce our prized possessions to mere atoms, we can begin to cut our attachment to them.

Material objects are very important to us in our daily lives. Whenever we are emotionally attached to something, it can generate many feelings for us. Our strongest attachments are to other people. Our personal relationships are the greatest source of feelings.

To counteract the feelings that arise in relation to an object, we should remember that feeling is also empty. The true nature of feeling is emptiness. Feeling arises when we are emotionally and karmically involved with an object or person. Our attachments are based on objects that are giving us pleasure and happiness. Our aversion arises toward objects when they give us more pain and suffering. We have neutral feelings toward everything else in our lives due to our underlying ignorance.

These feelings are part of our lives. We place so much value on the objects that bring us happiness. We love our houses, our cars, our property. We love our children, our partners, our friends. These same objects can suddenly bring us pain and aversion the minute they are no longer agreeable to us. The minute our house needs an expensive repair, or our child becomes a challenging teenager, we may suddenly feel very unhappy.

As we have discussed, feeling is interdependent. Feelings have no independent existence. The nature of feelings is emptiness. We place more value on the objects that generate positive feelings in us, but this does not mean those feelings will remain the same.

If we want to investigate feelings further, we must turn to the aggregate of ideation. The nature of ideation is also emptiness. We are unaware of this emptiness, so we cling to our idea of a subjective self. We believe this self has the power to measure the inherent worth of other people and objects.

We interact with beings and objects based on our karma. We can feel an affinity with someone based on shared karma. We can experience an instant closeness based on qualities we identify and find agreeable or familiar in the other person.

These identifications are based on characteristics. Due to the unique characteristics of a particular person, we value them. We feel some kind of natural connection to them.

If we look deeper into all the projections, we have placed on objects, we cannot find any inherent existence. There is no universal agreement on whether someone is good or bad. Our best friend could be someone else's worst enemy. Our projections are not based on any ultimate truth.

These ideations lead to the fourth aggregate of formation, which includes the karma of action and reaction. When you feel good, you desire more of that positive experience. If you are unhappy and suffering, you react by doing something to avoid or reject that experience. Karma starts with formation, but it is also empty of independent existence.

The main creator, according to Buddhism, is the fifth aggregate of consciousness. The first experience of consciousness arises from the six consciousnesses related with the six sense organs. This first sensory impression is nonconceptual. It arises from our defiled emotions, so even that nonconceptual state is not pure.

According to Buddhist psychology, consciousness is present in all our sensory experiences. Immediately following the first sense perception of an object, we develop an image in our head.

Our consciousness includes the past, present, and future mind. Mind is a continuum. At the present moment, whatever information we have collected through the senses can become the future. It is also based on the past. It continues at the mental level. Based on this timeline of the mind, we can prove that there were past lives and that there will be future rebirths.

Freedom from the four extremes means going beyond all form, feeling, ideation, formation, and consciousness of the past, present, and future. When we are emotionally involved with these aggregates, there is no freedom. I have used the example of my attachment to my mom, but you can think of any beloved object or person to understand the strength of this attachment. Even when objects or persons are long gone, we can find ourselves mentally attached to them for the rest of our lives.

All the conditioned things that we are attached to will decay in the end. Even if a person is gone, we can still see them in a dream, and they may appear completely real. Sometimes my mother appears to me in a dream. Although her body is dust, and her mind has already taken rebirth, I can see her clearly in my mind because of my love and connection. My connection remains a vivid image in my mind.

Although the object is gone, the mental image is strong in our memory. We may assume that this is what is meant by the second description of emptiness in the *Heart Sura* that says "emptiness is form." This is not the case though. The attachment that creates that form out of emptiness does not lead to freedom. You are not letting go. There is no emptiness there.

The main reason why the Buddha taught the first emptiness—"form is emptiness"—was to go beyond existence. Existence occurs because of our emotional involvement. Whether or not an object has been destroyed, its form has not become emptiness for us. We have not gone beyond the extremes of existence.

This is not just a scientific or philosophical theory. It is a direct experience in our lives. Our level of emotional engagement will have an impact on our transformation. As long as we have attachment to any person or object, it is proof that we have not transcended the first extreme of existence. If something still exists in our minds, feelings, ideations, or actions, then we have not gone beyond.

We are attached to outer objects because of our primary attachment to ourselves and to our bodies. Our bodies demand pleasure, comfort, and satisfaction. We have great appetite for things that will be agreeable to our aggregates.

One great Indian master said that the source of samsara is attachment to the self. This primary attachment breeds all other attachments to the outer world. We may think our attachment to others is a selfless kind of love, but until it is based on wisdom and compassion, it is very self-oriented.

We all want to live forever. We want our loved ones to live forever. When something threatens this eternalistic view, we feel terrible pain and suffering. The main reason we are trapped in samsara is because of our attachment to ourselves. We must engage in deep meditation practice before that self can begin to dissolve.

There is a Sanskrit saying, "Where there is faith, there is God." As long as you have faith, you will project some object of faith.

When you love someone, you want that person to be unchanging and to live forever. You may become attached to outer faith objects like statues. The greatest attachment will be to something created in your own mind. If you do not use faith to go beyond the first extreme of existence, then that faith has the potential to become fanatical and destabilizing. It can become the source of terrible conflict. But once you see the emptiness of the five aggregates, you can realize nirvana.

# 17

# Form Is Not Other Than Emptiness

AS DISCUSSED IN EARLIER chapters, there are four kinds of emptiness. To experience inner transformation, we must learn to see the emptiness of the five aggregates of form, feeling, ideation, formation, and consciousness. These five aggregates are also called the five skandhas. These include all conditioned things in the universe.

When we say "conditioned things," we are referring to phenomena that are created due to causes and conditions. These include everything that is interdependent and relative. These include not only our physical bodies but our feelings, ideas, actions, and consciousness. These actions include physical, verbal, and mental activities, which fall under the fourth aggregate of formation. We must understand the emptiness of ourselves as well as the emptiness of all phenomena in the universe.

Due to our habitual patterns and emotions, we assume that our aggregates are inherently existent. At the relative level, these aggregates do exist. We do have a house, a car, a body. We accomplish things with these objects. Since these material objects are valuable to us, we become emotionally involved with them. We become convinced that these objects exist independently.

Meditation is the best method to examine the true nature of the aggregates. The more meditation we do, the harder it becomes to find any form of independent existence. We can use the object of the cup to illustrate this point again.

A cup exists because the atoms that comprise it are still together. It has some utility. I can use it to drink water or tea. It has some monetary value or perhaps some sentimental value. If I grind this cup into dust, then I cannot find the cup. All I will find is the dust that remains, which itself is comprised of atoms. Between these two views of the cup, which one is more real, the cup or the atoms?

The atoms may seem more real because they remain even after the cup is reduced to dust. You can no longer find the cup in these atoms. We have to go even further and investigate the nature of the atoms. Atoms are the building blocks of all material objects. What we find is that even atoms exist interdependently. They are not independent or inherently existent. That is how we can prove that form is emptiness.

If we gain meditative realization, then we will begin to see the empty nature of the five aggregates. As a result, our attachment to the five aggregates will begin to decrease. Our attachment to ourselves and our possessions will diminish. This transformation can only happen through practice.

Scholars will often reduce everything to the first view of emptiness, the emptiness of form. There are some very well-known philosophers who study Buddhist philosophy and try to sum it all up as the negation of form, feeling, ideation, and consciousness. If we go further through the practice and free ourselves from the four extremes, then we can no longer conclude that emptiness is simply a negation of everything!

Here in the West, there is often misunderstanding about emptiness because people do not go beyond the four extremes. If you get stuck on the first emptiness, you may easily interpret it to mean nothingness. Nothingness, especially when viewed from the perspective of theistic religions, can be misconstrued as nihilism. That is very dangerous because when you have this view of nihilism and nothingness, then you may lose belief in everything. You may even lose your faith.

There is also a danger that this view of nihilism will make you very narcissistic. If you think that there is nothing to look forward to, there is nothing to achieve, and that everything ends in nothingness, then you may just pursue pleasure. You may think, "I might as well indulge my appetites and my desires since it is all meaningless anyway."

This view of nothingness can also cause people to not believe in karma. They may think that if everything ends in nothingness anyway, then cause and effect have no power. They may decide to act in whatever way they please since they do not believe there will be consequences.

Even some people who identify themselves as Buddhists may think only the present moment exists. If we could remain in one present moment all the time, then this would be perfect! During strong meditation practice we may remain in the present. Other times we are filled with thoughts of the past and future. These people may believe that there is no karma and no rebirth. If these Buddhists do not become a buddha in this lifetime, then they may face disappointment.

Even if we accept that form is emptiness but become attached to that emptiness, then we will not progress according to the Buddha's teachings. If you think emptiness is existent or nonexistent, then you are falling into an extreme.

The Buddha taught that even attachment to emptiness is an extreme. The purpose of the *Heart Sutra* is not to achieve nirvana. The purpose of the Prajnaparamita, the wisdom gone beyond, is to go beyond both samsara and nirvana.

It is possible that through meditating on the emptiness of the five aggregates we can achieve nirvana. The purpose of the *Heart Sutra*, however, is to achieve complete enlightenment by going beyond both samsara and nirvana. To attain that full realization, we have to go beyond our ideas related to attributes and characteristics.

In Tibetan there is the term *tsentok*, which means "concepts based on characteristics." We have to go beyond these characteristics that are projections of our ideas. We have to go beyond all four extremes. In one sutra, the Buddha said that even great yogis may move beyond their attachment to themselves but find it very challenging to go beyond attachment to emptiness!

Nirvana is a good example. For Theravada Buddhists, nirvana is the highest result one can achieve through practice. For Mahayana Buddhists who have achieved complete enlightenment—who have gone beyond both samsara and nirvana—even nirvana may appear to be an extreme.

The second emptiness, "emptiness is form," involves overcoming attachment to nothingness. This is to guard against nihilism. Our understanding of this second emptiness is related to our level of realization. There are many discussions and debates on the meaning of this second emptiness, but the primary purpose of this second emptiness is to go beyond the second extreme of nonexistence. This can help us go beyond our attachment to emptiness.

One of the very best methods for integrating our understanding of these emptinesses is through our daily sadhana meditation practice. The entire preliminary practice in the sadhana relates to how to personalize the understanding of "form is emptiness," through accumulation of merit and wisdom.

The purpose of the accumulation of merit is to make up for all the negative karma we have accumulated in the past. In our past days, months, years, and even in our past lives, we have committed many negative physical, verbal, and mental actions due to our negative emotions.

We have to bring a change to our habitual patterns. We have to create new positive karma based on faith, loving-kindness, compassion, and wisdom. By doing these practices repeatedly we accumulate merit. All the preliminary practices, the ngöndro practices, are based on faith and devotion. We cultivate love, compassion, and wisdom through repeating these practices again and again. Through this process our positive karma becomes stronger and purifies our negative karma. That is when we begin to experience a change within ourselves.

Only after purifying our negative karma and generating positive karma and merit will we be ready to see emptiness. We may have experienced countless lifetimes of negative karma and destructive emotions. We need a very strong practice to purify those negativities. Ngöndro practice is one of the best methods to see the emptiness of the five aggregates.

As a sign that we have purified some negative karma, we will notice our attachment to our five aggregates will decrease. We may get a glimpse of the inner space that is true emptiness. In that inner space, you cannot find your body, your feelings, your ideas, your actions, or your mind. That glimpse of the inner space between your thoughts is true emptiness.

At this point in the sadhana practice we recite the emptiness mantra *om svabhava shuddha sarva dharmah svabhava shuddho 'ham*. Out of that emptiness, we generate ourselves in the form of the deity we are practicing. If we are doing a Tara or Vajrayogini sadhana, then we generate ourselves into their forms out of that state of emptiness. This generation stage in the sadhana corresponds with the second emptiness, "emptiness is form."

According to Vajrayana Buddhism, all five aggregates have buddha nature. That is why we have the five dhyani buddhas who correspond to these aggregates and are visualized in many higher sadhana practices. The dhyani buddhas represent how your body has the empty nature of a buddha. Your feelings, ideas, mental activities, and mind all have that emptiness. They all have buddha nature.

If we learn according to the yogi's path, the practitioner's path, then emptiness is not merely a concept. It is not a dry philosophy. It is a personal transformational practice. It is a method for gaining awareness that we are already buddhas!

From that empty space, when you express yourself as a deity in the sadhana practice, that deity is called *empty form*. In that empty form you can include all five aggregates. The difference between "form is emptiness" and "emptiness is form" is that the first type of form, our physical bodies, is created by our egos. In the second statement, that form is generated by the wisdom of emptiness. In that second emptiness, the generation of the deity is not created by the ego. That second form is not based on the self. It is based on the wisdom of emptiness.

This is why when we engage in visualization meditation, these generated deities are called empty form. Empty form is the true nature of form. One form is created by the ego, and the other form is generated by wisdom. "Form is emptiness" is based on the ego. "Emptiness is form" is based on wisdom. This second emptiness is not a negation; it is an expression of emptiness based on wisdom.

When you gain more experience in generation-stage practices, you will become more certain that emptiness is form. You can read hundreds of philosophical texts, you can study all the commentaries on the *Heart Sutra* based on these four emptinesses, but without personal practice these concepts will not be integrated into your life. These concepts may still seem very paradoxical and confusing until we bring them into our meditation through sadhana practice. Sadhana practice is designed to carefully lead us beyond the four emptinesses and the four extremes.

The purpose of the wisdom trainings in the *Heart Sutra* is to go completely beyond our personal self, the phenomenal self, and all ideas and characteristics. When we are visualizing ourselves as a deity in the sadhana practice, it is much deeper than getting attached to our ordinary form. The whole purpose of visualizing ourselves as a yidam is to go beyond our self-clinging related to the ordinary five aggregates.

Right now, the self is the center of our universe. Whenever anyone is threatening our idea of a self, we experience aversion. That is the basis for conflicts between self and other. We have attachment and aversion, and these two reactions are present all the time. Our lives are dominated by love and hate. We love our egos. Whenever our egos are threatened, we feel anger. We also have pain and pleasure, happiness and unhappiness. We can see how our lives are filled with conflicting feelings. This is because these emotions are rooted in the ego.

If the ego is fulfilled, we are happy. We feel so much pleasure when the ego is supported by others. If our ego is unfulfilled, if it is threatened, we get angry. We feel pain and suffering when someone criticizes us.

Generating ourselves into empty form allows us to go beyond these conflicts. We can see ourselves in the pure form of a buddha. We can also train our minds to see others in that pure form. We can purify our minds to the point where we can see the purity of the universe.

This is no longer just a philosophical concept. The tantric meditation practice of the sadhana is designed to integrate these four emptinesses into our lives. It helps us experience this transformation and wisdom at a personal level.

# 18

# Nor Is Emptiness Other Than Form

UNTIL WE HAVE a meditative experience of emptiness, whatever we are studying is just intellectual knowledge. Emptiness is not something to study objectively. The purpose of study is to inspire experiential realization.

Whether we remain attached to existence or go beyond existence depends on how much emotion is involved. All conditioned things can be included in the five aggregates. Whether these aggregates exist for you or not depends on how much emotional involvement you have with them.

Due to our strong clinging to ourselves, we generate destructive emotions. Based on our destructive emotions, we create karma. The two main reasons we are cycling in samsara are destructive emotions and the activities of karma; these are both rooted in the self.

Yogis and practitioners have to examine whether the self and ego inherently exist. The deeper we look, the less we are able to find an inherent self. If we cannot find the self, then we may conclude that the self does not exist. This intellectual conclusion does not mean that you have successfully detached from your self and your ego. It is only through deep meditation practice that we can make this selflessness become an experiential realization.

The preliminary practices of the sadhana are divided into two sections, the accumulation of merit and the accumulation of wisdom. These accumulations of merit and wisdom are antidotes to the destructive emotions and negative karma that we have accumulated across many lifetimes.

When you have purified those destructive emotions and karma through your practice, you may begin to experience some inner space. When you begin to glimpse that inner space through your meditation, you will gain a much deeper experience of this emptiness of matter. When your merit is very strong, and you have purified all your negativities, then, for the first time, your self-clinging will be dissolved.

Those first glimpses of emptiness do not automatically lead to stable realization regarding the nature of our minds. We may have some very strong practice, we may catch a glimpse of that empty nature, but that can be lost. That can be easily disturbed by outer events or inner emotions.

This is why the sadhana includes the generation practice. This is a method for us to express that emptiness in a purer form. Out of emptiness we generate ourselves in the form of a divine deity. The empty form of the deity is another expression of that inner space. Through these advanced practices, that inner space will become fully integrated into our experience.

At our current level, we may have a glimpse of that empty space, but it can easily be overtaken by emotions. We may be having a wonderful experience meditating and suddenly thoughts of attachment, anger, or confusion may enter our minds. If we do not have a very clear visualization of ourselves as a deity, that is an indication that our karma and emotions are not completely purified.

The clearer your visualization becomes, the weaker your self-clinging will be. Your emotions will become weaker. Your habitual pattern of negative karma will become weaker. As your practice helps you to purify all these negativities, your visualizations will become vivid and pure.

When you can see yourself in that empty form of the deity, that corresponds with the second emptiness, "emptiness is form." Now we can see that the word "form" has a very different meaning between the first emptiness and the second emptiness.

"Form is emptiness" refers to form based on the ego. This first form is your physical body and the five aggregates. These are rooted in your emotional self. This first experience of form is called "impure vision."

Now the second emptiness, "emptiness is form," refers to a purer form. It is represented by the generation stage in the sadhana. This purer form does not arise from self-clinging or negative emotions. This divine form of the deity is an expression of your true nature. All phenomena become a pure realm around you because they are expressions of your inner wisdom. Everything is now being expressed from a place of selflessness. As a result, these expressions cannot become causes and conditions to increase your destructive emotions and negative karma.

Until you have complete realization, there remains a risk that you will become attached to your pure vision. There is a chance that you will become attached to the deity's form in the sadhana. This is why the third emptiness, "form is not other than emptiness," is so critical.

This third emptiness helps us to go beyond the divine form. The moment we feel attachment to a deity's form, that attachment can become an obstacle. We have to go beyond that divine pride—beyond that empty form.

The philosophical purpose of this third emptiness is to go beyond absolute dualism. Whenever we have some mental state in which we are attached either to the existence of the divine form or the nonexistence of the ordinary self, dualism is still operating. Dualism and emotional involvement are tremendous obstacles to liberation.

This is why the next stage of the sadhana after mantra recitation is the dissolution of the deity. This is where we do the meditation beyond thought, where we dissolve the deity. We are reversing that generation stage.

First we dissolve pure vision, the pure realm into the deity. Then we dissolve the deity into the mantra. Then, if we are doing the Tara sadhana, we dissolve that mantra into the seed syllable *tam*. We dissolve each part of the seed syllable respectively, the crescent into the *nada* and then into the emptiness.

At this stage, the sadhana is integrating this third emptiness, "form is not other than emptiness." Now we have gone beyond both existence and nonexistence. We dissolve the deity back into the empty state. We are doing the dissolution practice to transcend both the existence and nonexistence of that deity.

The fourth emptiness is "emptiness is not other than form." The fourth emptiness goes beyond absolute nondualism. There are some teachings that claim that nondualism is absolute. If we create concepts and ideas even related to nondualism, then we are still creating attachment.

This fourth emptiness may seem like a concept, but the sadhana provides us with a very clear way to integrate it. After we engage in the meditation beyond thought, if we are doing the Tara sadhana, we instantly manifest in Tara's form again. We carry this visualization during our post-meditation practice. We imagine ourselves in Tara's form while eating, walking, sleeping, and doing all of our ordinary activities.

The purpose of this post-meditation practice is to integrate our regular lives with the extraordinary outlook of the deity. You are Tara. You are a buddha. Everyone else is also a buddha. All your thoughts are wisdom. All your words are mantra. All phenomena are a manifestation of pure vision. When we experience our daily lives through the pure vision of the deity, then we are integrating that fourth emptiness. We are even going beyond nondualism.

Nondualism in this context has less to do with subject and object. Nondualism here has more to do with our meditative state. When we are in that state of buddha nature, in that state of wisdom, then we are one with wisdom. There is no longer a "self" or "other" to go beyond. Everything is whole in that emptiness. Outer space and inner space are unified.

When we gain more experiential realization based on our sadhana practice or based on our practice of the six perfections, then these four emptinesses will make sense as a progression. Until you understand emptiness through practice, you will be filled with doubts and questions.

As we have established, these four emptinesses will help us go beyond extremes. They will help us go beyond karma, destructive emotions, and ideas. They will help us transcend both the personal self and the phenomenal self. As a result, we often refer to these four emptinesses as *freedom from the four extremes*. What is the experience of going beyond the four extremes like? It is enlightenment. It is buddhahood.

Yet you may be wondering, "Isn't freedom from the four extremes similar to nothingness in the end? Doesn't it just cancel everything out? What is the need to elaborate on this fourfold emptiness?" These doubts can only be resolved through sadhana practice. These four emptinesses help us to reverse the way in which we have evolved in samsara. Sadhana practice has the power to undo these attachments.

These four emptinesses are not just true of matter. You can apply these same four emptinesses to the other aggregates. This is why we receive the five dhyani buddhas' empowerment to seal that wisdom into the aggregates. The five dhyani buddhas represent the five wisdoms related to the aggregates. The aggregates, by their very nature, are wisdom. These five wisdoms appear in Vajrayana practice as the five buddhas. They guide the transformation of each aggregate.

The five aggregates are the ground; they are the foundation we are working with. They are the soil we are cultivating. Through meditation practice these five aggregates can become the five wisdoms, and we can become buddhas.

These five wisdom buddhas represent how matter is wisdom, feeling is wisdom, ideation is wisdom, formation is wisdom, and consciousness is wisdom.

> Shariputra! In the same way, all dharmas are devoid of characteristics, unborn, unstopped, unsullied, unpurified, undecreased, unfilled.

The Sanskrit word *dharma* has many different meanings. When we refer to the Buddha, Dharma, and Sangha, the term *Dharma* in that case refers to the Buddha's teaching and practice. Dharma is related to the Sanskrit word *dharana*, which means "apprehending" or "grasping." Here in the sutra, *dharma* means "apprehending the characteristics."

*Dharma* has ten different meanings. It is most commonly used in the context of Buddhadharma, which refers to the holy teachings and to all the practices the Buddha gave us.

When we use the word Abhidharma, dharma here refers to all the phenomenal objects of the universe. These are objects that hold general and unique characteristics by which we can identify them. In the *Heart Sutra*, the phrase "all dharmas" means the objects that hold general and unique characteristics.

*General characteristics* are characteristics that apply to everything. *Unique characteristics* are qualities that we use to distinguish one object from another. It is the unique characteristics that distinguish the shape of a cup from the shape of a bell. This combination of unique and general characteristics allows for the identification of objects.

When the sutra says, "In the same way, all dharmas are devoid of characteristics," this may seem paradoxical to us at our level. If dharma means "apprehending the characteristics," then why is the sutra saying that they are devoid of characteristics?

There is a big distinction. In the interdependent world, all objects are identified based on their characteristics. If you look closely at both the unique and general characteristics of those objects, however, you will find the objects disappear. That is why this is paradoxical. According to relative truth, you can find characteristics; you can find the object. According to ultimate truth, when you examine something closely, you find it is devoid of characteristics.

In Buddhism we have two truths. We have relative truth and ultimate truth. A cup has an interdependent, relative side, where we can agree it is a cup. It also has an ultimate side in which its true nature is emptiness.

As a practitioner, when we gain realization, we can see both the form and the empty nature of a cup simultaneously. We can even go beyond all four extremes. Ultimately, all things are free from characteristics.

We may also find the term "unborn" very paradoxical in the sutra. In the relative world, of course, there is birth. That is how we are all here. Ultimately, if we look closely, where does birth exist? How does it arise? When we examine it from the perspective of ultimate truth, we cannot find birth. It is unborn.

Whatever is born in the relative world will decay and die. It will cease. From the view of ultimate truth, however, everything is free from death, free from decay, and free from cessation. It is "unstopped."

Furthermore, from the perspective of ultimate truth, all things are "unsullied." Since the ultimate nature of everything is pure, then all things are, by nature, unsullied.

From the perspective of ultimate truth, the sutra says all things are also "unpurified, undecreased, unfilled." These words refer to the true nature of things as seen through the wisdom of ultimate truth.

Here in the relative world something can be purified because it has become defiled. At the ultimate level, though, it was pure all along, so really it is unpurifiable. Its nature has always been purity.

These lines of the sutra may seem paradoxical to us right now. They are not paradoxical to a buddha who has seen ultimate truth through meditation. These lines seem paradoxical to us because we are still experiencing everything at the relative level. All dharmas still appear to us to have characteristics. They are born. They can be defiled, they can be purified, and they can decay. For those awakened yogis who have realized emptiness, none of the characteristics exist.

# 19

# Unsullied and Unpurified

IF YOU wish to study the *Heart Sutra* in great depth, I highly rec-
ommend the English translations of Prajnaparamita literature by
Edward Conze. His books are very useful for serious students of the
sutra. Conze has done wonderful translations and has written critical comparisons with other *shastras*. Many Indian scholars—the
*panditas*—wrote commentaries on the sutras. Those commentaries are
called shastras.

We are studying the concise version of the Prajnaparamita. As I have
mentioned, this short version is derived from a much more extensive
sutra. Edward Conze's translation is separated into eight divisions based
on the *Abhisamayalamkara*, which is a shastra that all Mahayana scholars study to increase their understanding of the perfection of wisdom.

Reading the sutra is important. The purpose of the Dharma teachings is to inspire our practice. Whenever possible, we should study the
Dharma teachings in their original language since so much is lost in
translation. Many Tibetan translations give credit to the Sanskrit and
include a title in Sanskrit or Pali. Sanskrit is the original language that has
kept all these rich spiritual resources intact for over two thousand years.

To become familiar with a language, we have to read it repeatedly.

After familiarizing ourselves with the language, we have to reflect on and contemplate the meaning of the teachings. This is where spiritual teachers are so important. Teachers help us decode the many layers of meaning hidden in spiritual texts. More importantly, though, teachers inspire us to practice.

How much meaning we will gain from the Dharma is dependent on how much meditation practice we do. The teachers cannot do all the work for us. If we never practice, then once the teacher and the books are gone, will we have gained any lasting wisdom? Students can become very dependent on the teacher. At some point we have to go beyond that relationship if we wish to achieve personal realization and freedom.

In a similar way, our lives start out with so much dependency on our parents. At some point in our adolescence, we begin to individuate and to break free from that dependency. We have to gain this freedom to be self-sustaining adults.

There are nine stages of learning according to traditional Buddhist training. The first three are listening, reflecting, and meditation. The next three are teaching, debating, and composing. The last three are the result that includes becoming wise or learned, becoming ethical, and becoming beneficial.

We do all these things so that we can become wise. Wisdom does not necessarily arise from knowledge. Wisdom has to come from our practice and from mastering the deeper meaning of the teachings.

If we are good with language and understand some of the meaning of the texts we are reading, but we have not practiced, then we only have knowledge. That knowledge has to become wisdom through practice.

When we gain more wisdom, we will also gain more confidence in our path. That confidence will help us to become better people and to be more beneficial to others.

If we look to all the Buddhist masters of the past, we see that they never learned anything to improve their resumes or get better job interviews! It was very different back then. Places such as Nalanda University had thousands of students coming from all over Asia. These students would spend thirty or forty years studying there!

Those of us who have studied Buddhism know that until we have reached buddhahood, there is so much to learn and practice. Once we become buddhas, though, there is nothing left to learn and nothing left to study!

Study is only one part of the process. Cultivating the wisdom within you takes a long time. Students at Nalanda were studying and practicing for so long because they wanted to become buddhas. Buddhahood should be the ultimate purpose of all our study. If we study Buddhism as an academic subject, then we are only trying to get a degree or to gather more information, and our study will not be very transformative.

The purpose of all our study and training is to cultivate some inner wisdom and experience. Practice is essential to integrating all that we are learning. I encourage you to read the sutras even if you do not know the meaning of the words. Reading the Sanskrit can be like reciting mantras. Often we do not know the meaning in the beginning. After we recite the mantra thousands of times, it becomes so familiar to us. Even in our sleep we will sometimes sing the mantra.

One time a student was driving me to receive a lama who was arriving from India. It was wintertime, and the roads were very icy. At one point we hit a patch of ice and the car began to slide. The cars all around us were spinning and crashing into each other. The car behind us pushed us into the car in front of us. The words that came out of my mouth were *om mani padme hum*. The mantra was so deeply embedded in my mind that it was my first response. If we do enough mantra recitations, it can be our response to traumatic accidents or fear and worry. With enough mantra practice it can become effortless and natural within our minds.

When I was studying in the monastic university as a young student, the first thing we had to do was memorize all the root texts. Before we could study the *Heart Sutra*, we had to memorize the root text of the *Abhisamayalamkara*. Before we could study the *Abhidharmakosha*, we had to also memorize the Abhidharma root text. In this way, we had to know all the root texts by heart.

As young students we did not necessarily know the meaning of the words we were memorizing. At times we questioned the purpose of memorizing something we did not yet understand. Later, when I wanted to study these texts more deeply, I was very grateful to know the root texts by heart.

The ancient methods of Buddhist study were all based on the student's intention of becoming a wise and beneficial person. The ultimate goal was to become a buddha. The aspiration was to cultivate all these positive qualities inside us so we could benefit other beings.

I say all of this to remind us that the true purpose of learning is inner transformation. When we study the *Heart Sutra*, we should not approach it as a method of learning about the outer world. Although it helps us to understand the nature of all conditioned things, it is primarily a method of getting to know our own true natures.

Our study of the five aggregates is really a method for coming to know the truth about ourselves and about how we function in the world. By knowing the truth about ourselves, we automatically begin to understand the truth of others.

We are not talking about knowledge based on our emotions and inner karmic conditions. We are talking about wisdom that is free from feelings and karma. We are learning about ultimate truth here in the sutra. We are gaining understanding that is not based on relativity.

If we continue to base our understanding of the sutra on our inner conditions and emotions, then there is no way we will know anything about ultimate truth. This true "knowing" must be based on a universal understanding, a universal wisdom.

Studying the four kinds of emptiness is not just about knowing the true nature of the universe. It is about realizing this true nature at a very personal, experiential level. When you have realized the nature of everything, then you have gone beyond all your conditioning. You have gone beyond your isms, your emotions, your karma, your identity; you have gone beyond everything.

These four forms of emptiness are a state within you. This is why the *Heart Sutra* refers to this as an inner space in which you cannot find any extremes. If you are attached to any extremes, then you do not have realization.

If you have true realization, then you are not at risk for misunderstanding emptiness. When you have some inner experience, you will no longer wonder if emptiness is some kind of ultimate negation. You will know that emptiness is freedom from all the extremes.

Emptiness is very subtle. We cannot really grasp it at the intellectual level or at the verbal level. The more we try to express this emptiness, the more misleading our ideas can become.

Although the *Heart Sutra* is not a tantric teaching, our tantric sadhana practice can guide us to a much deeper, nonconceptual understanding of the four emptinesses. Once you have realized that state of the wisdom gone beyond, then you have transcended extremes.

> Shariputra! In the same way, all dharmas are devoid of characteristics, unborn, unstopped, unsullied, unpurified, undecreased, unfilled.

"In the same way" refers to going beyond the four extremes. "All dharmas" includes both conditioned and unconditioned things.

Early in our study of the sutra, we may question whether the sutra is just a study of conditioned things. We focus so much on learning about the five aggregates, and these aggregates only include what is conditioned.

When the sutra says "all dharmas," it includes conditioned things such as the aggregates and unconditioned emptiness. The four forms of emptiness include all conditioned dharmas as well as unconditioned emptiness.

In the Abhidharma, "all things" refers to all conditioned things, all unconditioned things, and even nirvana. Here in the sutra, "unconditioned" includes space, nirvana, and the four kinds of emptiness. Everything can be included under "all dharmas." It includes both conditioned and unconditioned things.

In the relative world, we have the characteristics we have discussed. We have general characteristics such as impermanence, and we have unique characteristics through which we identify all objects in the universe.

Based on these characteristics we generate all kinds of ideas. We may think that characteristics are not that important. To achieve perfect buddhahood, though, we must go beyond characteristics. We must know them in order to go beyond them. When we see the selflessness of the person and the selflessness of phenomena, we achieve nirvana. To achieve complete enlightenment, though, we must go beyond all characteristics.

Characteristics are the basis for all concepts and for our attachment and aversion in samsara. We are such emotional beings. When we are attracted to someone, immediately we generate feelings for them. Based on their characteristics, we create extensive narratives. We project our hopes and fears. We carry this person in our minds constantly.

We also do this with other objects we become attached to. We are programmed to cherish things here in samsara. We are very sentimental. We cling to our good memories. We grasp onto objects that inspire pleasure and happiness in us. We long for that to be a permanent state.

Characteristics are very subtle. The characteristics that we cling to most intensely are often projections deep in our hearts and minds. Outer characteristics are very tangible. We may like a certain flower because of its color. We may like a particular food because of its flavor. We may be attracted to someone who we find very beautiful. Those are tangible reasons we are drawn to something.

When our experience becomes rooted in our memories, mental pictures, and emotions, the characteristics become the most subtle and most powerful. It is hardest to let go of our inner attachment to someone. As mentioned earlier, we still carry inner projections and memories of a person long after they die.

Characteristics that inspire love or hatred in us have the greatest power. It is most difficult to let go of our closest loved ones and our worst enemies. Even the characteristics that inspire a neutral reaction are considered objects of ignorance. We do not let go of them because we are not even aware of these neutral things. We easily forget such objects because they are not as emotionally active as objects of desire or anger.

Characteristics help us to identify each and every object. We have thousands of objects to which we are attached in our daily lives. If we look closely, if we meditate on the emptiness of those characteristics, then we find nothing to be attached to. If we look closely, we cannot find those characteristics. All objects by their true nature are devoid of characteristics. They are empty of characteristics. That is the ultimate side of the coin. Relative truth and ultimate truth are just two sides of the same coin.

Ultimate and relative truth may seem very paradoxical at our level. If characteristics are rooted in the form of an object, and if the nature of that form is emptiness, then there are no characteristics! These two truths are in union.

Until we become buddhas, we remain attached to form and therefore to characteristics. We do not see the other side of the coin, which is the true nature of the object. We continue to interact with the universe in a relative way. Only when we see characteristics and emptiness simultaneously do we go beyond the four extremes.

Avalokiteshvara is saying in the *Heart Sutra* that emptiness is free from characteristics. This refers to ultimate truth. Depending on our level of realization, this might not make much sense. We subscribe so fully to a world of characteristics here in samsara that it can be very challenging to see emptiness.

All things are produced due to causes and conditions. Birth and birthlessness may seem very paradoxical. Birth is based on relativity. We are conceived due to our karma, emotions, and parents. Then we are born. Every moment that we are living we are also changing and dying. That is our experience here in samsara.

If we try to find birth as something truly existent, we cannot find it. This may seem absurd to us now. Of course we think we were born! After nine months we came out of our mother's womb. We have our birth certificates, and we can prove the date this happened.

But what happened before birth? We already existed in our mother's womb for many months before we were born. We were alive already there. Before conception our minds already existed; something was there even before conception.

The sutra has gone beyond even this logical examination of birth to see emptiness. "Unborn" refers to the ultimate nature of things where everything is emptiness. In emptiness there is no birth. The empty nature of everything is unborn.

Relatively, of course, we were born. We celebrate our birthday every year. We believe in the reality of our existence. Only when we study relative and ultimate truth and see emptiness will this paradox be understandable.

The word "unstopped" in the sutra is referring to emptiness as death-lessness. At the relative level, we are born, and we are subject to death. We are living to die! If you need a reminder of impermanence, it is good to practice meditation and reflection in a cemetery.

We want to live forever because of our attachments. That goes against the natural laws of the universe though. We all know that those who are born will die. There has never been an exception. All that is produced will decay.

Realizing the ultimate nature of characteristics, birth, and death is called the *doors of the three great liberations*. When we have gone beyond all characteristics, beyond birth and death, then we have achieved the greatest freedom possible.

We may think that buddhas or bodhisattvas are not born and do not die. We need to make a distinction. None of us chose freely to be born. Our rebirth was forced by karma, by our desire, by our attraction to one of our parents. Birth is very painful for ordinary beings because it is forced by karma. Death is also forced on us and creates tremendous suffering.

Bodhisattvas and buddhas take rebirth out of freedom. They choose to take rebirth to benefit all sentient beings. According to the Mahayana teachings, the Buddha Shakyamuni demonstrated the twelve exemplary activities including the activities of birth and of passing beyond nirvana.

The Buddha was born without pain. He was reborn joyfully out of freedom. He passed away very peacefully and consciously and was reborn with similar peace and awareness. Buddhas do not experience these transitions as painful or frightening.

Buddhas were not conceived through desire and karma. They were conceived through wisdom. They chose to return here so they could help other beings. Even though buddhas were born, they are still considered unborn because they were not forced by karma and emotions to take rebirth. Birth and death are considered exemplary activities when they are performed by buddhas and bodhisattvas. They are acting to benefit us.

It is like a movie. Someone can be born in a movie, but that is not real. Buddhas have gone beyond characteristics. They have gone beyond birth and death. They have gone beyond the doors of the three great liberations.

We ordinary humans do not have that freedom. That is why we are mentally tortured by so many thoughts and feelings. Our minds are chattering all the time. If you have ever tried to meditate, you will be aware of how much inner noise and activity we have. Even when we are alone, and even when we are sleeping, our minds may still be chattering away.

This is all due to our concepts and characteristics. Birth is painful. Living is painful because we are trying so hard to distract ourselves from the truth of impermanence. That very denial causes us more suffering and restlessness.

For us, characteristics, birth, and death, are torture. They are very painful. These three have not become doors to liberation yet. They are the cause of so much suffering. Only when we realize ultimate truth will these become the three doors to liberation.

These three liberations are also known by different names in some texts. They can be called *liberation of emptiness*, *wishlessness*, or *signlessness*. The words *sign* and *characteristic* are synonymous here.

We should clarify the word *wish*. When we take the bodhisattva vow, like many of you have done during empowerments, we make the resolution to achieve enlightenment for the benefit of all sentient beings.

That resolution is similar to a wish. This wish is also called the *double aspiration*. You are wishing not only for your own awakening but also for your awakening to benefit all beings. But this wish is related to desire; it is still connected to passion. For this reason, it is considered *relative bodhichitta*. It is not ultimate because it is based on desire.

Once you have seen wisdom, then *wishing bodhichitta* becomes *ultimate bodhichitta*. Ultimate bodhichitta is the wisdom gone beyond.

The first five perfections in the training of the six paramitas are considered *entering bodhichitta*. The first paramita of giving through the fifth paramita of meditation are still considered relative bodhichitta. Only when these five are integrated with the sixth paramita of wisdom will they become perfections and ultimate bodhichitta.

When you take the bodhisattva vow it is considered *wishing bodhichitta*. Then, as you accumulate merit based on that wishing bodhichitta, it becomes entering bodhichitta. Through the accumulation of merit you realize the ultimate bodhichitta of wisdom. When you finally realize wisdom, then that wishing bodhichitta becomes *wishless* because it has become the nature of wisdom. It has gone beyond desire.

Bodhisattvas are benefiting other sentient beings all the time. At the ultimate level they are not operating out of their desire to help. Due to their accumulation of merit, positive benefits happen effortlessly. Their good deeds are like sunlight shining down on us.

Our sun does not have any wish to light our planet. When it is dark on one side of the globe, it is not because the sun has stopped shining; it is merely because the planet is in its own shadow.

Likewise, the wisdom of the buddhas and bodhisattvas is shining all the time. Whether we will receive their light or not depends upon our conditions. If we are not ready for that wisdom, we will not receive it.

Once we have achieved the wisdom gone beyond, it is wishless, without signs, and without characteristics. That wisdom is emptiness. The doors of the three great liberations are only achieved when we have realized wisdom.

In our relative lives we always have this dichotomy of defilement and purification. We are struggling in our practice to purify our negativities. We do ngöndro preliminary practices to remove these obscurations.

We are born with karma. This is like being born with dirty clothing. The cloth itself is not dirty by nature. When we are forced to be born due to our afflictive emotions, we start out with these karmic defilements. Our practice is an effort to wash away the dirt to reveal the inherent purity of that cloth.

The wisdom gone beyond is completely free from defilements and free from purifications. It has gone beyond both. When the sutra says "unsullied and unpurified," it is referring to going beyond both defilement and purification.

Between birth and death, we also have a period of living and abiding. While we are living, this dichotomy of defilement and purification can play out. It is still based on dualism.

The notion of defilement and purification is important for practitioners, but it does not describe the actual nature of our lives. Our basic nature is pure. The wisdom gone beyond is like space; it is like the sky. The sky is clear by nature; it is empty of clouds. Clouds come and go.

Relatively speaking, when a cloud comes it is considered an obscuration. It is negative. It is a defilement. When the cloud goes it is considered purification. This does not refer to the sky itself. The sky does not have any concept of cloud or emptiness. For the sky there is no defilement and no purification. By nature the sky is clear, and the clouds do not alter this true nature.

In the same way, our true nature is like that sky. It is clear. We all have buddha nature. We are purifying defilements based on our five aggregates. We are purifying based on the afflictive emotions through which we were conceived and with which we are now living.

According to Buddhism, we have been conceived interdependently based on the three destructive emotions of desire, anger, and ignorance. As I have mentioned, we have attachment to one of our parents. We have subtle aversion to the other parent. That desire and aversion exist because of our basic ignorance. Our lives begin with the three afflictive emotions. The active emotions of desire and anger create all our pain, pleasure, happiness, and unhappiness.

If our lives were free from suffering, then there would be no need to purify these root destructive emotions. But our lives are filled with unexamined suffering. For this reason, Buddhism has developed methods for working to overcome these afflictive emotions.

According to Buddhism, no matter how much pleasure and happiness we have, deep down we are still constantly dissatisfied. This leads to an underlying sadness. For this reason, Buddhism has developed purification methods so that we can achieve complete freedom and peace.

Without this purification, our feelings of restlessness will haunt our lives. No matter how much success we have, no matter how many worldly pleasures we experience, we will always be unhappy because everything is always changing. We cannot make the good experiences permanent. We cannot keep everything the same at our jobs. We cannot stop our family from changing. We cannot save our bodies from illness and aging.

We have so many dreams for our lives. When those dreams become a reality, it is amazing to discover that we are still not satisfied. Our dream homes will develop problems. Maybe disagreeable neighbors will move in next door. Maybe there will be flooding or forest fires. Even if the house is perfect, maybe we will start to wish we had an even bigger house.

Our dream families will change also. Our sweet children will become defiant teenagers. Our partners will become different people over the years. Even when our dreams become a reality, we are still never truly satisfied. This is why we have to turn to spiritual methods to treat this underlying suffering. Until we purify ourselves, we will just keep on changing the objects in our lives, but the result will be dissatisfaction.

When we fall in love there is a bit of delusional romanticism. For a while we think that our new partner is perfect. We are completely caught up and distracted by our new love. Over time, this freshness starts to fade. We may begin to see our differences, and we begin to have conflict. Now our romance is no longer distracting us from our under-lying destructive emotions. It may even be enhancing those negative emotions.

Here in our relative lives there are so many defilements that we need to purify. When the sutra says "unsullied, unpurified, undecreased, unfilled," it may again seem very paradoxical.

From the wisdom gone beyond, though, there is no beginning or end. Birth is unborn. Death is unstopped. If there is no life, then noth-ing is increasing or decreasing. The wisdom gone beyond is undecreased and unfilled because it is unconditioned. That unconditioned space is the same all the time.

Our lives are not like that yet. Our lives are always going up and down. We may climb the corporate ladder and become the most pow-erful CEO. Once we reach the top, others may threaten our security, and eventually we will fall back down that ladder. The fall will be even harder due to the success we experienced. We see this cycle play out very dramatically among our star athletes or entertainers. Celeb-rities often fall the hardest, and they have no privacy while they are suffering.

Whether this cycle is based on economic status, on celebrity power, or simply on happiness, we find that things are always rising and falling. Everything is subject to the suffering of change.

The wisdom gone beyond does not change because it is not condi-tioned. It does not increase nor decrease. These may sound like simple words, but we have to go beyond words to the deeper meaning. We must try to learn this based on our lives. These words in the sutra can become profoundly meaningful if we begin to integrate them into our experience. The sutra is rich with messages that can help us to gain emo-tional freedom in our lives. The purpose is to introduce us to that wis-dom inside us.

As we have established, this part of the sutra refers to going beyond the doors of the three great liberations. It shows us a way beyond birth, death, and characteristics. Only when we have seen the wisdom gone beyond will these become liberations.

The wisdom gone beyond is when you go beyond all four extremes: existence, nonexistence, both, and neither. It is when you go beyond all dharmas, all conditioned and unconditioned things, all birth and death, to achieve complete enlightenment. The *Heart Sutra* has the power to introduce us to this perfect wisdom.

# 20

# No Ayatanas and No Dhatus

No eye, no ear, no nose, no tongue, no body, no mind; no form, no sound, no smell, no taste, no touch, no dharmas.

THESE LINES OF the *Heart Sutra* list the twelve ayatanas. The ayatanas include the six sense objects as well as the six sense faculties. For example, the eye organ is a sense faculty, and form is the corresponding sense object. The ear organ is the sense faculty, and sound is the corresponding sense object. At the level of ultimate truth, when you have wisdom, you will have even gone beyond all twelve ayatanas.

In our current lives we are very attached to our five aggregates as well as to the twelve ayatanas. Our eye organ perceives a visual object that is part of the aggregate of matter. Then our aggregates of feeling, ideation, formation, and consciousness create complex reactions and concepts in relation to that sensory perception. This is how we interact with everything based on our attachment to the aggregates and ayatanas.

There is no element of eye and so on through the element of mind and the element of mental consciousness.

These lines refer to the eighteen dhatus. The dhatus are the result. The dhatus include the twelve ayatanas as well as the six corresponding sense consciousnesses related to the sense organs.

The word dhatu has two meanings in Sanskrit. The first meaning is "cause and result." The second meaning is "nature." Both meanings can be applied here in the sutra. When a healthy eye organ sees a visual object, eye consciousness arises. This is the cause and result meaning of the word dhatu. The six sense consciousnesses are the result of the six sense organs and the six sense objects.

When we become enlightened, we realize the wisdom of going beyond all our emotional involvement with the five aggregates, the twelve ayatanas, and the eighteen dhatus. Seeing their empty nature is the other meaning of the word dhatu.

We have not seen emptiness yet, and we are firmly attached to the five aggregates. Of the five aggregates, the Buddha taught most frequently about mental activities. The aggregates of feeling, ideation, and formation are all related to mental activities.

There is a basic mind from which we generate all kinds of emotions. We experience anger, attachment, jealousy, faith, compassion, and other mental activities that stem from this basic mind.

The Buddha explained that these aggregates related to mental activities give a comprehensive explanation of Buddhist psychology. The Buddha taught the five aggregates so that we could overcome misunderstandings related to our feelings, thoughts, and mental activities. Indian Buddhist works such as the *Abhidharmakosha* and the *Abhidharmasamucchaya* explore mental activities in great depth.

Studying the mental activities is an important step toward freedom. The main reason the Buddha taught the five aggregates was to help us overcome our ignorance related to our emotions and mental objects. The five aggregates are the foundation of all our self-clinging.

The word ayatana has a technical meaning of "arising to extend." This refers to the arising of the six sense consciousnesses to contact the six sense objects through the doors of the six sense organs.

Ten of the twelve ayatanas are part of the first aggregate of matter.

The sense organs of eye, ear, nose, tongue, and body are part of our material form. Their corresponding sense objects of visual form, sound, smell, taste, and touch are also part of the first aggregate of matter. These ten ayatanas become the conditions for consciousness to arise. The sixth sense organ is the mind, and the sixth sense object refers to dharmas, which here means phenomena.

Here in the sutra, "mind" refers to the basic mind as well as to the other consciousnesses. The objects related to the mind are all dharmas. These dharmas include mental thoughts as well as unconditioned things. So ayatana has this meaning of "arising and extending" in relation to these sense organs and sense objects.

We are conceived with the basic mind. As our fetus grows in our mother's womb, we develop sense organs. With each evolution of the organ, we are able to interact more and more with the universe. As our little ears develop, we can begin to hear our mother's heartbeat.

The only difference we will find between the five aggregates and the twelve ayatanas is the *dharma ayatana*. According to the ayatanas, the term dharma denotes an object of the mind organ. This includes our mental thoughts, including our dreams. It also includes all unconditioned things, such as space and nirvana. These unconditioned things can also become objects of the mind. Unconditioned things are not included in the fifth aggregate, and that is the big difference between the ayatanas and the aggregates.

The five aggregates only include conditioned things. The twelve ayatanas include both conditioned and unconditioned things. The Buddha taught the ayatanas to help us overcome ignorance related to material objects. According to the Buddha, form is not only an object we see. All sounds are form. All smells are form. All tastes are form. All these sense objects are still composed of atoms. The Buddha taught the ayatanas to help us understand more about this aggregate of form.

We have all these sense organs through which we experience the universe. The Buddha enumerated the first ten ayatanas to help us to overcome our ignorance related to the first aggregate of form. Form is the cause of many types of emotional involvement, especially when we are very attached to a person. Our attachment to loved ones or enemies generates so much karma. Form can be very limiting to us as a result of our ignorance. The ayatanas were primarily taught to help us overcome our ignorance related to the aggregate of form.

The Buddha taught the eighteen dhatus to help us overcome our ignorance related to mind and consciousness. So, we can see how the five aggregates, the twelve ayatanas, and the eighteen dhatus all have very specific functions in increasing our awareness.

By knowing the eighteen dhatus, we can learn how consciousness arises related to sense organ and sense object. We experience something only when these three factors come together. We need a healthy eye organ, a visual object, and an eye consciousness to see something.

The Buddha taught the eighteen dhatus to demonstrate how consciousness arises interdependently with the sense organ and sense object. By understanding how consciousness arises, we can overcome ignorance related to the mind and consciousness.

Consciousness is the present mind. As humans we have all five aggregates, we have all twelve ayatanas, and we have the eighteen dhatus. These are our basic ingredients. They are also the basis of cycling through samsara. The better we understand these ingredients, the clearer our path of transformation and wisdom becomes. If we want to relate to the *Heart Sutra* on a personal level, we can understand these basic ingredients or factors as the basis for both samsara and nirvana.

One of the great Buddhist masters said, "Samsara is nirvana, and nirvana is samsara." The only difference is that when we have ignorance, we remain trapped in samsara. When we have awareness and wisdom, the very same experience is nirvana.

If we have ignorance related to the five aggregates, the twelve ayatanas, and the eighteen dhatus, then we remain in samsara. If we see wisdom in all five aggregates, twelve ayatanas, and eighteen dhatus, then we are enlightened! Whatever practice we may be doing, whether it is shamatha and insight meditation, or the six paramitas, or a sadhana practice, the purpose is to see wisdom in the five aggregates, the twelve ayatanas, and the eighteen dhatus.

In Vajrayana Buddhism, we work with the wisdom aspect of the five aggregates, twelve ayatanas, and eighteen dhatus. We see these factors in the forms of buddhas and goddesses. Vajrayana practices are based on the result. We are transforming based on the result. We are visualizing ourselves as the deity to bring that wisdom into our ordinary lives.

The Buddha taught these three categories to overcome three kinds of ignorance: ignorance related to mental activities, ignorance related to matter, and ignorance related to the mind. The Buddha also gave us many different methods of practice to suit different practitioners.

People who are more interested in shamatha meditation prefer a simplified form of practice. If someone is very intelligent, then he or she can gain wisdom just by studying the five aggregates. Other people may study the five aggregates and still possess doubt and ignorance, so they also need to study the twelve ayatanas. Other practitioners may still have ignorance and need to study the eighteen dhatus.

The Buddha designed these different practice methods according to the interests and intelligence of practitioners. For the sake of our own understanding, we should try to avoid just studying these aspects objectively. Instead, we should try to study these in relation to ourselves and to our personal experiences. When we integrate these teachings into our own lives, they will offer more meaning to us.

> There is no ignorance, no elimination of ignorance; no death and decay, and no elimination of death and decay.

The Buddha has gone beyond samsara. The Buddha has gone beyond the wheel of life. These lines refer to the wheel of life and its twelve interdependent links.

In Buddhism there is no such thing as a first cause. We live in the present. The present exists because of the past. Due to the present, there will be a future. We cannot substantially prove that the past and future exist. We can only prove the present moment. We know that the present moment cannot exist without a past or a future. So, our proof of the three times is based on interdependency. This basic timeline also occurs because of karma. Karma depends on a timeline because cause and result play out across the past, present, and future.

At the moment, everything is changing mentally, physically, and emotionally. What we call the present is really just the tiniest measurement of time in this exact moment.

If we extend the present moment, we have minutes. Then we have hours, days, months, and years. Our lives are an accumulation of many moments of present time. We may experience this lifetime as linear, but it is not linear when we begin to examine where those moments first began.

The wheel of life is depicted as a circle. This represents the fact that there is no beginning. We cannot find the first cause in interdependency. When the sutra says "no ignorance, no elimination of ignorance," it is referring to the twelve interdependent links of the wheel of life.

The first link is ignorance. This does not mean that ignorance is the first cause. Ignorance is still interdependent with another link in this wheel. The twelve links in order are: ignorance, formations, consciousness, name and form, ayatanas, contact, feeling, craving, grasping, being, birth, and death and decay.

According to the Buddhist understanding, there are four things interdependently working together: mind, body, emotions, and karma. These are also operating across the three times: past, present, and future.

Sentient beings are constantly cycling interdependently from moment to moment. The past becomes the cause for the present. Then the present becomes the cause for the future. We are cycling based on the ignorance of not knowing our true natures. Until we are enlightened, we are cycling in this way through the wheel of life.

# 21

# The Twelve Interdependent Links: 1–5

IN THE LAST CHAPTER we explored the five aggregates, the twelve ayatanas, and the eighteen dhatus. These comprise the Buddha's foundational system for studying ourselves, objects, and the universe. They are known as the *ground* or the *basis*. When we understand the three categories of aggregates, ayatanas, and dhatus, we have an understanding of the foundation of the existence of life here in samsara. These categories are also the basis for liberation.

Whether we will be subjected to suffering life after life or whether we will become free depends on our inner conditions.

> There is no ignorance, no elimination of ignorance; no death and decay, and no elimination of death and decay.

These lines refer to the true nature of our minds, which is pure. Buddhists call that purity buddha nature. It is pure from beginningless time. In that purity there is no ignorance. Since there is no ignorance, there is no possibility of the elimination of ignorance.

We can see this constant purity only when we have realized the wisdom gone beyond. When we see the true nature of the mind, then we experience that purity. There are no destructive emotions or karmic accumulations that we need to eliminate.

Although this purity is our true nature, most of us have not discovered it yet. Our lives start with ignorance. Our lives follow the cycle described by the Buddhist wheel of life. The wheel demonstrates that there is no beginning in this cycle.

If we could find a first cause, then life would be linear. It would not be a circle. In theistic religions there is a creator God who is seen as the first cause of creation.

In the wheel of life, though, the Buddha taught that there is no beginning. It is just an ongoing cycle of interdependency between cause and result. Every cause needs another cause and condition.

Can we really say the chicken came before the egg? That chicken came from an egg! We cannot really say who came first in this cycle. That is how interdependency operates.

## THE FIRST LINK: IGNORANCE

When the sutra refers to ignorance, it is talking about the first link in the wheel of life. When it mentions death and decay, it is referring to the last link. Of course, these twelve interdependent links are all connected.

The Buddha taught the wheel of life based on a timeline. We define our present life as the time between the moment of conception and the moment of death.

Did anything exist before that first moment of conception? To answer that question the Buddha taught the twelve interdependent links based on the three times: past life, present life, and future life. These three are based on cause and result. Our present life is a result of the past. Our present life will cause our rebirth.

Although we may study ignorance as the first link in the wheel of life, if we keep in mind past, present, and future, then we cannot prove that ignorance is the first cause. Even ignorance has its own cause.

I think that interdependency is the most important concept in Buddhism. It is based on very clear principles and explains logically how things unfold in relativity.

Even in Buddhism there are many different interpretations of interdependency. All Buddhist schools agree on interdependent origination, but there are different interpretations among the four Buddhist philosophical schools. If we study the twelve links according to the durational interdependent origination of the Realist school, they will be more useful. Durational interdependent origination emphasizes the prominence of a specific link, although all five aggregates are present in that duration.

The word *ignorance* in the wheel of life represents the destructive emotions we have accumulated in the past. Ignorance includes desire and anger.

If we study the images of the wheel of life, we will see how the three destructive emotions are represented as animals. Ignorance is portrayed as a pig. Anger is portrayed as a snake. Desire is illustrated by a rooster.

These three are represented together in that first link of ignorance. This is to demonstrate how these emotions depend on each other. Due to ignorance, we have desire. Due to desire, we have anger. All three destructive emotions work together.

Ignorance is also symbolized in the wheel of life by a blind person. This is to represent being ignorant not only to outer objects but to one's own true nature.

Ignorance is the basis of all destructive emotions. In the interdependent links, it refers to past destructive emotions. Due to those past destructive emotions, we have the second link, which is formation.

## THE SECOND LINK: FORMATION

The second interdependent link of formation refers to mental activities. Just like the fourth aggregate, it refers to karma. In the wheel of life, this second link of formation is represented by a person making pottery. Physical, verbal, and mental activities are actions included in the second link.

Ignorance represents our past destructive emotions. Formation represents our past karma. So, these first two links refer to the past.

Recall that according to Buddhist cosmology, there are three realms: the form realm, the formless realm, and the desire realm. There are also six classes of beings: humans, animals, hungry ghosts, hell beings, demigods, and gods.

The form realm is higher than the desire realm. These form beings have more merit. They do not need to consume things out of strong emotions like we do.

Even higher than the form realm is the formless realm. This is filled with beings who have no bodies and have reached deep meditative absorption. They are still not enlightened beings though.

We know that there are limitless planetary systems. When we read the Noble King of Prayers or any of the Buddha's sutras, we see that the Buddha referred to limitless planets and realms. Even science is now starting to refer to the possibility of infinite universes. Imagine how many beings could exist on these infinite planets!

The Buddha said that throughout all these planetary systems, all sentient beings could still be classified into three realms: the desire realm, the form realm, and the formless realm.

I mention this because I want to make it clear that the twelve interdependent links do not apply to limitless beings. The interdependent links primarily refer to humans.

The Buddha taught that there are four different kinds of birth. There are beings who are born from a womb like humans and many animals. There are beings born from eggs like birds, turtles, and fish. There are beings who are born out of moisture and heat when they combine. The fourth type of birth is called *apparitional* birth. It is miraculous in the sense that beings appear instantaneously, without a mother.

The twelve interdependent links of the wheel of life are based on the stages of human life. The Buddha taught that human life is the most conducive to spiritual practice. The twelve links do not necessarily apply to the formless beings and those beings who appear miraculously through apparitional birth. These twelve links are discussed to help us humans.

The links of ignorance and formation are related to the past. These first two links are considered *past duration*. Whatever destructive emotions you have accumulated in the past due to your activities based on the five aggregates is represented by ignorance. Whatever karma you have accumulated based on mental activities and the five aggregates is represented by formation.

These two are the causes and conditions that determine your present life. There is a Buddhist expression that says, "If you want to know your past, then look at your present." We can look at our bodies, our emotions, our minds, our actions, and everything in our present lives as a window to the past. Our current experience is based on what we have done in the past. Our current actions will determine our future.

This is why these twelve interdependent links are divided into the past, present, and future. They are interdependently based on past life, present life, and future life. You can only prove interdependency as it functions in time.

We live in the present time. Our present is based on the past. We can infer the future because of the past and present. Otherwise, how would we know it exists? Without the reference point of the present moment, it would be very hard to prove past and future. The past has already gone. The future has not yet come. How could we prove they exist without the present?

As we get older, we gather many memories and experiences. As we reach old age, we carry all these years with us in our minds. Our past only exists because we are living in the present and remember it.

We plan for the future. We plan for our next vacation or for our retirement. We plan because we believe that there will be a future. We believe there will be a future based on the fact that the past and present have occurred.

You can see how time plays an integral role in understanding these twelve interdependent links of cause and result. In the wheel of life, we cannot say, "This is the first cause; this is the beginning." Something had to come before it in that wheel. The twelve interdependent links are based on the destructive emotions and karma that force us to cycle through samsara.

As we were discussing earlier, the nature of our minds is pure. Our buddha nature is free from destructive emotions. Since it does not have ignorance and destructive emotions, it also does not have karma. It is free! There is nothing to eliminate.

All of the Buddhist practices we do are methods to discover this true nature within us. Once we have discovered that, we have realized wisdom.

Right now, our lives are based on afflictive emotions and karma. As long as we have destructive emotions and karma, then we remain trapped in this cycle of suffering from life to life. Once we become aware of the suffering of samsara, we can begin to purify and reverse these negative accumulations.

Through practice we can purify ourselves enough to see our true nature. Once we see our true nature, our ignorance disappears. When we realize wisdom, ignorance has ceased. Karma has ceased. Our cycling through the wheel of life has ceased. At that point we have achieved buddhahood, and we are enlightened.

Through meditation practice and the accumulation of merit and wisdom, we can purify all our negativities and ultimately see our buddha nature. Only through this reversion process, when we come to see our true nature, will there be any freedom.

The fourth noble truth is the reversal method. It shows us how we can reverse the twelve interdependent links so that we can become free from pain and suffering. The noble eightfold path presented in the fourth noble truth shows us a way to reverse this process.

## The Third Link: Consciousness

Due to past ignorance, which represents the destructive emotions created by the five aggregates, and due to formation, which is the past karma created by the five aggregates, our present life is conceived in the third link, which is consciousness.

If you look at images of the wheel of life, you will see that consciousness is represented by a monkey! You will hear many Buddhist teachings that refer to the *monkey mind*. The monkey image in the wheel of life represents our minds from the first moment of conception. Our present lives start from the monkey mind.

How are we conceived? How does our consciousness enter into the egg and sperm? These days we can see all kinds of diagrams and simulations of how the egg and sperm meet. These explanations do not demonstrate the role of destructive emotions in our conception. These explanations cannot show us how the mind becomes entrapped between the mother's and father's elements.

Mind is immaterial. What we bring into that moment of conception is just the mind that remained after our previous death. To understand conception, we also need to understand the process of death.

If we could completely remember the process of death, we would understand how we are conceived. Most of the time, however, we do not remember how we died. Most of us die in so much pain and with so much suffering. This suffering is often overwhelming, and we lose consciousness during the dying process. When we die with so little awareness, we have very little memory of death.

These days most of us die numbed by painkillers. We are often placed on high levels of morphine and are so sedated that we are almost asleep. We do not remember anything.

When we die with a lot of ignorance, it is almost like entering a very deep sleep. When we wake up, we do not remember anything. Sleep is a very good analogy for death. Our dreams are a very good analogy for the bardo stage before we take rebirth.

Whatever habitual patterns are most strongly imprinted in our minds will dominate our experience. If we are very angry, that anger will remain in the mind. If we are attached, that attachment will remain strong.

Attachment is one of the emotions that follows us the longest. We are very sentimental about our families and our loved ones. If we look closely, we are often the most attached to the opposite gender.

Daughters are often most attached to their fathers. Sons are often most attached to their mothers. Couples have very strong attachments to each other.

This attachment to our loved ones is one of the strongest emotions after death. Our same mind continues to look for that love and attachment in the next life. We are looking for love because we want to experience happiness and pleasure again. Love makes us feel so happy.

When we have some habitual patterns and karma with someone from a past lifetime, we will often feel a deep sense of recognition and affinity. There are billions of people on this planet. Why are we only attracted to certain people? Why is one particular person drawing our energy toward them?

If we are going to be born as a girl, we are often attached to our father at the moment of conception. If we are going to be born as a boy, then we are often drawn to our mother at the moment of conception, and our consciousness will be conceived through the egg. Then the egg and sperm come together, and our minds become sandwiched there between the mother's and father's elements.

The Buddha could remember everything about the experience of birth and death and helped us understand how things evolve. Desire and love are the same at our level. We are looking for love through desire. Desire exists because we are not enlightened yet. We do not see the buddha nature inside of us because of our basic ignorance.

After a couple has their first child, I think many families will see a bit of tension arise. Three is an odd number, you know? Relationships often shift when a child is born. One parent will pay more attention to the child, and the other parent may feel a bit neglected and ignored! Some aversion may even arise.

The links of ignorance and formation determine how and when we will be conceived. This third link of consciousness is based on our past emotions and karma. Consciousness is based on our past mental, physical, and verbal actions, and the afflictive emotions related to those activities. Those factors determine where we will be conceived.

## THE FOURTH LINK: NAME AND FORM

From the moment of conception, the fourth link, which is called name and form, begins. Name and form is another term for the five aggregates. It is important to clarify that the five aggregates were already present in the third link.

The minute that our consciousness becomes imprisoned between the egg and sperm, all five aggregates are there. In that moment, one's consciousness is most prominent, but that does not mean that it exists independently. It still interdependently exists with the egg and sperm and with our emotions. Our karma is there. All five aggregates are there, but consciousness is the most prominent.

From this consciousness the present life begins. From this moment of conception the fetus begins to evolve. As the fetus develops, the sense organs grow at different intervals. They do not all appear in the first moments of conception.

If we study fetal development, we see that it takes many weeks for the organs to form. That period from conception until our organs have developed is the duration of the fourth link of name and form. This is symbolized in the wheel of life by the image of a passenger traveling in a boat. The boat and the passenger represent name and form, which includes the five aggregates. This represents the evolution from conception until the organs have developed.

Form refers to the first aggregate of matter. Name refers to the other four aggregates: feeling, ideation, formation, and consciousness. They are called name because they are immaterial.

When our organs have developed, we can interact with outer objects. Our eye organ allows us to perceive visual objects. Our nose allows us to smell. Even while we are still in utero, some of our sense organs have already begun to detect sense objects.

## THE FIFTH LINK: THE SIX AYATANAS

In the duration of this fifth link, the baby's sense organs fully develop. The sense objects are there too, but the baby is not ready to perceive objects. For this reason, the fifth link only includes six of the twelve ayatanas. It only includes the ayatanas of the sense organs but not of the sense objects.

We should try to bring these teachings directly into our personal experience instead of studying them intellectually. Bringing our understanding of these links into our meditation practice helps us to begin reversing them.

As mentioned, the first two links of ignorance and formation are related to the past. Links three through five, which are consciousness, name and form, and the six ayatanas, are related to our present lives. Our current life starts with the third link of consciousness.

In the wheel of life, the six ayatanas are symbolized by the image of a house with doors and windows. These doors and windows refer to the eyes, ears, nose, and so forth. They represent these portals through which we sense the outer world.

These twelve links are not just something the Buddha made up. They are based on the three times, on our evolution, and on interdependency.

Scientists are always trying to find some independent origination for human beings. They may say, for example, that the human race began somewhere in Africa. Science is always trying to find some starting point.

There is no origination in the twelve interdependent links. The cycle is beginningless and endless. It is also not based on a first cause. In the Buddhist understanding there is no creator who started everything.

# 22

# The Twelve Interdependent Links: 6–10

THE BUDDHA GAVE his teaching on the wheel of life in his sutra to a king named Udrayana. The wheel of life is called *bhavachakra* in Sanskrit. *Bhava* means "being." It implies that from beginningless time we have been reborn again and again. The word bhava is often translated as "life." The Sanskrit is a little more subtle than this translation and has more to do with the different stages of being.

When we hear the word "life," we may assume it refers only to this one lifetime. Most humans do not view death as being part of life. We often see death as something separate. The word bhava includes death as part of existence. At death we are still a *being*. Our consciousness has not ceased. Our mind has not vanished.

If death were the complete cessation of our lives, then after death, the mind would not exist. The bhavachakra, the wheel of life, includes birth, living, death, and the intermediate stages and momentary states in between.

The Buddha taught these twelve links so that we could understand how beings are reborn repeatedly. The links are a good way to study our present lives. They also remind us that we have been cycling through life from beginningless time and have assumed many different forms.

The bhavachakra illustrates the six different classes of beings: hell beings, hungry ghosts, animals, humans, demigods, and gods. The Buddha taught that although these beings may have different physical characteristics, the same potentialities exist in every one of them. We take these different physical forms in different lives based on our karma and emotions, but we all share the same buddha nature. We all share the potential for enlightenment.

At one time maybe our minds were in the body of a fish deep in the ocean. In another life maybe we were a cow or a yak out in the fields. At some point, maybe due to anger, we took the form of a hell being, suffering terribly in the hell realms. At another point due to greed and stinginess, maybe we were born as hungry ghosts.

These teachings are most pertinent to our human experience. The Buddha said that out of the six classes of beings, humans have the best opportunity for spiritual practice. Human life has the greatest potential for achieving enlightenment.

People who are new to Buddhism may assume that the gods in the heavenly realm must be closer to buddhahood. But those heavenly beings are experiencing so little suffering that they do not take interest in spiritual practice. Their lives are very long, pleasant, and comfortable. As a result, there is really no incentive to practice and to accumulate merit. Eventually they exhaust their good karma and are reborn in a lower realm.

When we talk about sentient beings, we must remember that these beings are limitless. They are infinite in number and are cycling endlessly in samsara with us.

The five aggregates, the twelve ayatanas, and the eighteen dhatus help us understand our experience of ourselves and others. The three trainings which include meditation, wisdom, and discipline, help us to awaken.

When the aggregates, ayatanas, and dhatus are still defiled by ignorance, we remain caught in the wheel of life. When we overcome that ignorance through wisdom, then we reverse that process, and we finally see the Buddha nature.

## THE SIXTH LINK: CONTACT

The sixth link is called *contact*. When our six sense organs are fully developed in utero, then at some point we will have contact with the six sense objects. When the mind, the organ, and the object all come together, there is contact.

Contact is that moment where those three factors come together. It is represented in the wheel of life by the image of a couple embracing to symbolize contact between all six sense organs and all six sense objects.

## THE SEVENTH LINK: FEELING

The seventh interdependent link is feeling. That first moment of contact is followed immediately by sensation or feeling. Feelings arise based on the three root destructive emotions. For this reason, we see feeling illustrated in the wheel of life by the image of an arrow piercing an eyeball! This demonstrates that feeling, by nature, is painful.

When our desires are fulfilled through that contact we feel pleasure and happiness. When our desires are not fulfilled we feel anger, pain, and unhappiness. Even neutral feelings are based on our destructive emotion of ignorance.

As we have discussed in an earlier chapter, desire, anger, and ignorance are the three root emotions that all five feelings are based on. All feelings can be included into agreeable, disagreeable, and neutral feelings.

At some stage of fetal development the fetus begins to have some feelings and sensations. My mom used to say that mothers have to be careful about what they eat and drink when they are pregnant. She said if they eat something which is very hot, it can make the baby uncomfortable.

At some point in our evolution that contact creates feelings. This duration of feeling lasts all the way until we become sexual beings and can engage in sexual union. The end of the stage is marked by the moment when the feeling reaches that peak level of consummation with another person. The highest level of consum-mation in the desire realm occurs between two people during sexual union.

Feelings are based on the sensations of the six organs. Each organ can experience pleasurable, painful, or neutral sensations. The sensations are based on the six sense organs, and how we experience those sensations is based on the three root destructive emotions of anger, ignorance, and attachment.

Whenever your desires are fulfilled, you experience pleasure and happiness. Whenever you have anger, then you experience pain and unhappiness. Whenever you do not have strong feelings, then that neutral experience is based on ignorance. We think that feeling is originating in the object. The object may have some influence, but mostly our feelings toward that object are coming from our own emotions.

We know this is true because the same object can bring us such different feelings. As long as we love someone and they are fulfilling our desires and meeting our needs, we feel so much happiness and pleasure in relation to them. If that person no longer satisfies us, or if they betray our trust, that same person can bring us so much pain and suffering. Even if that person does not bring us strong emotions, we may just grow tired and bored and wish to forget them.

In this way, we can prove how each object has the potential to inspire three feelings: pain, pleasure, and neutral feelings. We think that feelings are being caused by the objects, but really they are based on our inner conditions, emotions, and karma.

As we all know, feeling is blind, and it is very fickle. That is why the Buddha chose the image of the arrow piercing the eye. This is related to the first noble truth of suffering.

Underlying even feelings of pleasure and happiness is defilement. These experiences are still rooted in desire and ignorance. For this reason, pleasure and happiness are the cause and condition of all our future pain and suffering. Even neutral feelings are the cause of our future pain. The image of the eye being pierced by the arrow refers to the nature of feeling. By nature, feeling is pain. Even our feelings of pleasure and happiness are caused and conditioned by the root destructive emotions.

This is why all feelings are called dukkha or suffering. The noble truth of suffering includes pleasure, happiness, and neutral feelings. They are all a form of suffering because they are caused by destructive emotions and negative karma.

## THE EIGHTH LINK: CRAVING

The eighth link is desire or craving. The more pleasure and happiness you feel, the more you crave. That is why the teachings warn that feelings of pleasure and happiness are like drinking salty water. The more you drink, the thirstier you become.

At this stage of craving, we are generally in our teen years. We have all these feelings, and we are old enough to engage in sexual activity. We have such strong emotions at this age. Teenagers are very sensitive and volatile. They are often rebellious, and they want to be independent. Most of the time they are rebelling simply because they want to have the freedom to pursue their own happiness. This stage of craving is marked by the ability to consume things repeatedly.

The more we consume, the more feelings we will have. In this way, consumption can become addictive. Drugs are such a clear example of this. Drugs generate pleasurable feelings, but the minute those feelings fade, the craving is intensified.

In the wheel of life, craving is represented by a person eating or drinking. The more you eat and drink the more you want. Our lives are filled with many addictions. Craving leads to the next stage, which is grasping.

## THE NINTH LINK: GRASPING

The ninth link is called *grasping*. Grasping is a result of our habitual patterns. Due to our habits, we form addictions, and we develop increasing desire for those objects.

This link is represented by the image of a person or a monkey reaching to get some fruit. It is reminiscent of Eve reaching for the apple in the Garden of Eden.

Due to our consumption, we develop an increased need to grasp the objects of our desire. This link is very apparent in drug addicts. Once an addict experiences that high, he wants to repeat the feeling. An addict keeps increasing the amount until soon he is very dependent on that substance.

## THE TENTH LINK: BEING

The tenth link is called *being*. Our grasping creates more karma. We have discussed how the word bhava from bhavachakra means "being" in the wheel of life. We often think of birth as the moment that we come into being. In reality, we already exist during those nine months of pregnancy. This is the reason why this link is illustrated by a pregnant woman in the wheel of life. In the wheel of life, being starts at the moment of conception.

The moment of death is also considered a state of bhava or being. This is due to the Buddhist belief that even death is not a cessation of our minds. The period from the moment of death until our next conception is considered another state of being.

There are four intermediate states: birth, life, bardo, and rebirth. We have these four intermediate states of being because of our contact, our feelings, our desires, and our grasping for objects. This has increased our karma and emotions. This is how we remain trapped, cycling through these four different states. Although the states change, the mind always continues. That continuation through the four states is really what is meant by the word bhava.

As I have mentioned, the twelve links become an interdependent cycle due to the three times. The first two links of ignorance and formation are due to our past destructive emotions and karma. The third through the tenth links—from consciousness to being—refer to our current experience of life.

Although we refer to the past, present, and future, our same five aggregates continue through all three times. The twelve ayatanas and eighteen dhatus are based on the stages of our evolution, but the five aggregates are always there. The Buddha said that even after death, when the mind is looking for an opportunity for conception, subtle aggregates are present.

# 23

# The Twelve Interdependent Links: 11–12

There is no ignorance, no elimination of ignorance; no death and decay, and no elimination of death and decay.

THESE LINES from the *Heart Sutra* only include the first and last links of the twelve interdependent links, or *nidanas* as they are often called.

Ignorance is the first nidana, and death and decay is the twelfth nidana. The wheel of life is an ongoing cycle. Ignorance appears first in the wheel, but this does not mean that ignorance is the creator of everything. Even ignorance must have causes and conditions.

Ignorance is still part of interdependency. This is true of the twelfth link of death and decay as well. The twelfth nidana of death and decay is also not the end of the cycle. We need to remember that the first link of ignorance has a cause, and the last link of death and decay still has a result.

These nidanas are like profound clues. Through studying these twelve links we can discover so much about the nature of our own lives.

We have been cycling from beginningless time. There is no first cause, and there is no last result. We can see this verified across the three times of past, present, and future.

This current life is just a moment. Long ago, people used to measure time with drops of water. There were also measurements based on the movement of the sun. These days we have the invention of the standardized clock. Even within a minute we can snap our fingers sixty times or many more times if we are fast enough. What is the shortest time we can measure?

We can reduce the timeline to the very shortest millisecond, and we can extend the timeline on either side. Since we cannot remember very far into the past, the past remains very mysterious to us. Of course, the future is yet to come, so it is also quite mysterious. Due to this mystery, we have difficulty believing in rebirth.

We believe that there was a yesterday because we can remember the recent past. We can believe in the period of time from our birth until the present because we have some evidence of it. Maybe we have photos of ourselves as infants or family to tell us stories.

The twelve links are based on the three times: past, present, and future. We can prove karma—we can prove cause and result—because of these three times. Each result is a cause for a future result.

This can provide us with evidence of our past and future lives. Without this, the future is just a reference. We may even think the future is a lie because no one can bring the future into the present moment.

Rebirth is based on time and karma. Many students have asked me, "How can we believe in rebirth if we cannot see it? If we cannot prove it?" I always ask them, "Do you believe in tomorrow?"

We are all going through our lives planning on the existence of tomorrow. Each day we schedule things based on our belief that tomorrow will happen. We believe in tomorrow because today exists and because we remember yesterday.

The twelve links may sound rather complex when they are taught in a philosophical way. When we simplify the nidanas, we can see that they are just based on the three times. They are based on cause and result, which is based on natural law—on karma.

It is just like the age-old question, "Which came first, the chicken or the egg?" Or, "Which came first, the mango seed or the mango fruit?" The fruit becomes the seed for the future mango. The same is true for us humans.

The Buddha taught that our karma has created our reality. The planet is like a big house created by our collective human karma. We have created the planet; the planet has not created us.

The Buddha said very clearly in the *Abhidharmakosha* that the universe is limitless. As we know, science is proving this to be true. Astrophysicists are now seeing, even within our galaxy, over eight billion planets that could support life. There are countless other galaxies and universes we cannot even detect yet. There are limitless sentient beings.

Someday humans may finally meet an alien from a distant planet who does not look anything like us. To that alien we will be aliens. We will look so strange to them!

There are infinite possibilities because there are limitless minds and limitless forms those minds can take. We create limitless karma, and as a result there are limitless beings and limitless planets.

If you visit the Natural History Museum in New York, you can learn about creatures living in the deepest oceans. There are other creatures who can survive even in molten lava. Beings that can live in a volcano! Other beings on our planet can survive in the frigid ice and the extremely cold temperatures at the poles.

In the Buddhist hell realm there are cold and hot hells. It may be hard to fathom the hell realm until we go to a place like the Natural History Museum and see evidence of this vast array of life forms. We can see proof of these beings that live in such extreme conditions.

We can divide all twelve links into four categories: the defilements, karma, mind, and the physical body. Each of the links can be placed in one of these categories.

Due to interdependency, karma and defilements have created our present mind and body. Our present human body is due to the karma that we have created; it is due to our past emotions. The karma and emotions of our present life will also determine what form we take in future lives.

All of the links can be included into those four categories. The first, eighth, and ninth links can be included in the first category of defilements. The second and tenth links can be included in the category of karma. The third through the seventh and the eleventh and twelfth links are the base, which is the mind and body. In this way we can divide all twelve nidanas into these groups.

## THE ELEVENTH LINK: BIRTH

The eleventh link is called *birth*. It refers to future rebirth. Birth here is defined as "conceiving to be reborn." The way we are conceived is dependent on our emotions and karma. These factors will determine whether we will be conceived in a womb and born as humans.

As we have discussed, there are four types of birth: womb, egg, moisture, and apparitional. In the case of apparitional birth, beings just reappear. These are the four different types of conception. This eleventh link of birth has to do with how we will be conceived for our future rebirth. This is totally dependent on our karma.

Higher beings, like those in the heavenly realms, can have apparitional births. They are not conceived like us and born with pain and suffering. Even the form realm beings are not conceived like we are.

Most humans are conceived in the womb. Sometimes, though, a human who has very pure karma may take an apparitional birth—they may just appear. It is said in the Buddhist teachings that in the Golden Time, when people have fewer defilements and less karma, and when people are naiver and more innocent, there will be more apparitional human births.

There are also humans who have been born from eggs. There are Buddhist stories about this. Then there are accounts of apparitional births like Padmasambhava, who just appeared miraculously on a lotus one day. There are also humans born as a result of heat and moisture. Humans can be born in any of these four ways. All beings are born in one of these four types of birth.

This eleventh nidana refers to future rebirth. Due to our present karma and defilements, we will be conceived in one of these four ways and reborn in one of the three realms. The three realms are the desire, form, and formless realms. In the desire realm, we may be reborn as any of the six classes of beings. These six classes are hell beings, hungry ghosts, animals, humans, demigods, and gods.

This eleventh link of birth does not refer to birth in this life. We have already been born. That is in the past. This link is all about future rebirth. If we are reborn as a human, then the twelfth link of death and decay will apply to us.

## THE TWELFTH LINK: DEATH AND DECAY

The twelfth link is called *death and decay*. Death and decay includes four links in the future. It includes the fourth link of name and form up to the seventh link of feeling in future lifetimes.

The stages of name and form all the way up to feeling reflect a process of decaying. You are getting older during this time. The Buddha specifically called this link death and decay because some beings, due to karma and defilements, will die without getting older. Some beings may die as fetuses. Some may die while they are still in the womb. Others may die at birth. Other beings will get old and die.

That is why the Buddha gave this link the two names of death and decay. Technically death and decay refer to future rebirth. They refer to the duration from the time that you are conceived through the development of your aggregates all the way up to your teens when you experience so many feelings.

Whether we will cycle repeatedly through rebirths or whether we will reverse that cycle and achieve nirvana depends on our feelings.

Why is feeling so important? If we live only to pursue pleasure and happiness, then we will be reborn again and again in an endless cycle.

This pursuit of happiness and pleasure is based on fulfilling our desires. We are pursuing sensual, desirable objects, which forces us to take rebirth.

If we can practice meditation, if we can receive the trainings of wisdom and discipline based on the Buddha's teachings, if we can realize that the nature of feeling is suffering, and if this suffering can produce renunciation, then for the first time we may begin to reverse the wheel of life.

The *Heart Sutra* says:

> So too there is no pain, no origin, no cessation, no path; no wisdom, no attainment, no nonattainment.

These lines are referring to the four noble truths. The five aggregates, twelve ayatanas, eighteen dhatus, and twelve interdependent links are the base; these are the foundation of our lives. The four noble truths are the path and result. If we practice the path, the result is ultimate wisdom. Ultimate wisdom is beyond all pain and suffering. The buddhas are free from pain, free from origination; they are even free from the path and from cessation.

Right now, here in the desire realm, we have so much pain. We have so much suffering. That is why the first noble truth is the truth of suffering. To understand the first noble truth of suffering, we have to study the nature of feelings. We are so attached to pleasure and happiness. The noble ones, the buddhas, saw the true nature of pleasure and happiness. They concluded that pleasure, happiness, and even neutral feelings are all a form of suffering. Enlightened beings can see that pleasure only leads to more pain. As a result, they have practiced renunciation.

The Buddha taught that there are three kinds of suffering: the suffering of suffering, the suffering of change, and the suffering of conditioning. The suffering of suffering includes our feelings of physical and mental pain. The suffering of suffering is based on anger.

The suffering of change is rooted in our desire and attachment. The suffering of change is based on those feelings of pleasure and happiness. Happiness is the cause of future unhappiness. Everything is always changing. Nothing can stay the same. We have so much suffering when the feelings of happiness and pleasure do not last.

The third kind of suffering is the suffering of conditioning. This is rooted in our neutral feelings and based on our ignorance. All things are impermanent. All things are subject to age and decay. Death is inevitable in our conditioned existence.

All five feelings of happiness, unhappiness, pain, pleasure, and neutral feelings are considered part of the three kinds of suffering. They are a form of suffering because their root causes and conditions are defilements. The roots of all these feelings are the three afflictive emotions of desire, anger, and ignorance. Once we have this realization that the nature of feelings is suffering, we can produce some commitment to renunciation. For the first time we can practice the renunciation of our destructive emotions.

When the sutra says "there is no pain," it refers to the noble truth of suffering. The first two links in the wheel of life—ignorance and formation—are based on emotions and karma. These first two links are therefore related to the second noble truth of the origin of suffering. Links three through ten are based on the mind and body, and they are related with the first noble truth of suffering.

The second noble truth of origination is a study of the causes and conditions that create our suffering. That is what the sutra is referring to when it says "no origin." It is saying that those destructive emotions no longer exist, nor does the karma related to those emotions.

The first two noble truths relate to how we are cycling in samsara through the twelve interdependent links. The third and fourth noble truths of cessation and the path show us how to reverse the wheel of life. The reversion starts from realizing the nature of feelings.

Once we understand that all feelings lead to dissatisfaction, we can begin the process of renunciation. Renunciation starts when we take refuge. Refuge involves training in renunciation. For the first time we conclude that the nature of our lives is pain and suffering. To go beyond suffering, we must commit to the practice of renunciation.

We renounce the causes and conditions of our pain and suffering. Based on that renunciation, our spiritual practice becomes more effective. We then engage in wisdom training in order to overcome our ignorance. We train in meditation to overcome anger. We train in discipline to overcome desire.

The Buddha's teachings are divided into these three trainings to free us from the three root destructive emotions. These three trainings are considered the path. They correspond with the fourth noble truth which is the noble eightfold path.

We emphasize wisdom training because it is the most important. Wisdom training overcomes ignorance. It overcomes that first link in the wheel of life. To uproot ignorance, we need to train in wisdom. Training in discipline and meditation is also important. Ignorance is the base of both desire and anger. Therefore, wisdom training is the most important of the three trainings because it can guide discipline and meditation.

Discipline and meditation without wisdom will not help us go beyond the wheel of life. That is why the *Heart Sutra* is so vital. The wisdom gone beyond allows our meditation and discipline to go beyond.

When the three trainings are successful, they create the cessation of suffering. Cessation is nirvana. It is freedom. It corresponds with the third noble truth of cessation. We become free from all destructive emotions. We become free from all karma and will never be reborn. We will never again be forced to be conceived by karma and defilements.

When we are forced to be reborn by karma and defilements, we do not have any free will. No one wants to get old. No one wants to get sick, but we all get sick and die. There are no exceptions in samsara. When birth and death are forced on us by our karma, we experience so much pain.

The four noble truths are the backbone of all Buddhist trainings. The path is shared by Theravada Buddhists as well as Mayahana and Vajrayana practitioners. The methods may differ, but the core teachings are the same. The teachings create a healing methodology for our lives.

Pain is a very powerful experience. When we have a headache, it is all we can think about. When our pain becomes acute, we go to the doctor. We look for a medical explanation for our suffering. Once the doctor has found the cause, we accept that as the origin of our suffering. The headache is the result of causes and conditions.

In a similar way, when we experience deep suffering, we may turn to spiritual practice. Through this we also learn to diagnose the underlying truth of suffering. We discover that the causes and conditions are the three destructive emotions and the karma they produce. Just like in the medical model, once the issue is correctly diagnosed, then different kinds of medicine and different options for treatment become available to us.

The treatment in Buddhism is the path. Medicine is also the path. Sometimes Buddhist practice is even called "medicine" in Buddhist traditions.

The three trainings of wisdom, discipline, and meditation are like three different kinds of medicine. When you have taken these medicines and fully recovered, then your suffering has ceased—you have achieved nirvana. The path is the cause, and nirvana is the result of training and practicing on that path.

The causes and results that are experienced in samsara are demonstrated by the twelve links in the wheel of life. The third and fourth noble truths regarding the path and cessation teach us how to reverse these twelve interdependent links through the three trainings. The three trainings teach us how we can achieve nirvana.

I have only given you a very simple explanation of the four noble truths. Each truth can be studied in much greater detail. There are four aspects corresponding to each noble truth. These sixteen aspects can give you a much deeper understanding of how to reverse the wheel of life.

## 24

# No Pain, No Origin

So too there is no pain, no origin, no cessation, no path; no wisdom, no attainment, no nonattainment.

D UE TO OUR MIND, body, karma, and destructive emotions, we cycle through the twelve interdependent links. We cycle through the three times. The present is dependent on the past. The present is the cause of the future. Our mind, body, karma, and destructive emotions are constantly interacting throughout the three times.

This is how we continue cycling through the wheel of life. If we look at images of the wheel of life, we can see all three realms: the desire, form, and formless realms.

In Buddhist cosmology, even the higher realms are still part of samsara. Formless beings have excellent experience in worldly meditation. They have especially strong absorption meditation due to their shamatha practice. But they have still not gone beyond.

These formless beings are often called *heavenly beings* because they are in a very peaceful state. But when their good karma is finally exhausted, they will fall back into the lower realms. That is why the Buddha said that human life presents the very best opportunity for achieving enlightenment.

All six classes of beings in all three realms are still not free from suffering. The suffering of change, impermanence, and death will affect even the gods.

In illustrations of the wheel of life, we can see the Lord of Death holding the entire wheel. This is to illustrate that whoever is born must die. Whatever is created must decay. Everyone is subject to impermanence and death.

Impermanence and death are our greatest fears here in samsara. This is because we are so attached to ourselves and to our lives. No one wants to die. We are forced by our karma to die, and as a result it is often painful. There is so much suffering because it is happening against our will. Some people cannot let go at the time of death. They have very strong grasping and attachment, and this makes it extremely painful to die.

Chaplains have seen so many people through the dying process, and they can attest to how challenging it is for some people to let go. It is especially hard for people who have created heavier karma. People who led destructive lives, people who were violent and committed crimes, have an especially hard time with death. Hospice workers have said that they repeatedly see this struggle occur for dying people who have had more troubled lives and who have more unresolved issues.

Death is one of the greatest forms of pain and suffering in samsara, and we all have to go through it. We try so hard to distract ourselves from the truth of impermanence by constantly pursuing pleasure and happiness.

Whether we will keep on cycling endlessly or begin to reverse the wheel depends on how well we understand the nature of our feelings. If we have strong attachment to pleasure and happiness, we will not commit to the kind of renunciation that is needed to reverse the wheel of life. If we continue with our attachments and clinging, we will be reborn again and again.

In images of the wheel of life, we can also see a buddha on top of the wheel. Buddhas have achieved the wisdom gone beyond and have gone beyond birth and death. They are beyond pain and suffering.

As I have mentioned, when a buddha takes rebirth, it is through free will. Buddhas and bodhisattvas take rebirth to benefit other beings. As a result of this freedom their births are not forced and are not painful. They take rebirth out of compassion based on the bodhisattva vow. They have vowed to work for the benefit of all sentient beings, and for this reason they reincarnate. Their rebirth is not based on destructive emotions. They do not need to practice. They have already achieved enlightenment. With limitless compassion arising from wisdom, they return to help others.

The first noble truth of suffering can give us a complete understanding of how feelings have the nature of suffering. None of us want to suffer. Until we thoroughly understand the truth of suffering, we will keep thinking that we can avoid suffering through chasing after happiness and pleasure.

The problem is that the more we pursue pleasure and happiness, the more dissatisfied we become. Our desires increase. When we cannot consume the things we desire, we feel more restless and uncomfortable. When the sutra says "no pain," it means freedom from suffering—even the suffering that is connected with happiness and pleasure.

The word dukkha is translated as "dissatisfaction" or "suffering." No matter how much we count on an object, there is no permanent satisfaction. As I mentioned before, the Buddha taught that pursuing pleasure and happiness is like drinking salty water. The more we drink, the thirstier we become.

Of the three kinds of suffering—the suffering of suffering, the suffering of change, and the suffering of conditioned existence—we have the most difficulty understanding the suffering of change. This is because it is closely related to our feelings of pleasure and happiness, which we assume to be positive. We do not see these good experiences as another form of suffering. This is why we are always pursuing pleasure and happiness. We are blind to the ways in which this pursuit makes us more dissatisfied.

We are also ignorant about the suffering of conditioning. The suffering of conditioning means that even birth itself is the beginning of death. Every moment we are rushing toward death. Everything that is born must die. Even while we are sleeping, and even while we are having a wonderful experience, we are still moving closer to death. We are aging, and we are dying. This produces underlying suffering in our lives.

When we finally recognize these three kinds of suffering, we can come to the realization that the nature of all feelings is pain. All feelings will eventually bring dissatisfaction. All feelings are based on the three root destructive emotions of desire, anger, and ignorance.

"No origin" refers to the absence of the three destructive emotions. If we can purify the emotions of ignorance, desire, and anger, then we can go beyond all three kinds of suffering and the origins of that suffering: We can go beyond ignorance, which is related to the suffering of conditioned existence. We can go beyond desire, which is related to the suffering of change. We can also go beyond anger, which is related to the suffering of suffering.

When the sutra says "no cessation, no path," it is referring to the third and fourth noble truths. Since there are three kinds of suffering and three origins or causes of that suffering, the path offers us three trainings to overcome those origins. The path offers us the training of discipline, the training of meditation, and the training of wisdom. These three trainings can overcome the three sufferings as well as the three root destructive emotions that cause that suffering.

Wisdom training can overcome ignorance and the suffering of conditioned existence. Training in discipline can allow us to overcome our desires and the suffering of change. Training in meditation can allow us to overcome anger and the suffering of suffering.

The fourth noble truth is called the noble eightfold path. This path includes eight aspects: right view, right intention, right conduct, right speech, right livelihood, right effort, right mindfulness, and right concentration. Each of these eight branches of the path correspond to wisdom, discipline, or meditation.

Desire is the strongest emotion in our lives as human beings. All food that we eat is based on desire. Everything we want to look at or listen to, everything that we want to touch or consume in any way, is based on our craving and attachment.

In the Abhidharma it is said that since our desire is so strong, and since our attachment to sensual objects is so intense, meditation can be very difficult at first. We can all observe this if we try to go on retreat. When we leave all the physical comforts of our homes, it can be quite challenging. Just being with ourselves without any of the objects we are attached to can be quite frightening at first.

All we bring on retreat are our bodies and our minds. We begin to see how dependent our lives are on other objects. We miss our friends. We may miss our television programs. We miss our favorite music. We crave our favorite foods. For the first time we become aware of how dependent we are on all these outer objects.

The more dependent we become, the weaker we grow. Whenever one of those dependencies is taken away, we feel so restless. That is why the Buddha taught discipline.

Discipline allows us to follow the natural laws of karma. We refrain from killing. We refrain from stealing. We change our behavior and habitual patterns and find much greater peace in our lives. When we experience the peace of living according to natural laws, then so many positive qualities begin to grow inside us.

If we ignore the natural laws of karma, our suffering will increase. If we kill other living beings, our karma will become very heavy. We will have more enemies. We can see this vicious cycle illustrated by stories about the Mafia. The bloodshed and the family feuds get passed down from generation to generation. Violence begets more violence. People keep on killing each other in order to get revenge. There is no end to this cycle. When you have that heavy karma, you live in total insecurity. You are always scared for your life. You are always expecting to be attacked.

Here in the desire realm, in order to free ourselves from desirable objects, we have to undertake training in discipline. When we have more discipline, then our meditation practice will become stronger.

Without discipline, meditation will be very difficult. Our minds will always be busy. Even if we sit in a meditative posture, our monkey mind will still rebel. Our thoughts will race after desirable objects or fixate on destructive emotional states. Our thoughts become filled with inner chatter, or our minds get very sleepy and spaced out.

The more discipline we have, the more meditation we have. The more meditation we have, the more wisdom we cultivate. These three trainings are interdependent in this way.

Our lives have started with ignorance. For this reason, wisdom training is needed as an antidote. We have lived countless lifetimes cultivating patterns of addiction and attachment to objects. We need the training of discipline as an antidote to desire.

In the graduated path, the first step is the discipline required to overcome desire. The next step is the meditation required to overcome anger. Only after those two trainings can we begin to realize wisdom.

The methods of training may be different between Theravada, Mahayana, and Vajrayana Buddhist practitioners, but the basic practice is always divided into three trainings. This is because the same three destructive emotions operate in all practitioner's lives.

Once we accomplish all three trainings and come to the highest level of realization, then we realize cessation, which is nirvana. We must remember that this is not really an achievement. Enlightenment is not an outer achievement based on accumulated trainings.

Enlightenment is much more like cleaning a dirty cloth. We may work very hard to get the dirt out of the cloth. We may think that the newly cleaned cloth is wisdom we have gained. In actuality we have merely uncovered the wisdom that was already there. That wisdom is our true nature that was always pure and always there beneath the dirt. We have not achieved anything new. We have merely washed away all the obscurations and defilements that we have accumulated throughout countless lifetimes, and we have finally seen our true state.

This innate purity is just like the purity of outer space. The sky is there all the time. The clouds come and go, obscuring that sky temporarily. When the clouds dissolve, is the clear sky something new? The sky has been there from beginningless time! Only the clouds have changed.

Enlightenment is not something we create. That state has always been there infinitely inside us. Through the three trainings we purify our karma and destructive emotions so that we can see our true nature again.

This is what is meant when the sutra says "no wisdom, no attainment, no nonattainment." These lines refer to the wisdom that has been there all along. There was nothing to attain. That is the wisdom gone beyond, in which we cannot say whether we have achieved anything.

Up to this point in the *Heart Sutra*, we have learned about our lives as the *base* or the *ground* to be purified. We have seen how ignorance is forcing us to cycle repeatedly through samsara. We have studied how the integration of the four noble truths can begin to reverse the wheel of life so that we can achieve freedom.

The path is the method of reversion. To begin to reverse the wheel we have to recognize that the nature of all feelings is suffering. Only when we have that realization will we begin to let go. This recognition of suffering produces some renunciation. We stop feeling so attached to outer objects. We become a little bit more easy going. For the first time, we will begin to see some inner transformation.

Through the practice of the three trainings, the wheel of life can be reversed. The four noble truths are the antidote to the wheel of life. The four noble truths help us to free our minds from karma and from emotions. The path shows us a way to achieve freedom.

> Shariputra, because nothing is really obtained, all bodhi-
> sattvas who have no fear rely on and dwell in Prajnaparamita,
> for they have no mental obscurations.

Once you have achieved that freedom, you remain in that fearless wisdom. Fear is everywhere in our current lives. Every moment we have fear because we still have our egos. Due to the ego we have attachments. Our sense of "I" is so important. It creates our sense of possessiveness too. Since we are attached to the ego, it creates many other attachments to outer objects.

The more objects we have, the nicer the house, the fancier the car, the more afraid of loss we become. The more we have, the more insecure we feel. Capitalism breeds so much greed and so much fear of loss.

The stock market is a prime example of this high-stakes game of fear and greed. Every moment things are changing. When the market goes up, everyone starts buying, and the greed increases. When the market goes down, everyone starts panicking and selling. It can all change so quickly. This creates a frenzy of emotions and high blood pressure. Time is ticking away, just like your heart. You can feel the impact of all this fear and impermanence on your own heartbeat.

After the markets close, these traders may need to go drink beer, eat, and play loud music! Anything to unwind from the stress. The very next morning it all begins again. There is no relief in that cycle.

The more attachment we have, the more we fear loss. We are all attached to this life. Whatever threatens our safety is the scariest thing to us. We spend our whole life trying to avoid injury, illness, and death, and yet we are all going to die anyway! Our greatest fear is going to happen regardless of what we do.

If we have a lot of anger, we may become very aggressive. The more aggression we have, the more enemies we make. We can see this so clearly among politicians and corporate leaders. They are always struggling for power. The more they fight, the more insecure they become. Their power and aggression are based on their fear. This is not the strength of fearlessness.

When we have a lot of ignorance, we will have so much confusion. We will never know quite what to do, and that will create so much fear. We may feel like travelers in a place we have never been. We may often feel lost and disoriented.

We can see how all three root destructive emotions can bring fear. These three emotions are there because of our self-clinging. When we achieve complete freedom, we are egoless. We no longer have destructive emotions. We are free from fear.

Only those beings who are enlightened, who rest in the wisdom gone beyond, are free from fear. They are free from fear because they have achieved freedom from anger, freedom from desire, and freedom from ignorance. They have no mental obscurations.

There are two kinds of mental obscuration. Obscuration of the defilements refers to anger and attachment. Obscuration of knowledge refers to ignorance.

They are perfectly liberated and have gone completely beyond deception.

When one has achieved the wisdom gone beyond, one experiences perfect freedom. One is also free from all deceptions, ignorance, and negative karma. The word "deception" here in the sutra refers to the relativity of samsara.

Relying on the Prajnaparamita, all the buddhas of the three times are completely enlightened to that unsurpassable, noble, and perfect enlightenment.

Through training in wisdom, the buddhas of the three times—those who were enlightened in the past, those enlightened now, and those who will be enlightened in the future—attain enlightenment based on the Prajnaparamita

The Prajnaparamita, the wisdom gone beyond, is unsurpassable. It is the highest and the most noble and perfect enlightenment. It is perfect because it has gone beyond samsara and nirvana. It is free from the three circles, the self, samsara, and nirvana. It is noble because it has gone beyond all that is ignoble.

25

# Completely Beyond
# Deception

UNTIL WE CAN ACHIEVE the Prajnaparamita, the wisdom gone
beyond, we will be living in deception. Deception starts with the
ignorance in our lives. From the moment we are conceived, that deception starts. Ignorance obscures everything. Ignorance is what prevents
us from discovering our true nature.

We do not know who we really are. Since we do not see our own true
nature, we also cannot see the true nature of others. We may think we
know ourselves based on what society projects on us. We may think we
know ourselves based on our accomplishments and our personalities.
In reality, we are still completely blind to ourselves. As long as we have
that basic ignorance, we will also have desire. We will remain attached
to everything in our lives because we cannot see our empty nature.

This is most evident in our relationships. We can project so many
romantic feelings onto someone because we do not know who they
really are. These projections fade as we begin to see more clearly.

All desire is a form of deception. Desire gives us feelings of pleasure
that lead to more pain. Desire forces us to pursue objects of pleasure

and happiness. Meanwhile this pursuit only brings more restlessness and discomfort.

When our desire is not fulfilled, then we grow frustrated, and we feel pain. As a result of that suffering, anger arises. We feel anger toward other people, and we even feel anger toward inanimate objects! If our car will not start, we may feel anger at the car. If the weather is bad and ruins our plans for a nice day at the beach, we may feel anger at the weather.

We live in a time in which we have come to expect instant gratification. We become so impatient these days if things are not going according to our plans. We get so angry if our computers break or our phones die.

We may yell and throw things and take this anger out on objects. Really the anger is harming us. It is deceiving us. We blame outer objects for this anger, but really it is coming from inside us.

There are so many ways our emotions can harm us. If we have a lot of pride, we may stop learning. Our own arrogance can completely obscure wisdom. Pride can deceive us into thinking we know everything. This arrogance then prevents us from learning more. Our pride in our own intelligence often makes us more ignorant!

History shows us the destruction that egomaniacs create around them. The more powerful they become as rulers, politicians, or CEOs, the more blinded they are by their power. This hunger for power grows until they make so many poor decisions that they create their own downfall. Whole empires come and go based on this pattern.

Doubt can also deceive us. If we have too much doubt and skepticism, we may become very paranoid in our thinking. Doubt may lead to many intellectual debates, but it cannot lead to certainty. Without certainty our faith is compromised, and our practice is weak. If there is doubt, we become paralyzed and unable to make good decisions or commit to anything.

Wrong views are the greatest deceivers of all. This is especially true for people who are very well educated. When we have too much information and too much intellectual knowledge, we form so many opinions. We develop so many fixed views.

We need to see whether these views and opinions are correct. Our education is primarily based on material education. It reinforces our identity within a nation and establishes our sense of place in the physical world.

Our education often has nothing to do with natural laws. Most education involves no belief in karma. There is often some basic morality imprinted into us but rarely any real instruction on cause and result. Without this understanding of the natural laws of cause and effect, we may not gain much wisdom in our education.

Many spiritual traditions now say that although we think we have become more civilized, we are losing something integral. We are making huge progress in science and technology, but we are losing our wisdom and values. We are entering a dark age. We are losing something vitally important to humanity.

Hindu and Buddhist traditions refer to this dark age as the Kali Yuga. Externally our lives are getting brighter and brighter. The whole planet is now flooded with electrical light, but we seem to be losing touch with that inner light that is born through spiritual practice.

As a civilization we are becoming more gloomy, more depressed, more emotionally disturbed. If society is truly progressing, we should be seeing more transformation. We should see an increase in mental and physical health and positivity. That is not the case.

Developed countries show an even higher rate of anxiety and depression. We may think we have come so far in advancing our society, but modern people seem to have more mental illness.

If we are so civilized and our healthcare is so good, why are we becoming more ill? Why do we see this increase in psychiatric illness? Why is twenty percent of the American population on some type of psychotropic drug?

We have achieved a highly developed civilization, but something vital is missing. We are living in disharmony with the natural laws of karma. We want instant gratification, and we are willing to do anything to distract ourselves from our karmic pain. We cannot repress and ignore the roots of this suffering forever. The pain will be present in our lives, just beneath the surface. If we are not treating that pain on a deeper level, we will experience feelings of restlessness and anxiety.

Many people choose to ignore the natural law of cause and result because they do not believe in karma. There are even modern Buddhists who do not believe in karma. There are modern Buddhists who do not even believe in rebirth. If you do not believe in karma, then even if you are studying Buddhism and doing some meditation practice, you will be practicing to increase your relaxation and comfort in this life. There will be no deeper transformation.

That is why the Buddha discussed the wheel of life. It becomes so clear that if we do not believe in karma, we cannot begin to change. Our practice cannot be successful without some belief in karma based on the three times of past, present, and future.

If we understand that karma is created by the mind, and that the mind is a continuum, then we come to believe that there was a past life and there will be a future life.

If we do not believe in karma, then we cannot believe in rebirth. Without a belief in rebirth, it does not make much sense to practice patience and develop other positive qualities that do not immediately benefit us. If we cannot see the results right away, and if we have no belief in rebirth, then we become very lazy. We may think we are wasting our time if our efforts do not produce an immediate result.

Belief in the ego, which is based on the five aggregates, is also a great deceiver. We have developed a strong sense of self-clinging through countless lifetimes of identification with the five aggregates. We have such strong attachment to our body, feelings, thoughts, and mind.

The five aggregates are the basis of our self-clinging. When our wisdom training grows deeper, we realize that we cannot find independent existence in any of those five aggregates. We cannot find any independent existence in outer objects.

Right now, we have so much attachment to ourselves and to our lives. None of us wants to die. We want to make ourselves eternal, and we want to believe that the objects of our attachment will last forever.

This belief in a permanent self is a great deceiver. We project permanence on all the objects around us. This attachment is blinding. This attachment goes against nature. It is a state of denial.

We all know that whatever is born must die. Whether we like it or not, one day we will be forced to suffer. We will be forced to die. One day all the objects we are attached to will decay. We deceive ourselves constantly into thinking that all these things inherently exist.

Even becoming attached to the spiritual path can be a deception. Once there was a Buddhist nun. She was very attached to her shrine. She had a beautiful buddha statue. Whenever some other devotees came to the shrine with incense, she would scold them if smoke dirtied the statue. She would become angry!

As a practitioner I have seen this attachment to the spiritual path. There can be so much emphasis on ritual and so much attachment to the temple. There can be too much focus on how you look or the value of your offerings.

In beautiful temples you can become attached to the valuable brocades and colors and forms. You can also become attached to the rules. Many monastics have to observe the rule of eating their last meal before noon. If something happens to delay this meal, they may get so frustrated.

If you get too attached to discipline, it can become an obstacle. If you cling to the precepts, you are also obscuring the path. You may come to think that the precepts are the only training, and you may ignore training in wisdom and meditation.

On the other hand, if you only pursue scholarship and ignore the precepts, you will be missing something important. If there is no meditation or discipline, you will never gain real wisdom.

One of the great masters said, "If you want to climb a mountain, first you need to know all the skills." Without understanding the proper methods, you will be in danger. This is a warning to learn the methods of meditation thoroughly. If you go on retreat with no meditation training, you will make very little progress.

One can become an extremist in any of the three trainings. One must combine all three and train in them in order to go beyond. If you become too attached to any of the trainings, they will cease to be a method for attaining enlightenment.

Even within Buddhist philosophy, we have four different conclusions. Each school of Buddhist philosophy thinks that their conclusions are the best, and this can prevent them from going beyond. In the highest Buddhist school of philosophy, the Madhyamaka school, there are multiple conclusions. Some proponents of this school argue for self-emptiness. Some argue for other-emptiness. And some argue for a freedom from extremes.

If we use these conclusions to practice meditation, then there is a chance that we will find the wisdom required to go beyond. If we never practice meditation and simply become attached to our own views, then we become extremists and there is very little transformation.

If your philosophical conclusion is self-emptiness but you become attached to this conclusion, your ego is still involved. This view may be higher, but your ego defeats your view. Instead of liberating you, these views can keep you trapped in samsara.

As we have discussed, there are six realms in which we can be reborn. The causes of these six realms are the corresponding six destructive emotions: anger, greed and stinginess, ignorance, desire, jealousy, and pride. These are the six root causes of rebirth in samsara. If we die with great anger, that emotion may lead our consciousness to be reborn in an angry place. If we die with great ignorance, we may be reborn in the animal realm. If we die with stinginess and greed, we may be reborn as hungry ghosts. If we die with jealousy, we may be reborn as demigods who are constantly fighting.

Those who train in the Prajnaparamita, the wisdom gone beyond, have seen the nature of their mind. They have gone beyond all six destructive emotions. As a result, they are not forced by destructive emotions and karma to be reborn. Buddhas always remain and dwell in the Prajnaparamita.

We are still living with these destructive emotions. As a result, our lives may seem very exciting. Maybe for us the Buddha's life seems boring, since his life seems very peaceful.

We are not at peace. The more emotions we have, the more feelings we generate. We think these strong feelings give us a sense of being alive! If the Buddha were among us, we may find him to be boring. He would never go out to a bar. He would never care about sports, food, or entertainment of any kind.

I have tested this with some of my students. I have given them two contemporary biographies of two great masters. One biography is very exciting. It resembles our worldly life. The other biography is a more typical Buddhist biography. I asked my students to read both books and then report back to me. When they read the exciting biography, they said, "Oh, I finished the whole book." When they read the standard biography, the students said they lost interest. One student even said she had fallen asleep!

The original Tibetan word for deception is *chinchilok*. Some scholars translate this word as "false views." We have to go beyond such false appearances. We have to go beyond the six destructive emotions of the six realms.

The six root destructive emotions can be misleading. We can see that illustrated so clearly when we examine our relationship to objects of attachment. The saying, "Beauty lies in the eye of the beholder" is so apparent when we examine our close relationships.

When we have more passion and desire, we may find someone we are attracted to to be very handsome or beautiful. When we become angry, we may find that same person to be disagreeable and ugly! Or we may begin to have neutral feelings over time and find that person boring.

The person is the same. Our inner conditions determine how we view him or her. Have we not all experienced these three emotions of desire, anger, and ignorance or boredom?

Look how radically your feelings for someone change if you begin to have doubt. If you discover someone is unfaithful in a romantic relationship, your projections onto that person change instantly. We can project so many things onto the same object.

These six emotions of anger, greed, ignorance, desire, jealousy, and pride are always changing in relation to objects. These emotions deceive us into having such different experiences of these objects. But this is not our true nature. Our true nature is wisdom. In that true nature there is no ignorance, desire, or anger. There is no greed, jealousy, or pride.

When you see an object with wisdom, your experience will be completely changed. For the first time you will see that for years you have been delusional! When you are at the mercy of conflicting emotions, you assume that is the nature of life. You do not ever think outside that paradigm.

We need to understand that regardless of what we are experiencing in our lives, all our emotions are merely circumstantial. They are not permanent. They come and go like clouds in the sky. Our true nature is the space beyond the clouds, where it is always clear. That space is pure. That space is like the wisdom gone beyond. It has gone beyond all clouds, misconceptions, and delusions.

Buddhas always live in the wisdom beyond deception. We are not at that level of realization, and we still believe in false perceptions. These false perceptions are circumstantial and temporary. In order to go beyond them we have to practice.

In the *Heart Sutra*, Avalokiteshvara is sharing wisdom teachings in accordance with the Buddha's blessings. He is training us explicitly in the right view of wisdom. He is also training us implicitly in the practice of meditation and discipline.

## 26

# Gone Beyond

Buddhas are completely enlightened. They have gone beyond all five aggregates, twelve ayatanas, eighteen dhatus, and even beyond the wheel of life. These aspects are the base of our identity in samsara. Buddhas have also gone beyond the four noble truths, which are the path. When the *Heart Sutra* says, "no wisdom, no attainment," it is referring to the result. Buddhas have even gone beyond the result.

We may be confused by the double negatives in the statement "no nonattainment." In the relative world, all sentient beings are cycling endlessly through the wheel of life with the five aggregates, twelve ayatanas, and eighteen dhatus. If we have cultivated some spirituality and have an understanding of the four noble truths, then we are on the path. Through our practice, we can also achieve the result, buddhahood, which is the attainment. The words "no nonattainment" refer to that wisdom gone beyond, which has gone beyond the base, the path, and even the result.

Shariputra, because nothing is really obtained, all bodhisattvas who have no fear rely on and dwell in the Prajnaparamita, for they have no mental obscurations. They are perfectly liberated and have gone completely beyond deception.

These lines refer to the benefits of the results. Those who have gone completely beyond the base, path, and result, have achieved the Prajnaparamita. They have no fear or obscurations. They have gone beyond all deceptions.

> Relying on the Prajnaparamita, all the buddhas of the three times are completely enlightened to that unsurpassable, noble, and perfect enlightenment.

Buddhas are limitless just as sentient beings are. We cannot measure the number of sentient beings in the universe. Imagine how many beings there are even just in the ocean. And this is not to mention all the formless beings as well. Sentient beings are numberless. Buddhas are also numberless.

The buddhas of the three times include buddhas who have become enlightened in the past, buddhas who are becoming enlightened in the present, and buddhas who will be enlightened in the future.

The Buddha Shakyamuni appeared in a particular eon in which one thousand buddhas are to appear. When we consider the three times, however, buddhas are limitless.

Past, present, and future are so related to mind, karma, and concepts. But the wisdom gone beyond is timeless! When you have seen the wisdom gone beyond, such wisdom has gone beyond all three times. This implies that those buddhas who have been enlightened in the past, present, and future will have the same unsurpassable enlightenment. There is nothing greater than the wisdom gone beyond. It is noble because it has gone beyond all ignoble things to realize perfect enlightenment. All these qualities of enlightenment are achieved through the training of the Prajnaparamita or the wisdom gone beyond.

This is the highest training there is for buddhas. Many questions arise around this sutra related to the different schools of Buddhism.

The *Heart Sutra* is from the Mahayana tradition. The Theravada tradition does not accept this as their sutra. Mahayana Buddhists affirm that this is the only training in which all the buddhas of the three times are enlightened. This is the training in unsurpassable enlightenment. What about the tantric practice of the Vajrayana Buddhists? Usually the Vajrayana understand tantra as the highest unsurpassable training. Tantra is known as the quickest path to enlightenment.

In Vajrayana practice, tantra, mantra, and yantra go together because tantra is the natural continuum of the mind, mantra is the nature of speech, and yantra is all the essential physical practices.

Because we have body, speech, and mind, we need all three forms of practice. Mantra is generally practiced in the Vajrayana and is related with channels and chakras, but in the *Heart Sutra,* mantra is implicitly referring to practice and emphasizes the five graduated paths. In the *Heart Sutra* one can get the same mantra benefits of the Vajrayana.

You may be wondering, what is mantra? What is tantra? Tantra is also the wisdom gone beyond. Mantra is also the wisdom gone beyond. Although the word mantra is exclusive to tantric Vajrayana practice, the same realization and meaning is also incorporated into the *Heart Sutra.*

> Therefore, the mantra of the Prajnaparamita, the mantra of great wisdom, the unsurpassable mantra, the mantra equal to the unequalled.

The syllable *man* in mantra refers to the mind. The syllable *tra* refers to protection. Combined, these two words refer to a nonconceptual wisdom. The mantra of Prajnaparamita has gone beyond all ideations and concepts. Whether you call it tantra or not, the realization is the same.

We may be wondering why this is a Mahayana sutra that contains a mantra. The mantra has more to do with realization and the meaning of the sutra than it does with the tantric practice of mantra recitation. The *Heart Sutra* is explicitly a Mahayana sutra for which you do not need to receive empowerment. In order to practice the tantric Prajnaparamita, however, you do need to receive empowerment.

The Prajnaparamita is a mantra of nonconceptual wisdom. It is "the mantra of great wisdom." It has gone beyond ignorance. It has gone beyond the wheel of life. It is the "unsurpassable mantra" because there is no higher realization.

When the sutra says "the mantra equal to the unequalled," it is referring to buddhahood. Buddhas are unequalled, and this mantra is equal to buddhahood.

> The mantra that fully allays all pains, because it is not false, should be known as truth.

The wisdom gone beyond has transcended all pain and suffering. If we rely on something that is not true, then we will never achieve the result we are seeking. This Prajnaparamita as a practice is based on ultimate truth. When you practice it, you know that you will achieve buddhahood. When we rely on truth, we can reach our destination. If we are traveling a well-marked path, we will not get lost. But if we are traveling based on a misleading path, then we will never reach our destination.

> The mantra of Prajnaparamita is spoken thus:
> *Tadyatha om gate gate paragate parasamgate bodhi svaha!*

*Tadyatha* has a meaning of "thus," which also means the wisdom gone beyond. *Om* has a meaning of "auspicious," which represents the interdependency between right cause and right result. *Gate gate* means "gone, gone." This refers to going beyond samsara. *Paragate* means "gone beyond," which means going beyond nirvana.

What practices do we need to do in order to go beyond samsara and nirvana? As far as Prajnaparamita practice is concerned, the main practices are the six perfections after generating bodhichitta. Perfection has a meaning of going beyond, so *gate gate paragate* means we have gone beyond samsara and nirvana to achieve complete enlightenment.

In the beginning of ngöndro practice, we talk about the accumulation of merit and the accumulation of wisdom. Until these two become one, our accumulation of merit will not become perfect.

When we incorporate the first five paramitas or perfections into our practice, we are accumulating merit. We are overcoming negative karma. We are accumulating more good karma.

The first *gate*, "gone," also refers to the path of accumulation. The path of accumulation includes our practice of the first five paramitas: the perfections of giving, conduct, patience, diligence, and concentration. The more we practice these first five perfections, the more we decrease the destructive emotions and the negative karma they produce.

We practice giving to overcome our stinginess, greed, and desire. The perfection of giving should not be measured by the value of what we give. Giving always has three circles: the giver, the receiver, and the gift.

We are practicing the perfection of giving to transform something inside us. The receiver and the gift are secondary. The motivation of the giver is most important. Our lives are filled with constant give and take, constant exchange. We give our compassion to those in need. We give our love to our friends and families. We make offerings out of faith and devotion. Among all these motivations, what is the most transformative? In a similar way, each paramita can be studied in detail to deepen our practice.

The accumulation of merit that Vajrayana practitioners produce through their ngöndro practices are equivalent to the accumulation of merit that Mayahana practitioners produce through practicing the first five paramitas. The first five paramitas decrease our negative karma and destructive emotions and increase our positive emotions and good karma. When they are combined with the sixth paramita of wisdom, they have the potential to become perfections.

The first *gate* refers to overcoming our negative karma and accumulating merit. The second *gate* refers to the path of application. Application is how we apply the merit we have accumulated. It is as if we have accumulated enough wealth in our accounts; we have some equity, and now we can apply it. Without that capital, we have nothing to apply.

The accumulation of merit gives you some power and strength. We are generally so conflicted. We have love and hate. We have passion and compassion. We have ignorance and wisdom. For us right now, every positive emotion has a corresponding destructive emotion. These feelings are always in conflict inside us.

After the path of accumulation, our positive emotions have been strengthened. This merit gives us some amount of free will. We can apply those positive qualities where they are needed.

Before the accumulation of merit, even though we wanted to do good things, our negative emotions and karma were still ruling us. These conflicting emotions were still dragging us down. They were making us less effective.

The second *gate* refers to the point at which we have accumulated enough good karma and positive emotions and are ready to apply them. Application can completely overcome negative karma and destructive emotions.

*Paragate* means "gone beyond." We have overcome negative karma and active destructive emotions, and we are ready to go beyond. The simple translation of *gate gate paragate* is "gone, gone, gone beyond." We have gone beyond samsara and nirvana by achieving the path of accumulation, the path of application, and the path of seeing.

The path of seeing refers to the realization of your true nature. For the first time you have glimpsed the buddha inside you. You have also glimpsed the buddha inside other beings. *Paragate* refers to the path of seeing.

Right now, we do not see the buddha inside us, and we do not see the buddha inside others. Even though we may do many Vajrayana practices, and we may receive many empowerments, our karma and habitual patterns remain strong. As a result, we cannot see this purity in ourselves or in others.

The third path of seeing allows us to see the purity and emptiness in all beings and objects. We have come to see both the object and the empty nature of the object simultaneously. Emptiness has become our personal realization. It is no longer a philosophical or intellectual understanding. It has become a personal realization, which makes it very powerful.

At the level of the path of seeing, those first five paramitas are now integrated with the sixth paramita of wisdom. At this level, the first five paramitas become perfections. They are perfections once they join with the wisdom.

The perfection of giving is achieved when you realize that there is no giver, no receiver, and no gift. This means that you have seen the empty nature of all things. When you see the true nature of things, then there is no giver, no gift, and no receiver. This is true for conduct, effort, patience, and meditation. All of these become perfections when we see the true nature of things.

They become perfections when we see the true nature of things related with these three circles. This allows us to *go beyond*. When giving becomes a perfection, we no longer have any emotional involvement with ourselves, with the gift, or with the receiver.

Buddhas give us teachings that arise out of their limitless compassion. These teachings are the greatest gifts of all. When our gifts are rooted in wisdom, they have the power to "go beyond' and to free us.

If our giving is rooted in the ego, and in our desire and attachment, we will never be free. Even if we give something, we will always be expecting something in return. Even giving some spiritual teachings will not be a perfection if they are rooted in our emotions. We may not be demanding anything obvious, but deep down we may be expecting some attention, recognition, love, or devotion. To have *gone beyond* entails that all five perfections are integrated with the perfection of wisdom. That is only possible when we have a glimpse of the empty nature of ourselves, the receiver, and the gift.

Gaining this glimpse of the empty nature of things still requires more practice, however. The word *parasamgate* literally means "well gone beyond." We have to cultivate that path of seeing repeatedly through the path of meditation. By seeing the true nature of things again and again, our minds become one with this nature. Then we achieve *bodhi*, the awakened state. Through cultivating that realization repeatedly, we become awakened. At that point we are completely awakened from the ignorance of destructive emotions and karma. We are fully enlightened.

Our practice can be based on the six perfections of Mahayana Buddhism after taking the bodhisattva vow. Our practice can also be based on the tantric sadhana practices. Much of the sadhana practice is based on the six perfections. In some tantric instructions it says that when you are in the form of the deity, and you are also making offerings to the deity, that is one of the best ways to practice the perfection of giving.

As that deity, you have gone beyond yourself. Then, when you are making offerings with mantras and mudras, you are generating gifts from that realization of emptiness. You are visualizing the offering goddesses. These goddesses are making offerings to the buddhas and the deity who is visualized in front of you. These buddhas and the deity are also enlightened. So the methods of practice may differ, but the meaning is the same.

Vajrayana Buddhism is said to have more skillful means. Tantra is based on taking the result into the path. You visualize that you are already a buddha. As a buddha you then make offerings and perform many practices. The only difference is that in Mahayana, you are still an ordinary person who is trying to become enlightened.

Mahayana Buddhism has a more graduated path. There are five levels of realization that we can use to measure our experience. If our practice is going in the right direction, then we can use the path of accumulation to gather merit. When we apply this merit properly on the path of application, then we see the ultimate truth of emptiness and enter the path of seeing. When that emptiness becomes the nature of our mind through the path of meditation, we awaken to the path of wisdom. We see the clarity of the mind and its empty nature. That is *bodhi*.

*Svaha* means letting whatever awakening you have achieved become well established in you. The recitation of this mantra in the *Heart Sutra* helps us to experience such realization. Even if we are not gaining realization, mantra recitation can still help us practice the six perfections.

If we have proper training in wisdom, then this wisdom can become the guide to our practice of the six perfections so that we can go beyond. Mantras remind us to practice discipline and meditation. For someone who is very spiritually evolved, recitation of the mantra in the *Heart Sutra* can become all three trainings: discipline, meditation, and wisdom.

We are not at that level yet. This mantra should remind us to practice the six perfections according to Mahayana Buddhism. If we are Vajrayana practitioners, then this mantra can help us to achieve wisdom through our daily sadhana practices. This mantra refers to all the stages of realization.

> Shariputra! In this way, bodhisattvas should train in the profound Prajnaparamita.

Up to this point, the Buddha has not spoken. The Buddha has been in meditation for the entire duration of this teaching. From his wisdom in that state of meditation, he has been aware of everything. He is blessing Avalokiteshvara to train Shariputra. The teachings up to this point are called the "Blessed Sutra."

> Then the Blessed One arose from that meditation called Profound Vision and spoke to the bodhisattva Arya Avalokiteshvara.

Now the Buddha has arisen from his meditative state. "Arose" does not mean that he stood up. It means that he came out of that deep meditation to speak these words:

> Well said, noble son, well said! It is just so. One should practice the Prajnaparamita as you have taught, and all the tathagatas will rejoice.

These are the Buddha's actual words. The Buddha is now confirming that what Avalokiteshvara taught Shariputra is correct. This section of the sutra is called "the Buddha's Spoken Sutra."

> When the buddhas had spoken thus, the elder Shariputra and the bodhisattva Arya Avalokiteshvara, together with that assembly, as well as gods, humans, demigods, and gandharvas, joyfully praised the words of the Blessed One.

This section is called the "Rejoicing Sutra." All those beings who are on Vulture's Peak during this teaching are rejoicing now. There was a huge assembly including gods, humans, demigods (also called *asuras* in Sanskrit), and gandharvas or spirits. Everyone who was assembled there rejoices in response to the Buddha's words.

Although this is the concise version of the *Prajnaparamita Sutra*, you can see how it still includes the base, path, result, benefit, and closing practice. The deeper we study, the more we can gain from this brief version of the sutra.

In this short sutra we have been shown how we can go beyond the wheel of life. We have been shown how we can go beyond samsara and nirvana to achieve buddhahood. This is the training of *darshana*, the wisdom training.

The practice of the Prajnaparamita, the wisdom gone beyond, is to go beyond samsara and nirvana. The teachings may at first seem to be merely philosophical, so it is important to bring them into our practice. Our practice should be based on the three trainings of discipline, meditation, and wisdom. Once we have that foundation, then when we practice tantric sadhanas, including yantra and all the completion practices, they will make more sense. We will have certainty that these methods will be effective.

# The *Heart Sutra* Concise Practice

*(Recite the refuge and bodhichitta three times.)*

To the Buddha, Dharma, and Sangha
I go for refuge until I awaken.
By the merit of generosity and so on,
May I attain buddhahood to benefit all migrating beings.

*(Recite the four limitless prayers three times.)*

May all sentient beings possess happiness
and the causes of happiness.
May all sentient beings be free of suffering
and the causes of suffering.
May all sentient beings never be separate from the joy
free from suffering.
May all sentient beings remain in equanimity
free of attachment and aversion.

*(Recite the mantra as many times as possible.)*

*Tadyatha om gate gate paragate parasamgate bodhi svaha!*

*(Recite the dedication once.)*

Just as heroic Manjushri knows
and likewise, Samantabhadra
in order that I may train in following them in every way,
I fully dedicate all of these merits.

*This practice was compiled from traditional sources by Lama Migmar.*

# APPENDIX 2.

# Prajnaparamita Sadhana

*Namo ekaksharayai*
*Namo guru prajnaparamitayai*

*(Recite the refuge and bodhichitta three times.)*

To the Buddha, Dharma, and Sangha
I go for refuge until I awaken.
By the merit of generosity and so on,
May I attain buddhahood to benefit all migrating beings.

*(Dissolve all appearances into the state of emptiness while reciting the following mantra:)*

*Om svabhava shuddha sarvadharmah svabhava*
   *shuddho'ham*

*(Recite and imagine:)*

Instantly one arises from the state of emptiness as the great mother Prajnaparamita on top of a lotus and moon. One's body is the color of pure gold; it has one face and four hands. The first right hand raises a sword to the sky. The first left hand is in the mudra of meditative equipoise. The second right hand holds a counting *mala*. The second left hand holds a book. One is adorned with silks and all the jewel ornaments. One stands with two feet together.

Prajnaparamita cannot be spoken of, thought of, or
    expressed;
nonarising and unceasing, the essence of space;
the sphere of wisdom that must be known for oneself.
Homage to the mother of the buddhas of the three times.

Thus I heard at one time: the Bhagavan was residing on Vulture's Peak in Rajagriha together with one hundred and sixty-three bhikshus and trillions of bodhisattvas. At that time, the Bhagavan said to venerable Ananda, "Ananda, this so-called *Prajnaparamita in One Syllable* should be upheld for the well-being and happiness of all sentient beings in this way."

*(At the conclusion of the recitation, while recalling the meaning of the instruction heard in one's mind, train one's mind in the clear appearance and emptiness of the form of the deity. Focus the mind only on the A on the tip of the tongue:)*
अ ཨ A

*(Further, reflect on objectlessness and place one's mind in a state of emptiness free from proliferation and recite the A twenty-one times. After that, from a state of illusory dependent origination, recite the complete rejoicing:)*

After the Bhagavan said that, venerable Ananda, those bhikshus, and all of those great bodhisattvas realized prajnaparamita, rejoiced, and praised the Bhagavan's teaching.

*(Recite the dedication once.)*

Just as heroic Manjushri knows
and likewise, Samantabhadra
in order that I may train in following them in every way,
I fully dedicate all of these merits.

*This sadhana was compiled from traditional sources by Lama Migmar.*

# The *Heart Sutra* Repelling Practice

*(Recite the refuge and bodhichitta three times.)*

To the Buddha, Dharma, and Sangha
I go for refuge until I awaken.
By the merit of generosity and so on,
May I attain buddhahood to benefit all migrating beings.

*(Recite the Heart Sutra and repelling prayer as many times as possible.)*

## THE HEART SUTRA

Salutations to the Omniscient One.

This is what I once heard at the time the Blessed One was seated on Vulture's Peak in Rajagriha with a huge congregation of the exalted community of bhikshus and bodhisattvas. At that time, the Blessed One was dwelling in the meditation called Profound Vision.

Also at that time, the great being and bodhisattva Arya Avalokiteshvara was reviewing the profound characteristics of the Prajnaparamita and saw the natural emptiness of the five aggregates.

Then the elder Shariputra, moved by the power of the Buddha, addressed Arya Avalokiteshvara with these words: "Noble son! How should someone who wishes to perform the profound practice of the Prajnaparamita train himself?"

The great being, the bodhisattva Arya Avalokiteshvara replied, "Shariputra! That son or daughter of a good family who wishes to perform the profound practice of the Prajnaparamita should first rightly see that all the aggregates, by their very nature, are empty.

"Form is emptiness. Emptiness is form. Form is not other than emptiness, nor is emptiness other than form.

"So too all feeling, ideation, formation, and consciousness are empty.

"Shariputra! In the same way, all dharmas are devoid of characteristics, unborn, unstopped, unsullied, unpurified, undecreased, unfilled.

"Therefore, Shariputra, in emptiness there is no form, no feeling, no ideation, no formation, no consciousness, no eye, no ear, no nose, no tongue, no body, no mind; no form, no sound, no smell, no taste, no touch, no dharmas. There is no element of eye and so on through the element of mind and the element of mental consciousness. There is no ignorance, no elimination of ignorance; no death and decay, and no elimination of death and decay.

"So too there is no pain, no origin, no cessation, no path; no wisdom, no attainment, no nonattainment.

"Shariputra, because nothing is really obtained, all bodhisattvas who have no fear rely on and dwell in the Prajnaparamita, for they have no mental obscurations. They are perfectly liberated and have gone completely beyond deception. Relying on the Prajnaparamita, all the buddhas of the three times are completely enlightened to that unsurpassable, noble, and perfect enlightenment.

"Therefore, the mantra of the Prajnaparamita, the mantra of great wisdom, the unsurpassable mantra, the mantra equal to the unequalled, the mantra that fully allays all pains, because it is not false, should be known as truth. The mantra of Prajnaparamita is spoken thus:

*Tadyatha om gate gate paragate parasamgate bodhi svaha!*

"Shariputra! In this way, bodhisattvas should train in the profound Prajnaparamita."

Then the Blessed One arose from that meditation called Profound Vision and spoke to the bodhisattva Arya Avalokiteshvara: "Well said, noble son, well said! It is just so. One should practice the Prajnaparamita as you have taught, and all the tathagatas will rejoice."

When the buddhas had spoken thus, the elder Shariputra and the bodhisattva Arya Avalokiteshvara, together with that assembly, as well as gods, humans, demigods, and gandharvas, joyfully praised the words of the Blessed One.

This concludes the *Heart Sutra*.

## REPELLING PRAYER

*Namo!*
Prostrations to the Guru.
Prostrations to the Buddha.
Prostrations to the Dharma.
Prostrations to the Sangha.
Prostrations to the Great Mother, the Perfection of Wisdom.

Through relying upon the power and strength of prostrating to you, may the truth of our words be accomplished.

Just as the powerful god Shakra, previously having relied upon the power and strength of reciting the words and contemplating the profound meaning of the Great Mother, the Perfection of Wisdom, repelled Mara and the like, so likewise do we also rely upon the power and strength of reciting the words and contemplating the profound meaning of the Great Mother, the Perfection of Wisdom. Through the truth of the speech of the noble Triple Gem, may all opposing forces, abandonments, and unfavorable conditions for accomplishing the holy Dharma by ourselves and our circle be repelled. *(Clap your hands once.)*

May they be destroyed. *(Clap your hands once.)*

May they be allayed. *(Clap your hands once.)*

May they be thoroughly allayed.

Through method, refuge, purification, and the pure Mahayana, may the activities of Mara, which completely deceive sentient beings, be repelled.

Please pacify all the obstacles to the accomplishment of perfect awakening caused by outer and inner harm.

*(Recite the dedication once:)*
Just as heroic Manjushri knows
and likewise, Samantabhadra
in order that I may train in following them in every way,
I fully dedicate all of these merits.

*This repelling practice was compiled from traditional sources by Lama Migmar.*

# About the Author

LAMA MIGMAR TSETEN has served as Buddhist chaplain at Harvard University since 1997. He received both a traditional and a contemporary education in India, graduating from the Central Institute of Higher Tibetan Studies at Sanskrit University in Varanasi. His Holiness the Dalai Lama awarded him medals for achieving first position among his class of students from the Nyingma, Sakya, Kagyu, and Geluk schools for nine consecutive years, and His Holiness the Sakya Trichen awarded him with the title of *khenpo*. He served as the head of the Sakya Center in Rajpur, India, and the Sakya Monastery in Puruwala, Himachal Pradesh, India. Lama Migmar has supervised the editing and publication of more than fifty rare volumes of Sakya literature and is the author of many books, including *Play of Mahamudra*. As the founder of the Sakya Institute for Buddhist Studies in Cambridge, Massachusetts, Lama Migmar leads retreats throughout North America and Europe. Learn more at www.lamamigmar.net.

# What to Read Next
# from Wisdom Publications

ESSENCE OF THE HEART SUTRA
*The Dalai Lama's Heart of Wisdom Teachings*
His Holiness the Dalai Lama
Translated and edited by Geshe Thubten Jinpa

"Lovingly and wisely edited by Jinpa, the bulk of the book is consumed with a fairly meaty exploration of the *Heart of Wisdom* sutra, a classical Mahayana text, and as such will be useful to established practitioners as well as neophytes." —*Publishers Weekly*

LUMINOUS LIVES
*The Story of the Early Masters of the Lam 'bras Tradition in Tibet*
Cyrus Stearns

"A seminal manuscript history of its earliest practitioners and masters, and a detailed description of the Lam 'bras teachings." —*Tricycle*

THE FOUR NOBLE TRUTHS
*A Guide to Everyday Life*
Lama Zopa Rinpoche

*The Four Noble Truths* begins with an excellent elucidation of the nature of the mind and its role in creating the happiness we all seek. Lama Zopa Rinpoche then turns to an in-depth analysis of the four truths that are the cornerstone of Buddhist teaching.

SEARCHING FOR THE SELF
*The Library of Wisdom and Compassions, Vol. 7*
His Holiness the Dalai Lama
Thubten Chodron

"I am thrilled to see *Searching for the Self*. All the volumes in the *Library of Wisdom and Compassion* are highly cherished treasures—they are profound yet easily accessible. *Searching for the Self* will help to open your wisdom eye to investigate emptiness. With that understanding, you can fly in freedom without grasping at illusory objects."
—Geshe Lhakdor, director, Library of Tibetan Works and Archives, Dharamsala, India

THE PLAY OF MAHAMUDRA
*Spontaneous Teachings on Virupa's Mystical Songs*
Lama Migmar Tseten

"This new collected edition of Khenpo Migmar Tseten's *Play of Mahamudra* volumes constitutes a veritable treasure for all who are deeply engaged on the path to enlightenment. Khenpo Migmar's translation of Mahasiddha Virupa's *Treasury of Dohas* and of Sachen Kunga Nyingpo's *Praise to Virupa* makes us intimately familiar with the essence of these root texts, and his elucidation of the *Dohas* offers us a deep and clear understanding of their core meaning. Anyone who truly contemplates on Mahasiddha Virupa's words is certain to attain realization."
—His Holiness the Sakya Trichen

Ornament to Beautify the Three Appearances
*The Mahāyāna Preliminary Practices of the Sakya Lamdré Tradition*
Ngorchen Könchok Lhundrup
Translated and annotated by Cyrus Stearns
Foreword by His Holiness the Sakya Trichen

*Ornament to Beautify the Three Appearances* is the first book of a two-volume set of works written by Ngorchen Könchok Lhundrup (1497–1557) to explain the Lamdré teachings, the most important system of tantric theory and practice in the Sakya tradition of Tibetan Buddhism.

The Freeing the Heart and Mind Trilogy
His Holiness the Sakya Trichen

This trilogy is "required reading" for any Sakya practitioner and will also be deeply inspiring for Buddhists of all traditions.

# About Wisdom Publications

Wisdom Publications is the leading publisher of classic and contemporary Buddhist books and practical works on mindfulness. To learn more about us or to explore our other books, please visit our website at wisdomexperience.org or contact us at the address below.

Wisdom Publications
132 Perry Street
New York, NY 10014 USA

We are a 501(c)(3) organization, and donations in support of our mission are tax deductible.

Wisdom Publications is affiliated with the Foundation for the Preservation of the Mahayana Tradition (FPMT).